ARAMAIC 10-DAY JOURNEY IN ISRAEL

MINISTRY OF YESHUA MSHIHO

VOLUME II

ANDRE MOUBARAK
TOUR GUIDE, BIBLICAL EDUCATOR, AND BEST-SELLING AUTHOR
FROM THE HEART OF JERUSALEM

Copyright © 2025 by Andre Moubarak

All rights reserved. No part of this book may be reproduced or transmitted in any form or by any means— electronic, mechanical, photocopy, recording, scanning, or others- except for brief quotations in critical review or articles, without written permission from the author. *Internet addresses (websites, blogs, YouTube channels, etc.) are offered as resources. The publisher does not guarantee their continued viability over the life of this book.*

Learn more about the Author www.TwinsBiblicalAcademy.com

All Scripture quotations, unless otherwise indicated, are taken from the Peshitta Bible. Holy Bible, New International Version* and New American Standard Bible*...

...New International Version*, NIV*. ©1973, 1978,1984, 2011 by Biblica, Inc.*
All rights reserved worldwide.

...New American Standard Bible*, NASB*. ©
1960, 1962, 1963, 1968, 1971, 1972, 1973, 1975, 1977, 1995
by The Lockman Foundation. Used by permission.

Editor - Arthur Fogartie

First edition 2026

ISBN: 978-1-7348402-9-2 (print)

ISBN: 979-8-9911102-0-4 (hardcover)

ISBN: 979-8-9911102-1-1 (eBook)

Printed in the United States of America

Bulk purchases available. Contact the author: andremoubarak@gmail.com

Dedication

To every tour leader that crossed my path, and to every Spirit-filled, divine moment we shared together.

Your passion, love, and servant's heart I deeply admire. I dedicate this book to you. Thank you!

Contents

The Program: Andre's Signature Tour xv
    Volume I – Early Life of *Yeshua Mshiho* xv
    Day 1: Arrival in Israel xv
    Day 2: Bethlehem – The Birth of Jesus xv
    Day 3: Jordan River – The Ministry of John the
            Baptist xvi
    Day 4: Nazareth – Jesus as a Man xvi
    Volume II – Ministry of *Yeshua Mshiho* xvi
    Day 5: Sea of Galilee – Becoming a Disciple xvi
    Day 6: Golan Heights – The Roman Empire xvii
    Day 7: Light to the Nations – The Gentile Pentecost xvii
    Volume III – Last Week of *Yeshua Mshiho* xviii
    Day 8: In the Steps of Jesus – Crucifixion, Death,
            Burial and Resurrection xviii
    Day 9: The City of the Kings – God Establishes His
            Temple in Jerusalem xviii
    Day 10: Last Day in Israel xix

Introduction to Volume II 1
    Ministry of *Yeshua Mshiho* 1

Volume II 4
Day Five: Sea of Galilee – The Kingdom of Heaven 4

Arriving at the Mount of Beatitudes 5
The *Malkout Shmaya* 6
What is the *Malkout Shmaya*? 8
When Is the *Malkout Shamaya*? 11
Why did *Yeshua* teach about the *Malkout Shmaya*? 14
The Operation of the Kingdom of Heaven 14
Eremos Cave 16
Saint Peter's Primacy Church 19
Yeshua Calls His Disciples 21
    Stage One: Come and See 25
    Stage Two: To Follow 25
    Stage Three: Obedience and Surrender 29
Break Time 34
Kfar-Nahoum 34
Short History of *Kfar-Nahoum* 35
Inside the Synagogue 36
Why Is *Kfar-Nahoum* Known as the Hometown
of *Yeshua*? 38
Yeshayahu's Prophecy 39
The *Kfar-Nahoum* Synagogue in *Yeshua's* Day 42
Yeshua Teaches That He Is the Bread of Life 43
Kepha's House – *Dominus Ecclesias* 49
Do We Know Which Insulae Was Kepha's? 51
The Events That Took Place in *Kepha's* House 53
Archaeology of *Kfar-Nahoum* 55
Back to the Bus and Lunch 58

The Yigal Allon Center in Kibbutz Ginosar 59
Boat Ride on the Sea of Galilee 63
Names of the Sea of Galilee 65
Climate and Storm Patterns Around the Sea of Galilee ... 66
Saint Peter's Fish 67
Yohannon Hamatbil is Beheaded 69
Yeshua Walks on the Sea 70
Kepha's Reaction to Yeshua Walking on the Water 75
The Day Concludes 77
Being Anointed by the Spirit 78
    #1 – Live a King-Centered Life 78
    #2 – Read Your Bible 80
    #3 – Obedience of Faith 82
    #4 – Kingdom Productivity 83
    #5 – Connected to the Community of the Faithful 85
    #6 – Be Involved with the Community Conflict
         (Spiritual Warfare) 86
    #7 – Giving Evidence of God's Kingship in
         Your Life 87
Wadi Elhamam – Yeshua the Rabbi 89
Characteristics of a Rabbi's Lifestyle 92
    #1 - Rabbis Lived an Itinerant Life 92
    #2 - Rabbis Were Poor 96
    #3 - Make Disciples 98
    #4 - A Teacher of the Torah 101
    #5 - Rabbis Taught in Parables 103

Day Six: The Golan Heights Theme – The Roman Empire 110

Leaving the Hotel 110
The Roman Empire 112
The Golan Heights 114
The Lower Golan 115
The Upper Golan 118
Kiryat Shmona 119
Metula.. 120
The Good Fence 122
Israel–Hamas *War* 123
Our First Stop: Dado Observation Point............................ 124
Information about *Lebanon*.. 126
Praying for Lebanon and Learning about Hezbollah 128
Ceasefire & Aftershocks... 130
Lebanese Government's Stance 131
Tel Dan National Park 132
Biblical Period: The Relocation of Dan............................. 133
The High Place... 135
The Canaanite City Gate – *Ob-Rohom's* Gate................. 146
The Israelite Gate 147
The House of *Dawood* Inscription 151
Tel Dan - The Modern Period 153
The Bus Drive to Caesarea Philippi – Panias 154
Caesarea Philippi – The Roman Temple of Pan 156
The Sacred Niches... 158
Why Did Yeshua Bring His Disciples to Caesarea
Philippi? 161
The Temple of Pan Was Built on a Rock 163
Caesarea Philippi Was Located in Enemy Territory........ 164

Caesarea Philippi: The Gateway to Hades 164
Honor and Shame: What the West Misses 165
Today's Conflicts in Israel: Echoes of the Past 166
From Caesarea Philippi to the Transfiguration 168
Background to the Transfiguration 169
An Alternative Location in Morqos's Gospel 172
On the Bus to Mount Bental 174
Mount Bental – Overlooking the Borders of Syria 175
Modern Historical Divisions of the Middle East 181
The Six Day War 182
Yom Kippur War 182
Psalm 133 183
The IDF Bunker 185
Wine Tasting in the Golan Heights 186

Day Seven: Light to the Nations Theme – The Gentile Pentecost 188

Leaving the Sea of Galilee to *Tel Megiddo* 188
Driving Through the *Jezreel* Valley 189
Tel Megiddo – The Mountain Fortress 193
    1. *Sumerian Ur* (*Tel el-Muqayyar*, Iraq) 193
    2. *Urfa* (Orhāy in modern Turkey) 194
    3. *Urkesh* (*Tel Mozan*, Syria) 194
The Seal of *Megiddo* 197
King *Yeroba'am* – Historical Background 198
Maps of the Chariots 199
The Israelite City Gate 199
The View at the Top of the Fortress 201

Haar Megiddo 201
The Silo Lookout 203
The *Megiddo* Water System 204
The Spring of *Megiddo* 206
Mount *Kerem-El* 207
Elisha and the Two Bears 208
History of Mount *Kerem-El* 210
The Druze 211
Beliefs and Traditions of the Druze 213
Mount *Kerem-El* Overlooking the *Jezreel* Valley 215
The Prophet Eliyahu and Mount *Kerem-El* 215
Caesarea Maritima 228
Brief History of Caesarea 229
The Caesarea Theatre 232
Archaeology of Caesarea 243
The Biblical Story of Cornelius 245
Shawol Comes to Caesarea 246
Roman Procurator Porcius Festus 248
King Herodos Agrippa II 248
Shawol's Appeal 249
The Pontius Pilate Inscription 252
Crusader Fortress of Caesarea 254
Open Promenade and Crusader Marketplace 255
The Roman Aqueduct 256
Caesarea to Tel Aviv 259
Yuffi 262
Greek Mythology 262
Simon the Tanner's House 267

What is *Kosher* food? 270
The Drive up to *Or-Shlem* 275
The Land of *Yesrael* 276
Olives and Olive Oil 276
Grapes and Vineyards 278
Figs and Fig Trees 279
Pomegranates 282
Dates 283
Wheat and Barley 285
Summary of the Seven Species of the Land 286
Approaching *Or-Shlem* 287

What's Next? 291

Additional Information and Resources 292

Our Story 294

Twins Biblical Academy Online Courses 296
Why Another Online Course: "Twins Biblical Academy" 297
Some Background about the Maronite Community 298

What You Will Learn in the Online Courses 301
First C: Culture 301
Second C: Customs 303
Third C: Context 303
Acquired Learning 305
Clarity 306
Correction 306

Confirmation 307
How the Courses Work 307
Who Benefits from the Courses 308

More Books For Your Reading Pleasure 309

Invite us to share the Word with your ministry. 313

(Endnotes) 316

The Program: Andre's Signature Tour

Volume I – Early Life of *Yeshua Mshiho*

Day 1: Arrival in Israel

- Group flight arrives in Israel at Ben Gurion Airport (Tel-Aviv)
- Twins Tours guide and driver meet group at the airport arrival terminal
- Drive to Bethlehem (one hour)
- Check into the Bethlehem Hotel for two nights
- Dinner and stay overnight at the Bethlehem

Day 2: Bethlehem – The Birth of Jesus

- Herodion National Park – The discovery of the Tomb of Herod
- The Shepherds' Fields – The Angels appearing to the Shepherds
- Bethlehem and the Church of Nativity – A Messiah Is Born
- Dinner and stay overnight at the Bethlehem Hotel

Day 3: Jordan River – The Ministry of John the Baptist

- John the Baptizer – In the spirit of the prophet *Elyahu*
- Jericho – The City of Palms
- Qumran – The home of the Dead Sea Scrolls
- Baptismal Site *Qaser Elyhoud* – Bethany beyond the Jordan
- Jordan Valley – Descending through the Syrian-African Great Rift
- Check into the hotel in Nazareth (two nights)

Day 4: Nazareth – Jesus as a Man

- Kfar Cana – Jesus' first miracle
- The Annunciation Church – Where the Word became flesh
- Nazareth Village – A delightful recreation of a Galilean Jewish village in the time of Jesus, illustrating the parables
- Mount Precipice – Rejection of Jesus by His hometown
- Dinner and overnight stay in Nazareth

Volume II – Ministry of *Yeshua Mshiho*

Day 5: Sea of Galilee – Becoming a Disciple

- Mount of Beatitudes – Teaching on the Kingdom of Heaven

- Primacy of St. Peter – Tabgha, where Jesus had breakfast with the disciples
- Capernaum – Jesus' headquarters during his earthly ministry
- Lunch at St. Peter's Fish
- Boat Museum – Learn about the discovery of the ancient boat
- Boat Ride – Enjoy sailing on the Sea of Galilee
- Valley of the Doves – A short walk along the Jesus Trail
- Check into the Kibbutz hotel near the Sea of Galilee for two nights
- Dinner and stay overnight in Kibbutz

Day 6: Golan Heights – The Roman Empire

- Dado Observation point – Overlooking the Lebanese border
- *Tel Dan* – The fortress and altar of the tribe of *Dan*
- Caesarea Philippi – The Roman temple dedicated to the god Pan
- Mount Bental – Overlooking the Syrian border
- Dinner and stay overnight in Kibbutz

Day 7: Light to the Nations – The Gentile Pentecost

- Tel *Megiddo* – The mountain fortress and the site of Revelation's Armageddon

- Mount Carmel – Elijah versus the priests of Baal
- Lunch – Druze Village
- Caesarea Maritima – Home of Cornelius, the God-fearing Gentile and Peter's message
- Visit the water aqueduct along the beach of the Mediterranean
- *Jaffa* – A light to the nations
- Drive up to Jerusalem and check into the hotel for three nights
- Dinner and stay overnight in Jerusalem

Volume III – Last Week of *Yeshua Mshiho*

Day 8: In the Steps of Jesus – Crucifixion, Death, Burial and Resurrection

- Mount of Olives – Overlook and Palm Sunday Route
- Dominus Flevit Church – Where Jesus wept over Jerusalem
- Garden of Gethsemane – Church of Agony
- Cross the Kidron Valley to the Lions Gate
- Mount Zion – Cenacle and Upper Room
- Dinner and stay overnight in Jerusalem

Day 9: The City of the Kings – God Establishes His Temple in Jerusalem

- Dome of the Rock – An Islamic shrine located in the Old City of Jerusalem

- Pools of *Beth-esda* – Where Jesus healed a paralytic
- Garden Tomb – Alternative site of Calvary and Golgotha
- Davidson Center – The Southern Steps, Pentecost
- The Western Wall – The most religious site in the world for the Jewish people
- Dinner and stay overnight in Jerusalem

Day 10: Last Day in Israel

- Late Morning Checkout from Hotel
- The Road to Emmaus – Jesus appears to the two disciples
- Tel *Azeka* and the Elah Valley – David vs. Goliath
- Farewell Dinner
- Drive to Airport - According to Departure Times

Introduction to Volume II

Ministry of *Yeshua Mshiho*[10]

In the first volume of this series on the early life of *Yeshua*[1], we explored the first four days of our Holy Land journey and provided background on the Aramaic mindset during *Yeshua's* childhood.

Assuming readers have already familiarized themselves with the first volume, I will not repeat that information here. However, I would like to clarify a few points before you embark on this second volume book, "Aramaic 10-Day Journey of Israel. Ministry of *Yeshua Mshiho* around the Sea of Galilee."

Yeshua and His disciples spoke a dialect of Aramaic known as "Old Galilean." The Syriac dialect found in the New Testament is the closest to Old Galilean, though it is not identical. This difference is similar to the variation between Texan English and New York English.

For example, *Kepha*[2] was recognized as a follower of *Yeshua* when He was taken prisoner by the *Hayklo*[3] guards. Bystanders noted his distinct speech, as recorded in (*Mattai*[4]

26:73). "And a little later those who stood by came up and said to *Kepha*, 'Surely you also are one of them, for your speech betrays you.'" This indicates the noticeable difference between the Galilean dialect and the Jerusalemite dialect spoken in Southern Judea. Despite Galilee being about seventy-five miles north of *Or-Shlem*[5], its inhabitants spoke a more informal Aramaic Judean dialect compared to the more educated and cultured speech of the Southern region.

While our understanding of Old Galilean Aramaic is limited, we are more familiar with other Aramaic dialects, particularly Syriac. The Syriac version of the New Testament, along with other ancient documents, supports the present Aramaic Bible known as the *Peshitta*. I will refer to this version in all three volumes as the Aramaic text of the New Testament.

It's important to note that biblical scholars widely agree the inspired text of the New Testament was originally written in Greek, although *Yeshua* spoke a Northern Galilean dialect of Aramaic. The Eastern Church, however, believes the New Testament was inspired in Aramaic. Both *Koine*[6] Greek and Old Galilean Aramaic are now considered dead languages, but there is a greater understanding and abundance of early manuscripts in *Koine* Greek compared to any Aramaic dialect.

This holds that the inspired text of the New Testament was in *Koine* Greek, but that *Yeshua*, His Apostles, and the Apostle *Boulos*[7] spoke Aramaic. It's likely that many of their words were dictated in Aramaic and translated into

Greek by scribes. Translating from Aramaic to Greek can present challenges in finding equivalent terms.

I pray this book helps readers use the Aramaic text as a resource for a deeper understanding of problematic passages in the New Testament. Always remember, it is the *Roho-Kodsho*[8] who guides us into all truth.

Volume II

Day Five: Sea of Galilee – The Kingdom of Heaven

- **Mount of Beatitudes** – Teaching on the Kingdom of Heaven
- **Primacy of Saint Peter** – Tabgha, where *Yeshua* had breakfast with the disciples
- **Capernaum** – *Yeshua's* headquarters during His earthly ministry
- **Boat Museum** – Learn about the discovery of the ancient boat
- **Boat Ride** – Enjoy sailing on the Sea of Galilee
- **Migdal** – visit the first century AD synagogue in the hometown of *Miriam Magdalene*
- **Valley of the Doves** – A short walk along the "*Yeshua* trail"
- Check into the Kibbutz hotel near the Sea of Galilee for two nights
- Dinner and stay overnight in Kibbutz

Arriving at the Mount of Beatitudes

After breakfast, try to beat the crowds and leave a little early (7:45 am). A mere 15 minutes ahead of other groups will have a positive effect on the flow of the day. While on the bus, it is a good idea to go over the day's itinerary and the theme for the day, "The *Malkout Shmaya*".[9]

Personally, teaching about the Sermon on the Mount is my favorite, and I begin teaching it immediately after leaving with the bus. Because I prefer to take people on more scenic routes and provide a more authentic experience, we don't go to the main church parking lot where all the other groups are having their visits. There is another road on the same hillside before the main one that goes to the back of the church. There is a relatively unknown private dirt hiking road that takes you all the way to the bottom of the Mount of Beatitudes. Those unable to make the hike can remain on the bus and meet everyone at the bottom later.

After a 20-minute walk through banana fields, we will arrive at an elevated area lined with large basalt stones centered around smaller dark stones. There is an old altar located in the middle. This is the remains of a Byzantine church erected in the 4th century and used until the 7th century. It lies below the present-day church built higher up the mountainside.

Mount Beatitude Church

This is a good place to sit and teach and let people rest.

Remains of a Byzantine Church

The *Malkout Shmaya*[9]

One of the most important subjects in the New Testament that *Yeshua* taught is that of the Kingdom of Heaven. This was the most important topic to the heart and mind of *Yeshua*. He referenced it continually before, during, and even after his ministry. Consequently, the concept should be important to his followers.

Let's look at the cultural and geopolitical background of Galilee in the first century. The Romans controlled this part of the world. Herodos Antipas ruled Galilee. The Jews suffered under occupation and heavy taxes. It is hard to understand what life is like under an occupation unless you've experienced it. Many of the things you might take for granted would be outlawed and criminalized. You aren't even a citizen of your own country. You are nothing more than servants and slaves in the eyes of the occupiers. Your national identity, religion, and way of life are constantly under threat. You work very hard and you gain almost nothing. Yours is a subsistence level existence.

Herodos Antipas was a puppet king. Taxes crushed the people. Zealots rose in rebellion. The population lived in tension between Roman imperialism, Herodian ambition, and the Jewish yearning for *Mshiho*.[10]

During the time of *Yeshua,* the land of Israel (then part of the Roman province of Judea and surrounding regions) was a mosaic of different types of towns and villages, shaped by Jewish tradition, Roman administration, and Hellenistic culture. Each type had its own architectural features, population makeup, political role, and religious climate.

This is what *Yeshua* and his disciples had to endure. Everyone was looking for a *Mshiho*[10] who could free them from oppression. Into this environment comes a Jewish rabbi, a teacher, proclaiming the Good News of the Gospel and telling fellow Jews that if they follow him, they will have a new citizenship, gain a new identity, and have freedom not only from the Roman occupation but also from the source of every stronghold and oppression, sin. *Yeshua* always goes to the core the heart of the issue. He always digs deeper to bring freedom, which begins in the intentions of the heart. This is the backdrop of *Yeshua's* ministry. Every word He speaks is to a world of oppression, expectation, and fear.

Why was this an important message to the heart of *Yeshua's* ministry? What is the *Malkout Shmaya*[9] all about?

(*Mattai*[4] *4:17*):

> From that time on, *Yeshua* began to preach, Repent, for the kingdom of heaven has come near.

When *Yeshua* emerges from the wilderness, He is empowered by the *Roho-Kodsho*[8] and begins his public healing ministry. His message is often referred to as "The Good News" or "The Gospel of the Kingdom of Heaven" or "The Kingdom of God." Again, this is at the center of his heart and mind, and He spent three years teaching about it constantly.

What is the *Malkout Shmaya*[9] ?

Again, we understand it by the context of Scripture, understanding the Aramaic words, and knowing the customs of the first century rabbis. When we put all these pieces together, we can begin to see a clear picture of what *Yeshua* was talking about and why it was so important to his heart.

(*Mattai*[4] 4:17) speaks of the Kingdom of Heaven, but it

is called the "Kingdom of God" in *Morqos* and *Louko*. So, which is correct? Which did *Yeshua* mean, or is there any difference? There are some scholars in the West who claim the Kingdom of Heaven is *Yahweh* ruling in heaven in the spiritual realm and that the Kingdom of God is his rule on Earth in the physical realm. Unfortunately, when we understand the Aramaic, which *Yeshua* spoke, we get a better sense of what He meant.

In Aramaic, *Malkout*[9] comes from the same word as *Malko*[19], which means "king." So *Malkout* means "kingdom." *Shmaya* means "heavens," a term very popular among Pharisees in the first century.

How then can we be sure that *Yeshua* meant the Kingdom of Heaven and not the Kingdom of God? First, because it was a common sentence in the first century. Every religious Jew was using it, especially among the Pharisees in the Second Temple Period. Secondly, it is a typical Aramaic way of speaking, a common turn of phrase. Thirdly, the terminology "Kingdom of God" is a non-typical way of speaking. Why? Because the name of God was not allowed to be pronounced or spoken. It was holy, so Jews use synonyms for God. Instead of evoking his name, they said *Adonai, Yahweh,* or *Jehovah.*

Look at what *Yeshua* says in (*Mattai*[4] 5:1-3):

> Now, when *Yeshua* saw the crowds, he went up on a mountainside and sat down. His disciples came to him, and he began to teach them. Blessed are the poor in spirit, for theirs is the kingdom of heaven."

Yeshua uses the term, *Shmaya*[9]. Another example is the Parable of the Prodigal Son: "I will return to my father and say I have sinned against heavens and against thee." The young man is saying that he has sinned against Yahweh, who lives in the heavens, as well as against his father on Earth.

The writers of *Morqos*[12] and *Louko*[13], were addressing non-Jewish audiences. They did not want their readers (more likely to be Greek speakers) to misunderstand the meaning of the Kingdom of Heaven.

Yeshua is not speaking of a world to come, something in the future. He means there is a Kingdom of Heaven here and now on earth, today, this very moment.

Bottom line: the three synoptic writers all mean the same thing. One is simply an Aramaic way of speaking, the other is a Greek way.

When Jewish boys come to the age of accountability, they have a *Bar Mitzvah*. *Bar* is "son" in Aramaic – literally, "the son of the Commandments." It is said that they put on the yoke of the Kingdom of Heaven. In other words, they come under the rulership and the power of the Kingdom of God. They are now accountable for their actions. It is a very common expression. So, when *Yeshua* speaks of the Kingdom of Heaven, He means the present time, the kingdom of *Yahweh* today.

According to Talmudic teaching, the existence of *Yahweh* was more than an intellectual affirmation; it included moral obligation. The recital of the declaration in morning and evening prayers, *"Hear, O Israel, the Lord our Yahweh, the Lord is one,"* (*Dbarim* 6:4), outlines "the acceptance of the yoke of the Kingdom of Heaven." This is submission to the divine discipline, submission to the rulership of *Yahweh* every day.

When Is the *Malkout Shamaya*[9]?

Is it here now or is it in the hereafter? The King James translation says the Kingdom of Heaven is at hand. When speaking about the Kingdom of God, most evangelicals are referring to a future realm, something like *Yeshua's* second coming to establish his reign in the future.

There are many differences between an Aramaic mindset view to life (held by *Yeshua*) and the Greek view. The Roman and Evangelical Churches of today are a product of the Greek, but *Yeshua* held to a Jewish Hebraic/Aramaic perspective. One can draw many contrasts between the Aramaic and Greek approaches to life.

A person holding to the Greek perspective studies to comprehend. Aramaic and Hebrew studies intend to revere, to regard with respect about a relationship. *Yahweh*, Son, and the *Roho-Kodsho*[8] are all about relationships.

- The Greek worships the holiness of beauty; the Aramaic/Hebrew worships the beauty of holiness.
- The Greek seeks reasons and rationality to determine ultimate authority; the Aramaic/Hebrew says revelation is the final authority.

- To the Greek, self-expression and freedom is a virtue; to the Aramaic/ Hebrew mind, the perfect virtue is obedience.
- The Greek asks why something should be done; the Aramaic/Hebrew asks what must be done.
- Greek thought is primarily about the other world, the future world; Aramaic/Hebrew thought, by contrast, is primarily interested in this world at this moment.

In Greek philosophy, the spiritual world in the future, in the Aramaic/Hebrew mindset, the emphasis is upon the here and now, the moment. The Christian life can be summed up in two words: "pray here" and "obey now." We are intended to live in the present; it is all about here and now.

The Sermon on the Mount is the New Testament parallels the Hebrews' interaction with *Yahweh* at Sinai in the Old Testament. Mount Sinai is where the Jewish people receive instruction on how to live in the here and now. There is more to salvation than what comes after you die, and there is more to the Christian life. There was no need for *Yeshua* to teach for three-and-a-half years if the now wasn't important.

Do not misunderstand. *Shmayal* is our eternal reward for the faithfulness we have shown here. But heaven and the world to come are not our main focus. Salvation involves *Yahweh's* purpose, His will. He has a greater plan than simply taking you to heaven when you are done with your life. He has things He wants you to do for his name's sake, this to accomplish for his glory. He wants you to get involved.

He saves you, in part, to do his will, which is exactly what *Shawol* says in *Ephesyayeeta*. "You are saved by grace through faith." You do not earn it. It is God's gift. (*Ephesyayeeta*[17] 2:8-10) Explains why *Yahweh* has saved you:

> For by grace, you have been saved through faith; and that not of yourselves, it is a gift of *Yahweh*; not as result of works, so that no one may boast. For we are his workmanship, created in Christ *Yeshua* for good works, which *Yahweh* prepared beforehand so that we would walk in them.

Know then that the Kingdom of Heaven is at hand. (*Louko*[13] 10:8-9) says,

> When you enter a town and are welcomed, eat what is set before you. Heal the sick who are there and tell them, "The kingdom of God is near you."

"Near" meaning "at hand." You can reach it, you can touch it, you can feel it. It is here and now. It is real.

If you do not understand that the Kingdom of God is a present reality intended to transform, instruct, direct, and guide your life, then you are missing a lot of what it is to be a follower of *Yeshua*. You will go to heaven one day when you die…praise the Lord…but what about here and now? Don't be too busy living in this world that you miss the everyday presence of the Kingdom of Heaven. Do not live in your past or in your future. Live in the present reality. *Yeshua* said, "the Kingdom of heaven is at hand," which is an Aramaic idiom meaning live in the present reality, live day by day, hour by hour, minute by minute, this way you heal your past and secure your future because you trust in *Yeshua* completely.

Why did *Yeshua* teach about the *Malkout Shmaya*⁹?

Because it is absolutely essential to understand his mission, it is also essential in understanding yours. If you can grasp who He is and was and what He continues to do, then you can begin to understand who you are and what you should be doing. If you are part of the *Malkout Shmaya*, then *Yeshua* is your king and you will obey Him.

You will get this if you understand who He was, what He was all about. What mattered to Him will be much clearer to you as to who you are and what you should be about to do.

The Operation of the Kingdom of Heaven

When we speak of the Kingdom of God or the Kingdom of Heaven, we are really speaking primarily of three things:

1. *Malko* - *Yeshua* is our king
2. *Malkoutho* - *Yeshua* rules over the kingdom
3. *Neshe* - We are a "citizen" of the kingdom, a subject

Yeshua, in his humanity and humility, always speaks in roundabout ways of himself. He never comes out and claims to be the *Mshiho*[10]. He always uses synonyms. In

Louko 22 when the High Priest demands to know if *Yeshua* is the *Mshiho*, the response is, "You said it."

Regardless, *Yeshua* is king in the Kingdom of Heaven. And as *Malko*[19], He rules and reigns. *Yeshua* has the right to exercise dominion over his subjects – us. Since the *Malkout Shmaya*[9] is here and *Yeshua* is *Malko*[19], we must consider if we are a *neshe*[21] If so, does He rule in your life?

The concept of *Malkout* first appears in *Shemoth* 15:18, which says, "The Lord shall reign for ever and ever." In Hebrew, this says, "*Adonai yemloch leolam vaed*." This is said after the miraculous deliverance of the Jewish nation from *Metsrayin* and the people break out in prophetic praise of the One who saved them. They conclude the praise by saying, "To rule and reign, there must be a redemption." Biblically speaking, redemption comes before ruling.

First you redeem, and that act gives you the right to rule. Remember *Shawol's*[16] admonition: We are bought with a price. We are not our own. In other words, we are subject to someone else. *Yeshua* redeemed us so that He might rule over us. There was purpose in His redemption. He wants to rule in our lives. *Yeshua* proves this when He commands evil spirits to depart. This act of dominion and rule proved to the disciples that the Kingdom of Heaven is at hand.

The Kingdom of Heaven terminology was very popular in pharisaic thought. It was used all the time. However, *Yeshua* adopted this terminology to be a designation of his movement.

When *Yeshua* speaks about the Kingdom of Heaven, He is talking about those who submit to his kingship. These are the Kingdom subjects, those who have submitted to his rule. Who are these people? They are the poor in spirit, the mourners, the meek, those who hunger and thirst after righteousness, the merciful, the pure in heart, the peacemakers, and those who are persecuted for his name's sake. These are his subjects in the Kingdom of Heaven. This is what the Beatitudes mean.

But the Kingdom is not something we possess. We do not own the Kingdom; the Kingdom owns us. *Yeshua* redeemed us therefore He rules. And if we submit to is redemption, we must submit to his authority. He becomes our *Morio*[5]. Many know him as a Savior, but fewer acknowledge him as *Morio* and *Malko*[91].

Eremos[26] **Cave**

A short walk away in the *Eremos* Cave – one of the best kept secrets in the area, in my opinion.

Eremos Cave

Seen by only about 5% of the pilgrims who visit *Yesrael*[27], this tiny cave was a significant holy site in the early centuries of Christianity. It was preserved in the memory of *Yeshua's* followers as the "deserted place" where He would often come for prayer and rest from the crowds.

My favorite passage, likely referring to this location, is from *Morqos*[12].

> In the morning, a great while before day, he rose and went out to a lonely place, and there he prayed. And *Kepha*[2] and those who were with him followed him, and they found him and said to him, "Everyone is searching for you" (*Morqos*[12] 1:35-37)

(*Louko*[13] 11:1-4):

Imagine being one of *Yeshua's* disciples awakened by the *Morio's* movements in the pre-dawn hours and observing *Yeshua* slip away from the entourage to commune with his Father. It's glorious to consider that *Yahweh* the Son, who enjoys unbroken union and communion with his Father and the Spirit, still carved out specific times of prayer from his exhausting schedule (the earlier verses indicate He had been healing and ministering all day). Would you be tempted to follow him at a distance and listen to his prayers? It seems that some of the Apostles did just that, finally begging, "Lord teach us to pray."

Perhaps more events took place in the cave in the hillside of *Eremos* overlooking the Sea of Galilee:

Yeshua often went to a solitary place to pray (*Mattai*[4] 28:16; *Morqos*[12] 6:46). Perhaps *Yeshua* prayed at this lonely spot. It is mentioned that *Yeshua* went 30 times to an *eremos* place to pray.

Certainly, he prayed after his cousin *Yohannon*[28] was beheaded by Herodos Antipas (*Morqos*[12] 6:14). Some of *Yeshua's* followers wanted to make him a king even if it meant using violent methods. When *Yeshua* refused, some of his disciples did not understand. He will soon take his Apostles to Caesarea Philippi and announce to them for the first time that he is next to die. So, *Yeshua* spent like many hours praying with his father to receive strength to continue his journey. We all need to get away, pray, and spend time alone with our Heavenly Father.

Andre sitting inside the Eremos Cave

Both the *Eremos* Grotto and *Yeshua*'s instructions in the Sermon on the Mount invite us to set aside a special place in our home where we can pour out our hearts to the Father. We may choose to do our alone time anywhere: our car, outdoors, or a secluded spot at home. What makes the space priceless is that it's consecrated for communion with our Abba.

Here's some good news. You can carry your *Eremos*[26] Grotto with you wherever you go, reserved in the inner chamber of your heart, where the *Abba* is welcome and can commune with you. You can be sitting on an airplane, standing in line at a store, or waiting in a traffic jam, and still slip away to the *Eremos* Grotto deep within you.

Lower down at the foot of the hill lies the area of springs known as *Tabgha*.

The pilgrim Egeria, who spent three years in the Holy Land, sometime between 383 and 395 AD, tells of a cave in the hillside at the "seven springs."

> On the hill which rises nearby is a grotto, upon which the Lord ascended when he taught the Beatitudes.

The hillcrest of *Eremos* offers a beautiful view over the lake and surrounding towns.

Saint Peter's Primacy Church

After the hike down from the cave, the group will arrive at Peter's Primacy Church. A spot on the left side near the water offers a great place to talk, teach, and study.

From this vantage point, you can see *Via Maris,* Mount *Arabel*[86], and the city of Tiberias.

Straight south is the far side of the Sea of Galilee where the *Nahar Yarden* leaves the lake. To the southwest is a hill with white buildings on it. This is Hellenised Tiberias, with a mixed population of Roman and Jewish inhabitants in the first century. Today, it is the modern Jewish town of Tiberias. To the west of the lake is Mount *Arabel* and the *Via Maris*[31]. This is likely the road *Yeshua* took when He came from *Natseret*. You can also see *Magdala*[71], a very important fishing Jewish town on the far western side of the lake.

View of Mount Arabel from St. Peter Primacy Church

Much of *Yeshua's* ministry was here on the northwestern side of the lake (where you are located and touring today). This lies in what the scholars call the "Gospel Triangle":

Korazin, Beth-Saida, and *Kfar-Nahoum.* Seventy percent of *Yeshua's* teachings took place in this area. This is where *Kepha, Ya'coub*[39], and *Yohannon*[28] would have fished. The hot springs in the area attract a great many fish... and fishermen.

Saint Peter's Primacy Church

Yeshua Calls His Disciples

Yeshua invoked three levels of discipleship when he called his followers:

- Come and See
- Follow Me
- Obedience and Surrender

Let's set the stage by reading (*Morqos*[12] 1:14-19):

> After *Yohannon* was put in prison, *Yeshua* went into Galilee, proclaiming the good news of *Yahweh*. "The time has come," he said. "The kingdom of *Yahweh* has come near. Repent and believe the good news!"
>
> As *Yeshua* walked beside the Sea of Galilee, he saw *Kepha*[2] and his brother *Andreaos*[38] casting a net into the lake, for they were fishermen. "Come, follow me," *Yeshua* said, "and I will send you out to fish for people." At once, they left their nets and followed him.
>
> When he had gone a little farther, he saw *Ya'coub* son of *Zebedee*[40] and his brother *Yohannon*[28] in a boat, preparing their nets. Without delay, he called them, and they left their father Zebedee in the boat with the hired men and followed him.

This shoreline is believed to be the spot where *Yeshua* called *Kepha* and *Andreaos*. Just a little way to the east is where *Ya'coub*[39] and *Yohannon*[28], the sons of *Zebedee*[40] and partners with *Kepha* and *Andreaos*[38], likely had their own boats fishing. *Yeshua* calls them to follow him. At once, they leave their nets, and from this point on, they are disciples of *Yeshua*.

(*Yohannon* 1:35-51):

> But that raises the question: why would someone be willing to abandon their occupation at their

first interaction with *Yeshua*? Let me clarify. This is not their first interaction with *Yeshua*.

Again, the next day, *Yohannon* stood with two of his disciples. And looking at *Yeshua* as He walked, he said, "Behold the Lamb of *Yahweh*!" The two disciples heard him speak, and they followed *Yeshua*. Then *Yeshua* turned, and seeing them following, said to them, "What do you seek?" They said to him, "Rabbi" (which is to say, when translated, Teacher), "where are You staying?" He said to them, "Come and see." They came and saw where He was staying, and remained with him that day (now it was about the tenth hour).

One of the two who heard *Yohannon* speak and followed him, was *Andreaos, Kepha's* brother. He first found his own brother Simon, and said to him, "We have found the 'Messiah' (which is translated the Christ). And he brought him to *Yeshua*. Now, when *Yeshua* looked at him, He said, "You are *Shimon*, the son of *Yonnon*[147]. You shall be called *Kepha*," (which is translated, a Stone).

The following day, *Yeshua* wanted to go to Galilee, and He found *Philipus*[41] and said to him, "Follow Me." Now *Pilipus* was from *Beth-saida*, the city of *Andreaos*[38] and *Kepha*[2]. *Pilipus*[41] found *Nathanael*[46] and said to him, "We have found him of whom *Moshe* in the law, and also the prophets, wrote—*Yeshua* of *Natseret*[33], the son of Joseph."

And *Nathanael* said to him, "Can anything good come out of *Natseret?*" *Pilipus* said to him, "Come and see."

Yeshua saw *Nathanael* coming toward him, and said of him, "Behold, an Israelite indeed, in whom is no deceit!" *Nathanael* said to him, "How do You know me?"

Yeshua answered and said to him, "Before *Pilipus* called you, when you were under the fig tree, I saw you." *Nathanael*[46] answered and said to *him,* "Rabbi, You are the Son of *Yahweh*! You are the King of *Yesrael!*"

Yeshua answered and said to him, "Because I said to you, 'I saw you under the fig tree,' do you believe? You will see greater things than these." And He said to him, "Most assuredly, I say to you, hereafter you shall see heaven open, and the angels of *Yahweh* ascending and descending upon the Son of Man."

The key words in this section are the words "come and see." They are in the invitation in verses 39 and 46. The summary comes in the closing of verses 50 and 51: "You believe because you saw Me, but you will see greater things than that."

This is the first stage of *Yeshua's* discipleship:

Stage One: Come and See

In this stage, people are seeking the promises of *Yeshua*. They witness his miracles and great things happen around them. This is when you first start going to church. You watch and observe, checking everything out, especially when you are a new believer and hungry to learn more.

So, Stage One is observing and trying to understand.

Stage Two: To Follow

(*Morqos*[12] 1:1-19) represents a different call of *Yeshua*. After you see and observe, you must follow. *Morqos* not only skips all the information found in *Yohannon*[28], but he also condensed the longer story of *Kepha's* call. Let's go back and look at the scene that took *Kepha*[2] from a stage one disciple to a stage two disciple.

(*Louko*[13] 5:1-11) says:

> One day, as *Yeshua* was standing by the Lake of Gennesaret[43], with the people crowding around him and listening to the word of *Yahweh,* he saw at the water's edge two boats, left there by the fishermen, who were washing their nets. He got into one of the boats, the one belonging to *Kepha*, and asked him to put out a little from shore. Then he sat down and taught the people from the boat. When he had finished speaking, he said to *Kepha,* "Put out into deep water, and let down the nets for a catch.

Kepha[2] answered, "Master, we've worked hard all night and haven't caught anything. But because you say so, I will let down the nets.

When they had done so, they caught such a large number of fish that their nets began to break. So they signaled their partners in the other boat to come and help them, and they came and filled both boats so full that they began to sink.

When *Kepha* saw this, he fell at *Yeshua's* knees and said, "Go away from me, Lord; I am a sinful man!" For he and all his companions were astonished at the catch of fish they had taken, and so were *Ya'coub*[39] and *Yohannon,* the sons of *Zebedee*[40], *Kepha's* partners.

Then *Yeshua* said to *Kepha,* "Don't be afraid; from now on you will fish for people." So, they pulled their boats up on shore, left everything and followed him.

It is important to remember that the story of *Kepha's* call took place in this area around the Sea of Galilee where we are currently standing outside the church on the shoreline.

Let's examine the verses more closely. Let's start with verse 2:

He saw at the water's edge two boats, left there by the fishermen, who were washing their nets.

There are seven springs located near the north-western shore of the lake. This is where first century fishermen came to fish. The fresh springs were used by fishermen to wash their nets. In this area, many small dark basalt stones were found that have round shaped holes in them. They were used to add weight to the nets so they would sink when cast into the water.

The cold, fresh water springs (originating from *Mount Hermon*) mixed with the warmer water of the Sea of Galilee and the resulting lukewarm water attracted fish to the area.

Look at verse 3:

> He got into one of the boats, the one belonging to *Kepha's*, and asked him to put out a little from shore. Then he sat down and taught the people from the boat.

Why did *Yeshua* get into one of the boats and why *Kepha's*?

First, note that *Kepha*[2] owned a boat. This implies a degree of success in fishing. Secondly, *Yeshua* wanted the boat because the area acted like a natural amphitheatre, able to amplify his voice when He spoke to the people on the shore.

Note that the Bible says *Yeshua* sat down. This is a common action for a Rabbi. Sitting indicated the gravity of what he was about to say. *Yeshua* is preparing *Kepha* for the future readying him to listen and then to teach what the lessons He will deliver.

When *Yeshua* finishes, He tells *Kepha* to launch out in the deep. This is a metaphor, indicating that *Kepha's* turn to go into a deeper more personal relationship with *Yeshua* has come. Read verse 4:

> *When he had finished speaking, he said to Kepha, "Put out into deep water, and let down the nets for a catch.*

Kepha is full of pride. After all, he is a very successful fisherman. He knows what he is doing. He is likely thinking *Yeshua* should stick to teaching because, clearly, *Yeshua* knows nothing of fishing. He is a *Rav*[44] and not a fisherman. It is very possible that *Kepha* only complies to prove *Yeshua's* wrong.

Consider *Kepha's* mocking tone:

> *Kepha answered, "Master, we've worked hard all night and haven't caught anything. But because you say so, I will let down the nets."*

Verse 6 shocks *Kepha* completely out of his complacency:

> *When they had done so, they caught such a large number of fish that their nets began to break.*

This was the moment *Kepha* realizes he is wrong! How many times do we think we have it all together, we are completely self-confident, and we know it all, only to realize that we know nothing when hardships come. It is a humbling moment to realize we are wrong. This is what happened to *Kepha*. He realized *Yeshua* is much more than the average *Rav*[44]. He is the *Mshiho*[10]! *Kepha* immediately recognizes his own sin.

> When Kepha saw this, he fell at Yeshua's knees and said, "Go away from me, Lord; I am a sinful man!"

This is a moment of revelation to *Kepha*, and he follows *Yeshua* from then on.

> Then Yeshua said to Kepha, "Don't be afraid; from now on you will fish for people." So, they pulled their boats up on shore, left everything and followed him.

Kepha follows *Yeshua* for almost three years.

Stage Three: Obedience and Surrender

What happens to *Kepha* after *Yeshua's* death and resurrection?

(*Yohannon*[28] 21:1-11) tells us:

> Afterward, *Yeshua* appeared again to his disciples by the Sea of Galilee. It happened this way: *Kepha*, *Tooma*[45], also known as Didymus, *Nathanael*[46] from Cana in Galilee, the sons of Zebedee[40], and two other disciples were together. "I'm going out to fish," *Kepha* told them, and they said, "We'll go with you." So, they went out and got into the boat, but that night they caught nothing.
>
> Early in the morning, *Yeshua* stood on the shore, but the disciples did not realize that it was *Yeshua*.

He called out to them, "Friends, haven't you any fish?"

"No," they answered.

He said, "Throw your net on the right side of the boat and you will find some." When they did, they were unable to haul the net in because of the large number of fish.

Then the disciple whom *Yeshua* loved said to *Kepha*, "It is the Lord!" As soon as *Kepha* heard him say, "It is the Lord," he wrapped his outer garment around him (for he had taken it off) and jumped into the water. The other disciples followed in the boat, towing the net full of fish, for they were not far from shore, about a hundred yards. When they landed, they saw a fire burning coals there with fish on it, and some bread.

Yeshua said to them, "Bring some of the fish you have just caught." So *Kepha* climbed back into the boat and dragged the net ashore. It was full of large fish, 153, but even with so many, the net was not torn.

Doesn't this miracle sound just like the first miracle of catching fish? Again, as a reminder, this story here takes place after *Yeshua's* death, burial, and resurrection. *Kepha* returns to Galilee to his old fishing life. It is the same place and setting as the first miracle. They had gone back to the place where it had all started for them.

Kepha is a broken failure. He has denied *Yeshua* three times. He has forsaken what he knows is true, run away, and is, essentially, hiding. Ever feel like this? But just like before, *Kepha* has spent hours fishing and caught nothing. After you've been with *Yeshua*, there is no going back to your old life. It won't be the same. The fish are the same. The lake is the same. But *Kepha* is different, so it can't be the same for him, not ever again.

When you are at your most broken, *Yeshua* can truly work to rebuild your life. Your ego and pride are defeated, so the *Roho-Kodsho*[8] can take over. The more broken you are the more *Yeshua* will work on your heart. The Lord wants your destiny, your calling, and your vocation in life to be released, but this can only happen when you lose everything in life important to you so there are no distractions between you and him. This is the moment when your ministry is released.

This happened to me. When I was at my most broken, *Yeshua* revealed my calling. I authored a book about it: *One Friday in Jerusalem*. But be warned: do not compare yourselves to others. You have a destiny that *Yahweh* wants to reveal to you. It is unique and different from anyone else's. Surrender to *Yahweh* completely, for it is not about you or me at all. It is about the *Malkout Shmaya*[9].

Kepha is a gifted fisherman, but the Lord wants him to be a fisher of souls. *Kepha* has a greater calling and destiny than fishing. And this is true for all of us. Our destiny is bigger than we think. Once *Kepha* realizes this, *he* plunges into full-time ministry and never looks back.

Look what *Yeshua* said to *Kepha* in (*Yohannon*[28] 21:12-19):

> *Yeshua* said to them, "Come and have breakfast." None of the disciples dared ask him, "Who are you?" They knew it was the Lord. *Yeshua* came, took the bread and gave it to them, and did the same with the fish. This was now the third time *Yeshua* appeared to his disciples after he was raised from the dead.
>
> When they had finished eating, *Yeshua* said to *Kepha*, "*Kepha* son of *Yohannon*, do you love me more than these?"
>
> "Yes, Lord," he said, "you know that I love you."
>
> *Yeshua* said, "Feed my lambs."
>
> *Again, Yeshua* said, "*Kepha*, son of *Yohannon*, do you love me?"
>
> He answered, "Yes, Lord, you know that I love you."
>
> *Yeshua* said, "Take care of my sheep." The third time he said to him, "*Kepha* son of *Yohannon*[28], do you love me?"
>
> *Kepha* was hurt because *Yeshua* asked him the third time, "Do you love me?" He said, "Lord, you know all things; you know that I love you."
>
> *Yeshua said,* "Feed my sheep. Very truly I tell you, when you were younger, you dressed yourself and

went where you wanted; but when you are old, you will stretch out your hands, and someone else will dress you and lead you where you do not want to go." *Yeshua* said this to indicate the kind of death by which *Kepha* would glorify *Yahweh*. Then he said to him, "Follow me!"

The first time *Yeshua* asks *Kepha,* "Do you love me," *Yeshua* uses the Aramaic word *hobo*[47]. The second time, *Yeshua* uses *rahmani*[48]. On the third occasion, *Yeshua* uses *ahab*[49]. This is why *Kepha* is so hurt. He finally understands it is not about him anymore. It is all about a relationship of love with the Master.

There is a difference between being a fisherman and being a shepherd. Fishing is a task, but shepherding is an activity of the heart. *Yeshua* was giving *Kepha* a new vocation. *Kepha's* heart needs to be healed, and only after that healing can *Kepha* serve *Yahweh*.

Kepha has to surrender all and then obey. Once he does, he completes his discipleship training and he serves *Yahweh* for the rest of his life. We have to surrender all, give *Yeshua* the priority of everything over our own lives, and only then can we walk in the spirit and change other people.

The Rock where according to tradition Yeshua and the Apostles ate breakfast

Break Time

At this point, it's a good idea to take a break to pray and reflect on the stages of discipleship that changed the life of *Kepha.*

Kfar-Nahoum[36]

After a bus ride, you will arrive in *Kfar-Nahoum.* It is a very important Franciscan Catholic site, so it is important to follow their rules. They are very strict, especially about modest dress, holy dress, so the ones who have short sleeves or shorts will need to cover up. Everyone should bring Bibles, sunglasses, and water – and try to be as quiet as possible. It is a five-minute walk to the main entrance, a great place for photos.

Kfar-Nahoum – The Town of Yeshua

Short History of *Kfar-Nahoum*[36]

Kfar-Nahoum is known as the hometown of *Yeshua*. *Nahoum* means "comfort" in Aramaic. This is the village where *Yeshua* found rest and comfort. *Kfar-Nahoum* was one of the most important cities on the north-western side of the lake in the first century, because it was a border city between Herodos Philippi and Herodos Antipas.

Kfar-Nahoum was a fishing village established during the time of the Hasmonean Dynasty, around 100 BC, among other Jewish villages in Galilee, like *Korazin*[34], *Beth-Saida*[35], *Natseret*[33], *Kanna*[50], and so on. *Kfar-Nahoum* is located on the northern shore of the Sea of Galilee. With a population of between 1,500 and 2,000, it was considered large, hence the Aramaic word *kfar* ("large"). But if any name of a village starts with *Beth*, which means "house," it is a small town, usually with 200 to 400 people, for example, *Beth-Lhem*[63], *Beth-Saida*, etc.

Be sure to notice the first century basalt stones of the original synagogue. Looking to the east, the group can see a modern church, beneath which is a house that was converted into a church during the Byzantine period. It is believed this house belonged to *Kepha*.

The town of Kfar-Nahoum

Inside the Synagogue

Obviously, the most important building in a Jewish town was the synagogue. In Hebrew, the word for synagogue is *Beth-knesset*[51]. The synagogue was discovered in 1838 and excavated by Heinrich Kohl and Carl Watzinger, two German archaeologists who researched ancient synagogues in Galilee. It was built in the 4th to 5th centuries atop the ruins of a first century synagogue.

The white limestone and the ornaments indicate that a wealthy Jewish community thrived here in the Byzantine Era. Archaeological excavations have revealed two ancient synagogues built one over the other. The original *Beth-knesset,* dating from *Yeshua's* time, is under the one that stands today. You can see the basalt stone if you look to the right side and down inside a square-shaped opening, called the *genizah*. It was a storage area in a *Beth-knesset,* perhaps designated for the temporary storage of worn-out, Hebrew/Aramaic language religious scrolls.

Two Synagogues – basalt on top of limestone

This is a large *Beth-knesset,* indicating a large town. The size of the *Beth-knesset* reflects the size of the population of the city. To the south is a long iron beam above which is a doorframe. This means the *Beth-knesset* had two floors. To the left of the doorframe, there is the base of a pillar that once supported the second floor.

Second floor door frame

Yeshua preached many times in the *Beth-knesset*[51] of *Kfar-Nahoum*[36]. While in Galilee, this city is where *Yeshua* stayed.

Why Is Kfar-Nahoum Known as the Hometown of *Yeshua*?

Consider (*Mattai*[4] 4:13-16):

> And leaving *Natseret*[33], He came and dwelt in *Kfar-Nahoum*, which is by the sea, in the regions of Zebulun and Naphtali, that it might be fulfilled

which was spoken by *Yeshayahu*[52] the prophet, saying:

"The land of *Zebulun* and the land of *Naphtali*, By the way of the sea, beyond the Jordan, Galilee of the Gentiles: The people who sat in darkness have seen a great light, And upon those who sat in the region and shadow of death Light has dawned."

Though *Yeshua* was from *Natseret*, he moved to *Kfar-Nahoum*. This is his hometown. When *Mattai* 9:1 says, "*Yeshua* stepped into a boat, crossed over and came to his own town," he is not referring to *Natseret* but to *Kfar-Nahoum*.

A boat on the Sea of Galilee

Yeshayahu's[52] Prophecy

In *Yeshayahu* chapters 7 through 12, the prophet is dealing with what could be called "The Assyrian Crisis."

One of the kings in *Yeshayahu's* time was *Ahaz* of Judah. During his reign, he was worried that *Yesrael* and *Syria* would join forces to conquer Judah. *Yahweh,* through *Yeshayahu,* had something to say about all this. *Yahweh* sent word to King *Ahaz*, telling him not to worry about the Northern Confederation, "Take heed, and be quiet; do not fear or be fainthearted" *Yeshayahu* 7:4. *Yahweh* said about this confederation or plan, "It shall not stand" *Yeshayahu* 7:7. *Ahaz* should have believed *Yahweh,* but he didn't pay much attention to the Lord's Word and hired the nation of Assyria to come over and crush the Northern Confederation. He paid them well in silver and gold from the house of *Yahweh.*

When *Ahaz* didn't pay attention to *Yahweh* and devised his own plan, he was guilty of unbelief, for which he would be punished. After the Assyrians crushed the Northern Confederation, they just kept right on coming south, right into *Yehudia*[53] and *Or-Shlem*[5]. The King got more than he bargained for because of his unbelief.

Yeshayahu[52] chapters 7 and 8 tell us about these things. Chapter 8 recalls how *Yahweh* used Assyria to punish both kingdoms of *Yesrael* and *Yehudia.* At the end of chapter 8, there is a picture of the coming gloom and darkness as the Assyrians roll through with their devastating military force. The last verse of chapter 8 shows the people looking around and seeing trouble, darkness, and anguish.

In chapter 9, *Yeshayahu* speaks to both *Yesrael* and *Yehudia* before the Babylonian Exile. *Yesrael* and *Syria* are pressuring *Yehudia* to form a coalition against Assyria.

King *Ahaz* of *Yehudia* is afraid to go against Assyria, so he sends an enormous sum to Assyria, asking for their help.

Yehudia was feeling powerless. As their enemies only seemed to grow in strength and tighten their grasp, they didn't know if *Yahweh* was for them or against them or if He had simply abandoned them.

As chapter 9 opens, the prophet claims that the gloom will not last forever. The pessimistic picture of chapter 8 gives way to brilliant light in chapter 9. Things will be bad in the aftermath of this Assyrian crisis, but not forever.

There is still reason for hope. *Yahweh's* plan will be carried out! A time will come, *Yeshayahu* says, when darkness will be dispelled by the Light. Gloom will be replaced with joy and *Yahweh* will have a nation of people ruled by a perfect king:

> Nevertheless, there will be no more gloom for those who were in distress. In the past, he humbled the land of *Zebulun* and the land of *Naphtali*, but in the future, he will honor Galilee of the nations, by the Way of the Sea, beyond the Jordan.
>
> The people walking in darkness
> have seen a great light;
> on those living in the land of deep darkness
> a light has dawned.
> You have enlarged the nation
> and increased their joy;
> they rejoice before you
> as people rejoice at the harvest,

This makes sense as to why *Kfar-Nahoum*[36] was a place of darkness. It was in the region that was constantly being overrun by foreign powers, sitting right along a natural invasion corridor, the *Via Maris*[31]. It had been invaded so many times that it became known as the "Galilee of the Nations" or the "Galilee of the Gentiles."

The Via Maris leading to Kfar-Nahoum

The Kfar-Nahoum Synagogue in Yeshua's Day

Let's examine some events that took place in this location. Read (*Louko*[13] 7:1-9):

Interestingly, this *Beth-Knesset*[51] was built by a Roman centurion, which is indicative of the influence of the Gentiles in Galilee. And though the man had faith that *Yeshua* could heal, he clearly didn't think he was worthy to have *Yeshua* enter his house, possibly believing that *Yeshua* would be in some way defiled by a Gentile. Note that he sent Jewish elders to *Yeshua* but did not come by himself.

Read (*Morqos*[12] 1:21-28):

> A demon is cast out, having entered into the *Beth-Knesset* itself. This was part of the fulfillment of *Yeshayahu's* prophecy.

Demons are a force of darkness. But there is more to it than this. Where is the man with the demon? Inside the *Beth-Knesset*. Is he there to meet *Yeshua*? No. What is a possessed man doing inside a *Beth-Knesset*? The darkness in the region was so great that in many cases, the people did not even know the hold *Shaitan*[54] had on their lives. Is this man foaming at the mouth or screaming out at the top of his lungs? No. Is he asking for help or are others asking *Yeshua* to cast out the *Shaitan*? No. The *Shaitan* is hidden.

Likewise, there are many people in church every Sunday who are demonically influenced and no one is aware of it, including those who are being influenced. Darkness is deceptive. I have many personal stories regarding *Shaitan*. When the anointing comes on you, the *Shaitan* is exposed. In *One Friday in Jerusalem*, I mention a few of these stories. If you are interested and not scared, you can read the book; you can find it on Amazon.

Yeshua Teaches That He Is the Bread of Life

Read (*Yohannon* 6:35-4):

> "I am the Bread of Life" in *Yohannon* 6:35 is one of the "I Am" statements of *Yeshua*. *Yeshua* used the same phrase, "I am," in seven declarations

about himself. In all seven, He combines "I am" with tremendous metaphors expressing his relationship toward the world. All appear in the book of *Yohannon*.

In (*Yohannon* 6:35), *Yeshua* says, "I am the bread of life; whoever comes to me shall not hunger, and whoever believes in me shall never thirst." In Aramaic, it reads:

Eyneno: I am
Lahmo: bread
Dhayo: of life

Bread, a staple, represents a basic dietary item in the Middle East. It is so important in the local culture that it is expected at every meal. A person can survive a long time on only bread and water. Bread becomes synonymous with food in general. We use the phrase "breaking bread together" to indicate the sharing of a meal with someone. Bread also plays an integral part of the Jewish P*hischa*[5] meal. The Jews were instructed to eat unleavened bread during the *Phischa* feast and then for seven days following as a celebration of the Exodus from *Metsrayin*[24].

Yeshua used terms, idioms, and analogies most people understood especially in the light of *Phischa*. He knew the Jewish leaders and *Yahweh's* people would follow his reference to bread. Through the human comprehension of hunger, a physical need, *Yeshua* explained how our every desire (not just for physical food but for everything spiritual) would be satisfied in him.

Andre guiding a group in Kfa-Nahoum Synagogue

All of this plays into the scene being described in *Yohannon* chapter 6 when *Yeshua* uses the term "bread of life." The day before *Yeshua* says these things, he feeds the five thousand. He was trying to get away from the crowds, but to no avail. He had crossed the Sea of Galilee. The crowd followed Him. *Philippos*[56] wonders how they will feed everyone because they do not have enough money. *Yeshua* chides *Phillipos* for his lack of faith. Finally, *Andreaos*[38] brings a lad to *Yeshua,* a boy who has five small loaves of bread and two fish. With that amount, *Yeshua* miraculously feeds the throng with lots of food to spare.

Afterward, *Yeshua* and the Apostles cross to the other side of Galilee. When the crowd sees that *Yeshua* has left, they follow him again. *Yeshua* takes this moment to teach them a lesson. He accuses the crowd of ignoring his miraculous signs and only following Him for the "free meal."

(*Yohannon*[28] 6:27):

> *Yeshua* tells them in the synagogue, "Do not labor for the food that perishes, but for the food that endures to eternal life, which the Son of Man will give to you. For on him *Yahweh* the Father has set his seal." In other words, they are so fascinated by the miracle that they have missed the fact that their *Mshiho*[10] has come.

So, the Jews ask *Yeshua* for a sign that He was sent from *Yahweh* (as if the miraculous feeding and the walking across the water weren't enough). They tell *Yeshua* that *Yahweh* gave them manna during the desert wandering. *Yeshua* responds by telling them that they need to ask for the true manna, the life-giving bread from heaven. When they ask *Yeshua* for this bread, *Yeshua* startles them by saying, "I am the bread of life; whoever comes to me shall not hunger, and whoever believes in me shall never thirst."

This is a phenomenal statement! First, by equating himself with bread, *Yeshua* is saying He is *essential* for life. Second, the life *Yeshua* is referring to is not physical but eternal. *Yeshua* is trying to get the Jews' thinking off the physical realm and into the spiritual realm. He is contrasting what He brings spiritually as their *Mshiho*[10] with the physical bread He miraculously created the previous day.

Third (and very important), *Yeshua* makes another claim to deity, the first of the "I am" statements in *Yohannon's* gospel. The phrase "I AM" is the covenant name of *Yahweh*, revealed to *Moshe* at the burning bush in *Shemoth*²² 3:14. The phrase speaks of self-sufficient existence (what theologians call "as deity"), which is an attribute only *Yahweh* possesses. Those present automatically understand his comment as a claim to deity.

The word "*Yahweh*" is formed by combining the Hebrew words *Haya* ("past"), *Hoven* ("present"), and *Yehyeh* ("future"). "I am the past, present, and future" – the deity of *Yahweh*. His character and identity are revealed in the name. Here, *Yeshua* is declaring that he is *Yahweh*.

Fourth, notice the words "come" and "believe." This is an invitation for his listeners to place their faith in *Yeshua* as the *Mshiho*¹⁰ and Son of *Yahweh*. This invitation is found throughout *Yohannon's* gospel. Coming to *Yeshua* involves making a choice to forsake the world and to follow him. The people are encouraged to follow the light and not the darkness. Believing in *Yeshua* means placing our faith in him – understand that He is who He says He is…He will do what He says He will do…and He is the only one who can. He is everything past, present, and future.

Finally, there are the words "hunger and thirst." It must be noted that *Yeshua* isn't talking about alleviating physical pangs. The key is found in another statement *Yeshua* made, back in his Sermon on the Mount. In *Mattai*⁴ 5:6, *Yeshua* says, "Blessed are those who hunger and thirst for righteousness, for they shall be satisfied." When *Yeshua* says those who come to Him will never hunger and those who believe in Him will never thirst, He promised to satisfy our hunger and thirst to be made righteous in the sight of *Yahweh*. Again, it is in the spiritual realm and not the physical world.

If we learn anything from the history of human religion, it tells us that people seek to earn their way to heaven. This is a basic human desire. We are created with eternity in mind. The Bible says *Yahweh* has placed (the desire for) eternity in our hearts.

The Bible also tells us there is nothing we can do to earn our way to heaven because we've all sinned (*Roma'yeh*[57] 3:23), and the only thing our sin earns us is death *Roma'yeh* 6:23. No one is righteous in themselves (*Roma'yeh* 3:10).

Our dilemma is a desire we cannot fulfill, no matter what we do. That is where *Yeshua* comes in. He, and He alone, can fulfill the desire in our hearts for righteousness through the Divine Transaction: "For our sake he made him to be sin who knew no sin, so that in him we might become the righteousness of *Yahweh*" (2 *Karinthaus*[58] 5:21). When Christ died on the cross, He took the sins of humankind upon himself and made atonement for them. When we place our faith in him, our sins are imputed to *Yeshua,* and his righteousness is imputed to us. *Yeshua* satisfies our hunger and thirst for righteousness. He is our Bread of Life.

Around the town of *Kfar-Nahoum, Yeshua* performed twenty-one healing miracles. Despite that, few Jews believed in him. They were stubborn. But *Yeshua* was focused. He came to the lost sheep of *Yesrael*. He lived among them. He was the light, but they did not believe in him. Look at what *Yeshua* said in the gospels of *Mattai* and *Louko.* "Woe to the unrepentant cities of *Korazin*[34], *Beth-Saida*[35] and *Kfar-Nahoum*!" These are all Jewish towns located around the northern shore of the Sea of Galilee. This is a prophecy that these three cities would be cursed. Those cities were eventually destroyed and have not been rebuilt.

Read (*Mattai*[4] 11:20–24).

Kepha's House – *Dominus Ecclesias*

You might be wondering where *Yeshua* lived in *Kfar-Nahoum*. (*Morqos*[12] 1:29) says, "As soon as they left the *Beth-knesset*[51] they went with *Ya'coub*[39] and *Yohannon*[28] to the home of *Kepha* and *Andreaos*[38]." So, as we are standing here, let's do what they did. Let's walk over from the *Beth-Knesset* to the house of *Kepha*.

The house is not what you think. A house, in Greek, is called "*insulae*[59]," which means a "compound." Excavations revealed that the houses of the Second Temple Period were arranged in "*insulae*" (blocks) with streets running between them. Generally consisting of a large courtyard surrounded by rooms, the houses were constructed of local basalt stones, and their walls were covered with light colored plaster. Each house had only one entrance, from the street. Inside each *insulae* is a "*kataluma*[60]," which means "guest room." This is the biggest room inside the *insulae* compound, usually kept free for guests and to supply them with food.

The Bible says there was no room in the inn, regarding *Youseph*[61] and *Miriam2* when they travelled to *Beth-Lhem*[63], but this is a weak English translation. There were no inns in the first century – at least not in the way we think of them. The text should read that there was no place in the *kataluma,* the guest room. The Last Supper took place in a *kataluma*. People gathered to pray in a *kataluma*. Families discussed their daily lives and solved family issues in a *kataluma*. It was the most used room in the compound and was likely the site of the earliest gatherings of the Church, for where two or three gathered in *Yeshua's* name, there He is with them.

Whenever you read in the Book of *Ma'aseh*[64] about a church, it is mistranslation – rather, it is misconstrued. Do not think of a church building. The Early Church met in guest rooms, like home groups with no more than 30 people at a time. In the first century, 30 believers was a mega church.

The courtyards were paved with basalt, and staircases were built along their walls, which gave access to the second story or roof. Many ovens have been uncovered in the courtyards, and the houses contained numerous grinding stones made of basalt. Each *insulae*[59] could have around 40 extended families living together in different rooms. There are many such structures in *Kfar-Nahoum,* for the people lived in communities like a tribal would.

It was in *Kepha's insulae* that *Yeshua* also lived.

An insulae with a kataluma in the Center

Do We Know Which Insulae[59] Was *Kepha's*?

There are some hints. The *insula* traditionally held to be *Kepha's* has plastered walls unlike all the other rooms in the area. And it is the only house with a plastered guest room on the west side of the city. Here are some other indicators:

Pottery – At the same time there was a shift in the use to which the room was put. Broken pottery excavated from the floors of mid-first century dwellings indicate normal family use. Thereafter, however, only storage jars and lamps were found. These would be used for public gatherings.

Graffiti – Visitors will see a lot of Aramaic graffiti scratched in the plaster walls, some of which mention *Yeshua* as *Mshiho*[10]. *Kepha* is also mentioned in Aramaic. That is highly unusual in the middle of the first century AD.

By the fourth century, this room had become the centrepiece of a house church that was visited by Egeria, a Christian pilgrim who toured the Holy Land and wrote about it. She tells us that "in *Kfar-Nahoum*[36], the house of the Prince of the Apostles has been made into a church, with its original walls still standing."

By the sixth century, another Christian pilgrim writes and tells us that the house church had been expanded to a basilica, which is the octagonal church. Archaeologists have found all this right here, and so we are confident that this is, in fact, *Kepha's* house where *Yeshua* lived.

Kepha's house – Dominus Ecclesias

The Events That Took Place in Kepha's House

Yeshua healed many people from *Kepha's* house.

Read (*Morqos*[12] 1:29-34):

Notice again the light overcoming the darkness, fulfilling *Yeshayahu's*[52] prophecy. *Yeshua* prays in a solitary place.

Read (*Morqos* 1:35):

What house did *Yeshua* leave? This house. Notice that the light of the world got up to pray while it was still dark so He could bring light into the darkness.

Yeshua forgives and heals a paralysed man.

Read (*Morqos*[12] 2:1-12):

The first verse ends with, "He had come home." In Aramaic it says, "That He is in the house." Which house? Once again, this is probably the house of *Kepha*, which means that the story where people dig out the roof and let down the paralytic man happened right here.

In Jewish culture, people were not allowed to enter the house from the roof. It was not appropriate, because it did not honor or respect the owner of the house. Typically, you entered from the door, and there was often only one entrance into the compound. Roofs were often constructed with a network of branches covered with straw and dirt. First-century roofs in Galilee were usually flat, consisting of timber beams (usually sycamore or cypress) set into the walls about 2-2½ meters or 78–98 inches over the floor, supporting branches or reeds which retained thick layers of earth plaster.

This is what the paralytic man was lowered through. *Yeshua* saw the faith of the friends who had carried the paralysed man. Look what he said in verse 5: "When *Yeshua* saw their faith, he said to the paralysed man, 'Son, your sins are forgiven.'"

But the teachers of the law objected. What did this have to do with darkness and light? This man was brought from the world of darkness to the house, the Church, and the light. He is home. *Yeshua's* light brings life and healing. He is the light that forgives sins, but the darkness hates the light and is confused by it so much so that the teachers of the law accuse *Yeshua* of blasphemy.

Read (*Morqos*[12] 2:13-17):

Yeshua calls *Mattai* and eats with sinners. Once again, *Yeshua* is beside the lake when a large crowd comes to Him, and He begins to teach. As He walks, he sees *Mattai*, the son of *Alphaeus*[65], sitting at the tax collector's booth. "Follow me," *Yeshua* tells him, and *Mattai* gets up and follows.

We don't know where *Mattai's* house was, but it was in this area in one of the *insulaes*. *Yeshua* goes to *Mattai's* house and eats dinner with him in the "*kataluma*[60]." How do the Pharisees respond? They don't like it. What does this have to do with darkness and light? The light is reaching tax collectors like *Mattai*, but the Pharisees can't see what is happening because they are deceived by the dark. Religiosity is darkness.

Yeshua preached every Saturday, every Shabbat, in the *Beth-Knesset*. He walked to and from. The *Beth-Knesset* was likely in easy view of the house where *Yeshua* lived. It is only about thirty meters or a two minute walk. But it probably took *Yeshua* a minimum of 20 minutes to get there! Why? Likely because of the many friends and people who wanted to be in his presence.

Archaeology of Kfar-Nahoum[36]

In the city, there is a stone featuring a carving of the Ark of the Covenant. This is the only stone inscription ever discovered in the Middle East that shows an image of the Ark on wheels. It is a replica, of course, not the original. This stone was found inside the *Beth-Knesset,* which means Jews lived and worshiped *Yahweh* there – proof that *Kfar-Nahoum* was a Jewish town.

The Ark of Covenant on wheels

Look at the pillar with the Jewish symbol of a menorah. One of the oldest symbols of the Jewish faith is a seven-branched candelabrum that was used in the *Hayklo*[3]. It has been said that the menorah is a symbol of the nation of *Yesrael* and its mission was to be "a light unto the nations" (*Yeshayahu*[52] 42:6). The sages emphasize that light is not a violent force; *Yesrael* is to accomplish its mission by setting an example, not by using force. This idea is highlighted in the vision of the Prophet *Zechariah,* who sees a menorah, and *Yahweh* explains: "Not by might, nor by power, but by My spirit" (*zechariah*[66] 4:1-6).

At the center of the menorah (the lowest branch) is a hidden cross. This is the first reconciliation in history between Jews and Christians. At one point in the Byzantine Period, there was a *Beth-Knesset* functioning alongside a church.

The menorah symbol with the hidden cross

Look at the milestone. The inscription on it is in Aramaic.

This was the internet of the first century. The community would write the news of the city, the amount of taxes you had to pay, the distance to make, and other information on it. Milestones are mentioned in the Bible. In the Roman Empire, milestones were originally stone obelisks made from granite, marble, or white limestone – whatever local stone was available. At the center of Rome, the "Golden Milestone" was erected as the presumed center of the Roman Empire. The saying, "All road leads to Rome," came about because the Romans were the first to create a large network of roads to connect their territory. They used milestones to mark the distances.

A milestone in Kfar-Nahoum

> חפיברוכזרחלריוח
> כרחדןמורה
> תיאנרלחח

The Aramaic inscription on this 5th c. column reads: "Alphaeus, son of Zebedee, son of John, placed this column here. May it be ascribed to him as a blessing." Apostolic names like these persisted in the region over the centuries — five of the Apostles were from Capharnaum.

The translation of the Aramaic script written on the milestone

Back to the Bus and Lunch

When we walk back to the bus, I like to take groups to try the *falafel* and *shawarma* sandwiches. (Organize ahead of time.) *Falafel* is a deep-fried ball made from ground chickpeas, fava beans, or both. Herbs, spices, and onions are commonly added to the dough. It is a well-known Middle Eastern dish that most likely originated in *Metsrayim*[24]. It comes inside a pita bread with a lot of salad. It is a vegetarian sandwich.

Shawarma is a Middle Eastern dish consisting of meat cut into thin slices, stacked in a cone-like shape, and roasted on a slowly turning vertical rotisserie or spit. Originally, it was made with lamb, which is now very expensive. Today it is made of turkey or chicken. Lamb is very expensive. It also comes in a pitta bread sandwich with a lot of salad.

I recommend the *falafel* first and then the *shawarma*. There's a great *falafel* song you can find on YouTube.

> Everybody eat the falafel
> all the other food's gonna topple
> everybody's head's gonna bobble
> when they put in their mouth falafel
> Everybody eat the falafel

After lunch, it's time for the Boat Museum.

The Yigal Allon Center in Kibbutz Ginosar[43]

Yigal Allon was born on October 10, 1918. One of the founders of Kibbutz Ginosar, Allon was a pioneer, Commander in Chief of the Palmach and Operational Commander of the Southern Command in the War of Independence 1948. During his political career, he served as Minister of Labor, Minister of Immigration and Absorption, Minister of Education and Culture and Minister of Foreign Affairs. He had strong ties with Israeli Arabs and was a comrade and friend. He believed in coexistence. Yigal died February 29, 1980.

After 6 Years after his death, in 1986, the Sea of Galilee almost dried up completely. Its level dropped to historical lows as a result of a severe drought and exposed its silted bottom.

Moshe and *Yuval*, two brothers who are residents of the same Kibbutz, had a feeling that one day the Sea of Galilee would give them a gift. Both of them were fishermen. One morning in the same year, 1986, when they were walking on the beach, one of the brothers stepped on a rusty nail. They knew it was an archaeological find. They became excited and started to look for more nails. They discovered an old piece of wood under the mud and then another nail. Eventually, they uncovered an ancient boat dating back to the second temple period. This discovery became a turning point in our understanding of first-century life.

A double rainbow appeared in the sky the day of the boat's discovery.

A jar for the fisherman's food and rusty nails

A visit to the museum begins with a movie about the discovery. Then groups have a chance to see the craft. Photography is okay as long as there are no flashes used. Along with the boat, researchers found other artifacts dating back to the first century: ancient nails, a jar where the fishermen preserved their food, and an oil lamp.

The boat's construction conforms to other boats built in that part of the Mediterranean during the period between 100 BC and 200 AD. Constructed primarily of cedar planks joined together by pegged mortise and tenon joints and nails, the boat is shallow drafted with a flat bottom, allowing it to get very close to the shore while fishing. However, the boat is comprised of ten different types of wood, suggesting either a wood shortage or that the boat was made of scraps and had undergone extensive repairs. The boat features four staggered rowing stations as well as a mast.

The boat has been carbon dated to 40 BC (plus or minus 80 years). The evidence of repeated repairs shows the boat was used for several decades, perhaps for nearly a century. When its fishermen owners thought it was beyond repair, they removed all useful wooden parts, and the hull eventually sank to the bottom of the lake where it was covered with mud, which prevented bacterial decomposition.

The Galilee Boat is historically important to Jews as an example of the type used by their ancestors in the first century AD for both fishing and transportation across the lake. Previously, only references made by Roman authors, the Bible, and mosaics had provided archaeologists insight into the construction of these types of vessels.

The boat is also important to Christians because it was the sort used by *Yeshua* and his disciples, several of whom were fishermen. Boats such as this played a large role in *Yeshua's* life and ministry, and are mentioned 50 times in the Gospels, though there is no evidence connecting the Sea of Galilee Boat directly to *Yeshua* or his disciples.

First-Century Boat

Boat Ride on the Sea of Galilee

A boat ride is located outside the museum at the docks. After the group is finished with the museum, the group will walk to the docks. Twins Tours has fashioned a great relationship with the boat crews over the last twenty years. There is often worship music playing in the background as we board the boat. Typically, you begin teaching the moment the boat casts off.

According to the Gospels, *Yeshua's* earthly ministry was centred around the Sea of Galilee. While important events occurred in *Or-Shlem*[5], *Yeshua* spent most of the three years of his ministry along the shore of this freshwater lake. Here, He gave more than half of his parables, and performed most of his miracles.

Most of this area was inhabited by simple, kosher Jewish towns under Herodos Antipas's rule. On the east side of the lake is where the Decapolis used to be, the ten Roman cities that represented the power of Rome. *Hippos*[67] is a mountain where a Roman garrison was built directly to the east of the lake. To the north of *Hippos* is a valley that comes down to the lake in a V-shape. This is the site of *Gedera*[68] where *Yeshua* met the demon possessed man. The east side of the lake was not kosher. It was pure Roman under the control of Herodos Philipus. To the south is where the Jordan River exits the lake heading toward the *Yam-Hamelah*[69] and *Or-Shlem*. That southern region was ruled by Herodos Archelaus, the third brother.

When *Yeshua* mentions in Scripture that they need to cross to the "other side," He was referring to the Roman side of the lake, the pagan side, the Gentile side, which is to the east. This was often scary for the disciples, for they knew what wickedness and idolatry existed there. Every time *Yeshua* wanted to go to the "other side," the disciples grew nervous. But some lessons can only be learned when one steps out of their comfort zone.

To the southwest side of the lake is the town of Tiberias. In the first century, it was a Roman Hellenised town, which means it had a Jewish population. Hellenised Jews had adopted and accepted the Roman way of life. Archaeologists found a *Beth-Knesset* in Roman Hellenised Tiberias with a zodiac calendar pictured on the floor along with many other Roman symbols. What was such a Roman thing doing in a Jewish synagogue (*Beth-Knesset)*? This is the result of Hellenism.

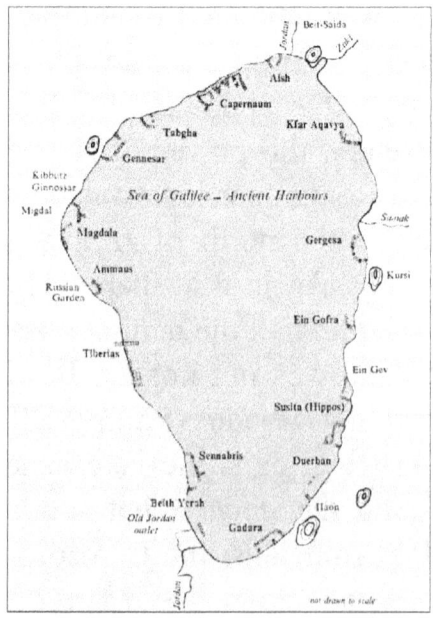

Map of the Sea of Galilee

Names of the Sea of Galilee

Other names for the Sea of Galilee in the Bible are…

1. *Chinnereth,* which is used many times in the Old Testament,
2. *Chinor,* which means "a harp" because of the shape of the lake,
3. *Gennesar,* the Hellenized name that *Josephus* used, which comes from the *Gannei Sarim*, meaning the "gardens of the kings." This refers to the Hasmonean kings who ruled Galilee from 167 BC to 67 BC. This reign converted most of the area to the Jewish faith and established the Jewish towns of *Kfar-Nahoum*[36], *Korazin*[34], *Beth-Saida*[35], and *Magdala*[71]. *Louko* uses the term *Gennesar*[43] in his gospel.
4. The more common New Testament designation is the familiar "Sea of Galilee."
5. *Yohannon*[28] twice refers to it as the "Sea of Tiberias."

Names were used based on the era of history and the location where you lived. For example, first century Jews would use *Gennesar*. A Roman of the period would use the Emperor's name: Tiberias. Let's use the Sea of Galilee, which is the lowest freshwater lake on Earth at approximately 700 feet (210 m) below sea level. At its widest points, the lake measures 13 miles (21 km) from north to south and 7.5 miles (12 km) from east to west. The lake's total area is 64 sq. miles (170 sq. km), and its circumference is about 32 miles (51 km). Its deepest point has been variously estimated between 140 and 200 feet (44-60 m), and its capacity is approximately one hundred billion cubic feet of fresh water, which makes it the largest freshwater lake in the Middle East.

View of the size of the Sea of Galilee

Yam Kinneret is the name used today in *Yesrael*. *Yam* in Hebrew means "any body of water not necessary a sea." Greek translators used their word for "sea." And the wrong translation of the same word is used till today, despite the fact that it is a lake and again not a sea. This lake is the primary source of water for the nation and as such, its outward flow to the Jordan River is carefully regulated by the government. In the southern part of this lake there is a dam, called the *Dagania*[70] dam. It was built in 1932 to control the water level. When the lake fills after good winter rainfalls, operators open the dam for the water to flow into the Jordan River to the *Yam-Hamelah*[69].

Climate and Storm Patterns Around the Sea of Galilee

The climate around the Sea of Galilee is temperate year-round, largely owing to its location below sea level. The average mean temperature in August is 95° F (35° C) and January's average mean temperature is a mild 57° F (14°

C). The relative humidity averages 65 percent and the lake receives about 16 inches of rain annually.

The Sea of Galilee is known for its violent storms, which can come up suddenly and be life-threatening for anyone on its waters. These tempests are caused by the situation of the lake in the Jordan Rift Valley with steep hills surrounding it on all sides. Cooler air masses from the surrounding mountains collide with the warm air in the lake's basin. Winds sometimes funnel through the east-west-oriented valleys in the Galilean hill country and rush down the western hillsides of the lake. The most violent storms, however, are caused by the fierce winds blowing off the *Golan*[102] Heights from the east. One such storm in March 1992 sent waves 10 feet (3 meters) high crashing into downtown Tiberias and causing significant damage to the shores of the city. A storm on the Sea of Galilee is described in (*Morqos*[12] 4:37). A furious squall came up, and the waves broke over the boat, so that it was nearly swamped.

Saint Peter's Fish

The presence of numerous, large harbors attests to the commercial importance of the lake during *Yeshua's* life. (By contrast, today there are only five harbors on the lake, and these are used primarily for tourist boats.) *Magdala*[71] apparently was the industrial center of the fishing trade, and fish to be exported were first salted there. In *Yeshua's* time, there were 12 harbors around the lake; *Kfar-Nahoum*[36] had two. *Magdala, Beth-Saida*[35], and *Tiberias* were among the others.

Saint Peter's fish

Today, thirty-five species of fish make their home in the waters of the Sea of *Yam Kinneret* and the *Yarden*[32] River, but three types seem to be most common in the New Testament record. Sardines were a staple of the locals' diet and these were probably the "two small fish" *Yeshua* used to feed the multitude. The *"Musht"* fish has a long dorsal fin that resembles a comb. It is popularly known as "Saint Peter's fish." This tasty fish can measure up to a foot-and-a-half long (0.5 meters) and weigh 3.3 pounds (1.5 kilograms). The third type is the catfish, which is not considered kosher because of its lack of scales. These are probably what *Yeshua* referred to "the bad fish" that would be thrown away in *Mattai*[4] 13:48, "When the fishing boat was full, the fishermen pulled it up on the shore. Then they sat down and collected the good fish in baskets but threw the bad away."

Yohannon Hamatbil[74] is Beheaded

Yeshua hears of *Yohannoa Hamatbil's*[72] beheading by Herodos Antipas here at the lake, and it doubtless had an impact on what He did. According to *Josephus*, sometime after baptizing *Yeshua*, *Yohannon Hamatbil* was killed at the palace-fortress of Machaerus, located near the *Yam Hamelah*[73] in the modern country of *Yarden*[74]. Built by King Herodos the Great, the palace was occupied at the time by his son and successor, known as Herodos Antipas.

You can read about it in (*Mattai* 14:1–12).

Read (*Morqos*[12] 6:14–29):

> The Gospel of *Morqos* records that Herodos Antipas had *Yohannon Hamatbil*[72] arrested and imprisoned after the preacher condemned the king's marriage to his wife, Herodias, as illegal because she had previously been married to his own brother, *Philipus*. Herodos Antipas initially resisted killing *Yohannon* because of his status as a holy man. But after his stepdaughter danced for him at his birthday party, he offered to give her anything she desired. Prompted by her mother, who resented *Yohannon's* judgment of her marriage, Herodias's daughter requested the prophet's head on a platter. In *The Antiquities of the Jews* (Book 18:116-19), *Josephus* confirms that Herodos Antipas "slew" *Yohannon* after imprisoning him at *Machaerus,* because he feared the prophet's influence might enable him to start a rebellion. Josephus also identified Herodias's daughter as Salome (the Gospels Gospels don't

Gospels don't mention her name) but didn't state that *Yohannon* was beheaded on her request.

Yeshua Walks on the Sea

Read (*Morqos*[12] 6:45-52):

> Immediately He made his disciples get into the boat and go before him to the other side, to Bethsaida, while He sent the multitude away. And when He had sent them away, He departed to the mountain to pray. Now when evening came, the boat was in the middle of the sea; and He was alone on the land. Then He saw them straining at rowing, for the wind was against them. Now about the fourth watch of the night He came to them, walking on the sea, and would have passed them by. And when they saw him walking on the sea, they supposed it was a ghost, and cried out; for they all saw him and were troubled. But immediately He talked with them and said to them, "Be of good cheer! It is I; do not be afraid." Then He went up into the boat to them, and the wind ceased. And they were greatly amazed in themselves beyond measure, and marveled. For they had not understood about the loaves, because their heart was hardened.

Just before this, the disciples had witnessed the miracle of the feeding of the five thousand. *Yeshua*, on purpose, put the disciples in a boat and told them to cross to the other side, while he went apart to pray.

View from the boat

During the trip, a storm arises, putting their lives in danger. The Christian life is not free of storms. We will all face storms. Suffering is part of our Christian Walk; suffering brings discipline to our lives. Sometimes, *Yahweh* allows us to be in the storm for a reason, just as He made His disciples to cross the lake in a storm.

(*Yohannon*[28] 6:15-21) is the parallel story to the one mentioned earlier in *Morqos*:

> *Yeshua*, knowing that they intended to come and make him king by force, withdrew again to a mountain by himself. When evening came, his disciples went down to the lake, where they got into a boat and set off across the lake for *Kfar-Nahoum*[36]. By now it was dark, and *Yeshua* had not yet joined them. A strong wind was blowing and

the waters grew rough. When they had rowed about three or four miles, they saw *Yeshua* approaching the boat, walking on the water; and they were frightened. But he said to them, "It is I; don't be afraid." Then they were willing to take him into the boat, and immediately the boat reached the shore where they were heading.

Notice in (*Yohannon*[28] *6:15*), *Yeshua* is sitting on a mountain to pray. He can see his disciples. Doubtless, He sees them fighting the storm even as night begins to fall. The disciples can only see the storm. They think they were alone and likely to die. How often have we been in similar situations where we thought we were fighting a storm alone?

But then *Yeshua* appears. Only, He isn't stopping to help. He is passing by. Why would He watch from a mountain and then pass by without helping? Because He wants them to call out to him. He wants us to cry to him. Sometimes, when we are desperate, we complain and blame others and murmur instead of calling upon the name of *the Morio*[25] and say, "*Yeshua,* save us. *Yeshua,* help me!"

The key verse here is that *Yeshua* was passing by! (*Morqos*[12] 6:48) says:

> *Then He saw them straining at rowing, for the wind was against them. Now about the fourth watch of the night He came to them, walking on the sea, and would have passed them by.*

The Aramaic word for "passing by" is *abar.* If you are so much in distress and suffering, can you recognize when

Yeshua is passing? Are you able to cry out for him? Or do you think that *Yeshua* has no intention of helping you?

(*Ayoub*[75] 9:8-11) might help. The key verse is 11:

> He alone stretches out the heavens and treads on the waves of the sea[6]. He is the Maker of the Bear and Orion, the Pleiades and the constellations of the south. He performs wonders that cannot be fathomed, miracles that cannot be counted. **When he passes me, I cannot see him; when he goes by, I cannot perceive him.**

Ayoub "strains" against the situations of his suffering; he wonders if *Yahweh* even cares enough to come and help. *Ayoub* wouldn't know because *Yahweh* is invisible. When He passes by, no one can see him.

In (*Shemoth*[22] 33:19) we read something interesting regarding *Yahweh's* passing by:

> And the Lord said, "I will cause all my goodness **to pass in front of you,** and I will proclaim my name, the Lord, in your presence. I will have mercy on whom I will have mercy, and I will have compassion on whom I will have compassion.

And we see the same thing in (*Shemoth*[22] 34:6), which says:

> And he passed in front of Moshe, proclaiming, "The Lord, the Lord, the compassionate and gracious Yahweh, slow to anger, abounding in love and faithfulness."

Abar is used in reference to *Yahweh's* passing by *Moshe*. In *Shemoth*[22] chapters 33 and 34, *Yahweh* is revealing himself. *Ayoub*[75] strains against his suffering. The children of *Yesrael*[27] strain against bondage in *Metsrayin*[24]. In both cases, *Yahweh* reveals himself when He passes. He reveals his character and his name, *Yahweh*. At the heart of *Yahweh's* name is the idea that the Lord is compassionate and gracious, full of mercy and love to help those who are crying out in distress.

What do we see in (*Morqos*[12] 6:49-52)?

> ... but when they saw him walking on the lake, they thought he was a ghost. They cried out, because they all saw him and were terrified. Immediately he spoke to them and said, "Take courage! It is I. Don't be afraid." Then he climbed into the boat with them, and the wind died down. They were completely amazed, for they had not understood about the loaves; their hearts were hardened.

What does *Yeshua* say to them in the middle of this lake? Don't be afraid. "It is I." *Yahweh* comes, reveals his name, demonstrates his power over the water, and tells his people do not be afraid for "I AM."

Yeshua is *Yahweh's* presence with us. What are you afraid of currently? Is there chaos in your life? Are you straining at something? Know this: *Yahweh* has sent you into the middle of the storm so He can appear to you, to walk with you. When you are in the storm and you are desperate, cry out to *Yeshua*, because He will speak to you through his words. No matter how many times you fall into trouble, you can call on his name, and He will show up and give you comfort as He walks beside you in the storm.

Kepha's Reaction to Yeshua Walking on the Water

Read (*Mattai* 14:28-33):

> "Lord, if it's you," *Kepha* replied, "tell me to come to you on the water." "Come," he said.
>
> Then *Kepha* got down out of the boat, walked on the water and came toward *Yeshua*. But when he saw the wind, he was afraid and, beginning to sink, cried out, "Lord, save me!"
>
> Immediately, *Yeshua* reached out his hand and caught him. "You of little faith," he said, "why did you doubt?"
>
> And when they climbed into the boat, the wind died down. Then those who were in the boat worshiped him, saying, "Truly you are the Son of *Yahweh.*"

Kepha asks *Yeshua* to call him out on the water. *Yeshua* replies simply, "Come." Then *Kepha* gets down out of the boat, walks on the water, and approaches *Yeshua*.

Kepha walks on water, but then he doubts and begins to sink. *Yeshua* immediately catches him and asks why he doubted. But *Yeshua* is also looking at the disciples who have not gotten out of the boat. They too have doubted. *Yeshua* wants to know where their faith is.

If you want to be a real disciple, you need to give it all, not only on Sundays at church, but every day of your life. Trust Him completely. That is my challenge to you all. Maybe *Yahweh* allows a storm to come at a specific time in your life. Those are the times to call upon *Yeshua*. He is there in the midst of your trial. The important thing to remember is that you are not alone. *Yeshua* is with you even if no one else is. These trials will teach you to grow up in your faith – not wealth. Your money will not help you. Only walking with *Yeshua* will help to heal your heart.

One of my favorite songs is called "Oceans." Out on the lake is a good time to sing it:

Oceans (Where Feet May Fail)
Verse 1
You call me out upon the waters
The great unknown where feet may fail
And there I find You in the mystery
In oceans deep my faith will stand
Chorus
I will call upon Your Name
And keep my eyes above the waves
When oceans rise
My soul will rest in Your embrace
For I am Yours and You are mine

Now, absorb the lesson, enjoy the rest of the boat ride, and experience spiritual life on the Sea of Galilee.

Andre Moubarak | 77

Dancing on the boat ride on the Sea of Galilee

The Day Concludes

After the boat ride you will conclude to your final destination for the day: The *Wadi Elhamam*[77].

Back to teaching

- Why is it important for Jews to read the *Torah* every day?
- Why is reading the *Torah* a core value for religious Jews?

Even today you will see Jewish people in the streets holding their books and reading all the time – walking, riding local buses, or shopping in the markets. It happens everywhere, but mostly in the *Beth-Knesset*. Why? Religious Jews believe the first thing *Yahweh* will ask them when they meet him will be? How much time they spent reading and studying the *Torah*.

In the Hebrew mindset, loving *Yahweh* is the same as reading his words. Reading Scripture, to the Jewish mind, is a lifestyle, something they do all the time. *Yeshua* studied the *Torah* every day of his life, growing up learning about and memorizing Scripture. In the book of the *Mishnah*[78] we learn how rabbis studied the *Torah* around 100 AD. They did so on their knees in a closed room inside their houses. In their minds, this was the proper way, behind closed doors, humbled before *Yahweh*. They believed five minutes on your knees was more powerful than two hours of preaching in front of someone else.

For the Christian, this is also important. Our study demonstrates how we are filled with the anointing of the *Roho-Kodsho*[8]. Here are seven points regarding how to operate under the authority and the anointing of the *Roho-Kodsho* to be part of the Kingdom of God. You cannot jump from one point to the another; you have to follow them in order.

Being Anointed by the Spirit

#1 – Live a King-Centered Life

This is *Yahweh*-centered life. Living this way requires you to put the King's priorities before your own. This is the Middle Eastern way of living, from an Aramaic way of thinking. What matters to the King is what matters to you. This is the first step to living under the anointing of the *Roho-Kodsho*.

Was the Kingdom important to *Yeshua*? Look at (*Louko*[13] 4:42-43).

> At daybreak, Yeshua went out to a solitary place. The people were looking for him and when they came to where he was, they tried to keep him from leaving them. But he said, "I must proclaim the good news of the **Kingdom of God** to the other towns also, **because that is why I was sent.**"

Yeshua was sent *specifically* to preach the Good News of the Kingdom of God. *Yeshua*'s earthly mission was to make it clear that He was the King and that He was ruling and reigning over those who submitted to him. He set the captives free to find a new life and transformation in *Yeshua*. Over one hundred times in the Gospels *Yeshua* speaks of the Kingdom of God.

To walk in your anointing, you need to make the Kingdom the center of your world just as *Yeshua* did. This is how *Yeshua* taught his disciples to pray: "Thy kingdom come Thy will be done." In Aramaic the statement is redundant. Thy kingdom come and Thy will be done mean exactly the same thing. A better translation might be: "May Your kingdom keep expanding. May *Yahweh* reign over you more and more." It is continuous and progressive, growing ever deeper and more meaningful.

If you want the King's will to be done in your life, then it begins in you! That's why *Yeshua* says to seek first the Kingdom of Heaven and only then will everything else be added to you. The priority for every Christian is to do *Yahweh's* will first, to make *Yeshua* king over your life.

This is the heart of the Christian life. If you could ever simplify your life in *Yeshua* to the extent that your number one priority seven days a week, 24 hours a day where all of your finances, everything you eat, all that comes out of your mouth, everything you let come into your eyes and ears, your entire existence is about seeking first His Kingship in your life, then you are going to be set free and walk under the anointing of the *Roho-Kodsho*[8]. Only then will *Yeshua* be glorified – not you or anyone else.

Yeshua explained that the Kingdom is like finding a pearl of great value. You discover it in the field, so you go and sell all you have to buy the field, so you can possess the pearl. That is what the Kingdom is like. You make the King's priorities your priorities.

#2 – Read Your Bible

Reading Scripture is essential to walking in your anointing of the *Roho-Kodsho*. It will humble you. These are the peacemakers, the meek, those that mourn, and those that yield to the Spirit. Instead of reigning over your own life, you allow *Yeshua* to reign over you. That is how the Scriptures help.

(*Morqos*[12] 10:14-15) says:

> When *Yeshua* saw this, he was indignant. He said to them, "Let the little children come to me, and do not hinder them, for the kingdom of God

belongs to such as these. Truly I tell you, anyone who will not receive the Kingdom of God like a little child will never enter it.

Who is in charge of your life? This is one reason *Yeshua* says in (*Louko*[13] 18:18) while counseling the rich young ruler:

A certain ruler asked him, "Good teacher, what must I do to inherit eternal life?"...[*Yeshua*] said to him, "You still lack one thing. Sell everything you have and give it to the poor, and you will have treasure in heaven. Then come, follow me."

Why is it difficult for the rich man to enter the Kingdom of God? Because the rich tend to rely on their riches rather than upon *Yahweh*. This makes it difficult to let *Yahweh* rule and reign in their lives. But the situation represents more than just money. Some feel they are rich in intellect, talent, strength, or resources, so they tend to rely on those qualities instead of *Yeshua*. But until you humble yourself and submit to him as King in your life, you will not be able to receive the anointing of his Spirit.

Yahweh wants you to prosper. Unfortunately, prosperity in the minds of so many is associated with materialistic wealth, but that is the furthest thing from the truth. There are ten or so words in the *Aramaic* Bible that talk about prosperity, but not one of them refers to the accumulation of material possessions. In original Aramaic prosperity, it is to be "content" with what *Yahweh* has given you according to his will at that moment. The more possessions you own, the more enslaved you are to them. When *Yeshua* went to the cross, He owned not a single thing, but He was the most prosperous man on earth!

It's not what you own that matters. It is doing what He wants you to do that truly matters.

#3 – Obedience of Faith

To operate in the authority, power, and anointing of the *Roho-Kodsho* is to live a life characterized by what *Boulos*[7] calls "obedience of faith." Obedience is the hallmark of a disciple who wants to be part of the Kingdom of God.

Look what is written in (*Mattai*[4] 7:21):

> Not everyone who says to me, "Lord, Lord," will enter the kingdom of heaven, but only the one who does the will of my Father who is in heaven.

What is *Yeshua* saying from his Aramaic mindset? He is saying that it takes more than just words to be part of his movement. It is not a prosperity gospel. Naming it does not claim it. Just because you call him King or Lord does not mean you are his disciple. Attending church every Sunday or being involved in ministry is not a guarantee. If you are not *obeying* Him, then you are not part of the Kingdom of Heaven. That only comes by obeying his words. You must crush your own will and walk under the will of the *Roho-Kodsho*! Let him see the obedience of your faith.

In (*Mattai* 11:29), *Yeshua* says:

> Take my yoke upon you and learn from me, for I am gentle and humble in heart, and you will find rest for your souls. For my yoke is easy and my burden is light.

Yeshua's yoke is easy to bear. It is easy, but it is a yoke. What does that mean in *Yeshua* culture?

A. You must yield to put a yoke on your neck. You must humble yourself and obey.
B. If you are going to "yoke up" with *Yeshua*, you will be busy plowing. You will do a lot of work because *Yeshua* has saved you, and He has things prepared for you to do.

In (*Louko*[13] 11:28), *Yeshua* says: "Blessed rather are those who hear the word of *Yahweh* and obey it."

To be in the Kingdom means to live a life of obedient faithfulness.

How many of us like to talk but do not walk with *Yahweh*?

#4 – Kingdom Productivity

Read (*Louko*[13] 4:18-19):

> To operate under the anointing and the power of the Kingdom of God means you will become productive. A Kingdom life is a productive life. *Yeshua* explained that the proof of discipleship is to bear much fruit.

"The Spirit of the Lord is on me, because he has anointed me to proclaim good news to the poor. He has sent me to proclaim freedom for the prisoners and recovery of sight for the blind, to set the oppressed free, to proclaim the year of the Lord's favor."

The Spirit of *Yahweh* was upon *Yeshua*, anointing Him to proclaim the Good News, to set and free the captives, and to liberate the oppressed. That is our mission too. Look at (*Mattai* 10:8): "Heal the sick cleanse the lepers, raise the dead cast out demons freely you have received, freely give."

Yeshua says on another occasion that the Kingdom is suffering violence. In an Aramaic way of thinking, *Yeshua* is referring to how the Kingdom of Heaven is breaking loose like the energy of a huge atomic reaction. Those who are in the Kingdom are being set free, bringing people from the darkness to the light. This doesn't happen without a fight. It is powerful and explosive.

(M*ikha*[79] 2:12-13):

> I will surely gather all of you, *Ya'coub*[39]; I will surely bring together the remnant of *Yesrael*. I will bring them together like sheep in a pen, like a flock in its pasture; the place will throng with people. The One who breaks open the way will go up before them; they will break through the gate and go out. Their King will pass through before them, the Lord at their head."

In a first-century context, consider the sheep in a pen at night. They are restless and anxious. They are disturbed and want to get out of the pen. But when the dawn comes and the light breaks forth, the shepherd comes, opens the door, and leads the sheep out. The sheep go through the gate, bumping, bleating, and making noises as they go out to the green pastures to drink of living waters. That's what the Kingdom is doing. You are breaking loose from your bonds of captivity, and because of that, you are given new authority and power. You are set free.

(*Mattai*[4] 10:7):

> As you go, proclaim this message: "The kingdom of heaven has come near." Heal the sick, raise the dead, cleanse those who have leprosy, drive out demons. Freely you have received; freely give.

The Kingdom of God is freedom and productivity. When you are walking in your anointing, you will bear fruit. You will reproduce yourself. You will help set others free in *Yeshua*.

#5 – Connected to the Community of the Faithful

To be in the Kingdom of God and operating under the anointing and power of the *Roho-Kodsho*[8] means you are connected to the community of the faithful. To operate in the Kingdom of Heaven, you must be connected to your family and church. You must be a part of *Yeshua's* movement. You must be involved with others and not function as an individual.

You can't do it all alone. You cannot take on the enemy by yourself. Even if you have the full armor of *Yahweh* from (*Ephesyayeeta*[170] 6:10-18), your back is undefended. You need to have others to watch out for you.

(*Ma'aseh*[64] 1:8) says:

> But you will receive power when the *Roho-Kodsho* comes on you; and you will be my witnesses in *Or-Shlem*, and in all Judea and Samaria, and to the ends of the earth.

You become part of *Yeshua's* movement by connecting to the community of faithful. It is all about the community and not the individual. In *Kfar-Nahoum*[36], every time *Yeshua* healed someone, He told them to return home. It all starts at home, because if you have a healthy home, you will have a healthy family, and when you have a healthy family, you will have a healthy community, and when you have a healthy community, you will have a healthy church, and when you have a healthy church, then you will have a healthy society, and we you have a healthy society, you will have a healthy government, and when you have a healthy government, the world will become a better place and *Yahweh* alone will be glorified! Only then can his name spread in the Earth as it was meant to be.

#6 – Be Involved with the Community Conflict (Spiritual Warfare)

To be in the Kingdom of God means you will be involved in conflict with the community. The Middle East is all about conflict. The Kingdom is a matter of conflict because you are dealing with people's personalities in the community. I am speaking of spiritual warfare. There is somebody who gets really irritated when you get into the Kingdom of Heaven.

Shaitan[54] is the one who opposes the things of *Yahweh*. He wants to ascend higher than *Yahweh*. He wants to rule and reign, and he will oppose you when you have the anointing on your life. When the Kingdom of *Yahweh* breaks into the world, the captives are set free. It is a battle from darkness to light, spiritual resistance that becomes very real and tangible.

To be under the anointing of the Spirit is to be in part of the army of *Yahweh*. That's why you need to be equipped for the fight. To be equipped in Aramaic means "to prepare," "to be ready" for something for later use. You need to operate in *Yeshua's* authority and in the power of His Spirit. *Yeshua* says the mission of the church is to equip the saints for ministry and for the conflict we will all face spiritual warfare.

(*Evraye*[81] 2:14-16) explains:

> Since the children have flesh and blood, he too shared in their humanity so that by his death he might break the power of him who holds the power of death, that is, the devil, and free those who all their lives were held in slavery by their fear of death. For surely it is not angels he helps, but *Ob-Rohom's*[82] descendants.

The Son of *Yahweh* came to destroy the works of the devil. To be in the Kingdom of Heaven is to be part of a community that is engaged in a spiritual conflict with the forces of this world. Do not function alone in this battle or you will lose, walk together in battles with your mentors and friends.

#7 – Giving Evidence of God's Kingship in Your Life

The final point of walking under the anointing of the *Roho-Kodsho*[8] is when you give evidence of God's kingship on your life. Who is the Kingdom? It is the King, King *Yeshua*. What is the Kingdom of God? It is the King ruling and reigning over people who submit to his authority. When will the Kingdom come into being? It is a present reality. It is breaking loose now; it is breaking free. It is something that is here and now. How does the Kingdom operate? Under the authority of *Yeshua's* name and the power of his *Roho-Kodsho*. Why is the Kingdom expanding? Because *Yahweh* has a purpose for planet Earth. There are things He wants to accomplish with you, which may shock you! but it is vitally important for you to realize that *Yahweh* needs you.

He needs you to give evidence of his kingship in your home, in your workplace, in your schools, in your offices, and in your society. He wants his name to fill the earth with his glory. So, yes, He has a purpose for your salvation!

But where is the Kingdom? Look what *Yeshua* says in (*Louko*[13] 17:21):

> "Nor will people say, 'Here it is,' or 'There it is,' because the kingdom of God is in your midst."

This can also be translated "among you" or "in you." The

Kingdom is not only among you collectively but also in you individually."

Where is the Kingdom? In you. *Yeshua* is in you. Who is *Yeshua*? He is King; He is *Morio*[25]. There needs to be evidence of his Kingdom in your life.

You now have everything you need to operate and walk under the anointing of his *Roho-Kodsho*. Simply follow the seven steps. It takes years for the anointing to stay on your life. Have patience. You cannot jump from one stage to the next; you have to walk through them one by one.

Now it's time to be on the move again.

Wadi Elhamam[77]– *Yeshua* the Rabbi

It is a short hike along the Valley of the Doves, part of the *Via Maris*[31], the first century route that *Yeshua* took from *Natseret*[33] to *Kfar-Nahoum*[36]. As you walk, pay attention to the landmarks. On the left is Mount *Arabel*[84]. Notice the beauty of Nature – birds, colorful plants, etc. This place is probably the most unchanged since the time of *Yeshua*. Not many groups visit the Valley of Doves as it is off the beaten track.

The Zealots lived in the surrounding caves to avoid paying taxes to the Romans. The hike continues until you reach a spring. Feel free to sit on one of the many stones. The area is shaded by a large tree, so it is perfect to continue teaching and learning.

The Valley of the Doves – Wadi Elhamam

This final lesson takes about an hour. It's good for everyone in the group to be prepared.

There are a variety of verses that refer to *Yeshua* as a rabbi. Here are some:

> Just then a man came up to *Yeshua* and asked, **"Teacher,** what good thing must I do to get eternal life?" (*Mattai*[4] 19:16)

> Asking, "Teacher, *Moshe* said, If a man dies having no children, his brother as next of kin shall marry his wife, and raise up children for his brother." (*Mattai* 22: 24-26)

> Someone in the crowd said to him, "**Teacher,** tell my brother to divide the inheritance with me." (*Louko*[13] 12:13)

> Some of the Pharisees in the crowd said to *Yeshua*, "**Teacher,** rebuke your disciples!" (*Louko* 19:39)

> Then came to him certain of the Sadducees, which deny that there is any resurrection; and they asked him, Saying, "**Master,** *Moshe* wrote unto us, If any man's brother dies, having a wife, and he dies without children, that his brother should take his wife, and raise up seed unto his brother. – (*Louko* 20:27-28)

"Rabbi" comes from the Hebrew root "*Rav,*" which means "great" and points to someone with "great knowledge" about the *Torah*. If you know any Hebrew, you probably know the expression *Todah,* which is the word for "thanks" or "thank you." But if you want to emphasis the word, you say, *Todah, Raba* – "Thanks a lot."

Thus, the term *rabbi* (with an "i" at the end) indicates that the individual is a great one or more specifically "my teacher." The "i" at the end points to possession. Thus, *rabbi* means "my great teacher," which means "he belongs to me," "he is mine."

In *Yeshua's* time, the term had essentially two meanings. The first one meant "master" as it is translated in some of the Bible. The other term is "teacher," because it includes a connotation of respect. It is not a formal title. That has changed today. A Jewish rabbi today, for example, is like an ordained minister. *Rabbi* became a title. But in *Yeshua's* day, it was a term of respect.

This began to change some 40 – 50 years after the death of *Yeshua* and after the destruction of the *Hayklo*[3] in *Or-Shlem*[5] in 70 AD. At that time, many of the Jewish sages made their way to a place called *Yavneh*[85], where they set the standards for Judaism for the next several centuries since they no longer had a *Hayklo* as the center of Jewish practice. Somewhere around 80 – 84 AD they set the standards for a person becoming a *rabbi*, thus changing the term into a title.

It begs the questions:

- What are the implications of being a rabbi?
- Who were the rabbis?
- What did rabbis do?
- How did they do it?
- Who followed the rabbis?
- How did the rabbis make disciples?

In truth, the best example we have is of the rabbi *Yeshua*. We have more literature and more information about *Yeshua* than any other rabbi of this period. *Yeshua* could be seen as a rabbi in the style of his time, yet in reality, he was unlike any rabbi who ever lived.

Characteristics of a Rabbi's Lifestyle

#1 - Rabbis Lived an Itinerant Life

Living an itinerant life means they walked about from place to place. They did not live in one location. They moved around. *Yeshua* was like this. He didn't have a home to call his own.

(Morqos[12] 6:5-6):

> He could not do any miracles there, except lay his hands on a few sick people and heal them. He was amazed at their lack of faith. Then *Yeshua* went around teaching from village to village. (Morqos 6:56):

> And wherever he went—into villages, towns or countryside—they placed the sick in the marketplace. They begged him to let them touch even the edge of his cloak, and all who touched it were healed.

Yeshua was always moving around. In fact, the pattern seen here is really a repetition of an Old Testament pattern of the prophets, like the prophets *Yeshayahu*[52], *Yermyahu*[86], and others. The prophets did a similar thing, traveling about from place to place. Sometimes they did so with their disciples, often known as the Sons of the Prophets:

> And it came to pass, when the Lord was about to take up *Elyahu*[87] into heaven by a whirlwind, that *Elyahu* went with *Elisha* from *Gilgal*. Then *Elyahu* said to *Elisha*, "**Stay here,** please, for the Lord has sent me on to Beth-el."

> But *Elisha* said, "As the Lord lives, and as your soul lives, I will not leave you!" So, they went down to Bethel.

> Now the **sons of the prophets** who were at Bethel came out to *Elisha*, and said to him, "Do you know that the Lord will take away your master from over you today?" (2 *Melachim*[88] 2:1-3)

The rabbis of *Yeshua* day in the first century were like that. They would go from place to place, often going into people's houses to teach.

> Now it happened as they went that He entered a certain village; and a certain woman named Martha welcomed Him into her house. (*Louko*[13] 10:38)

They also taught in the synagogues and the *Hayklo*:

> And *Yeshua* went about all Galilee, teaching in their synagogues, preaching the gospel of the kingdom, and healing all kinds of sickness and all kinds of disease among the people. (*Mattai* 4:23)

> Now when He came into the *Hayklo*, the chief priests and the elders of the people confronted him as He was teaching, and said, "By what authority are you doing these things? And who gave you this authority?" (*Mattai* 21:23)

The *Hayklo*[3] was a huge complex, and there was an area where rabbi would go to teach, known as the portico. Many people would gather there to listen. *Yeshua* showed up, found a place to sit, and people gathered around him to listen to his teachings.

But rabbis weren't exclusively indoor teachers. They often

taught outside, in the wild. A classic example of this occurred in Galilee when *Yeshua* taught the Sermon on the Mount. Imagine hundreds of people filling the slopes of the hill leading down to the Sea of Galilee. *Yeshua* sat near the shore and taught the people.

But He would also teach in solitary places:

> When *Yeshua* heard it, He departed from there by boat to a deserted place by himself. But when the multitudes heard it, they followed him on foot from the cities. And when *Yeshua* went out, He saw a great multitude; and He was moved with compassion for them, and healed their sick. When it was evening, his disciples came to him, saying, "This is a deserted place, and the hour is already late. Send the multitudes away, that they may go into the villages and buy themselves food." (*Mattai* 14:13-15)
>
> Then He got into one of the boats, which was *Kepha's*, and asked him to put out a little from the land. And He sat down and taught the multitudes from the boat. *(Louko* 5:3)

In the last example above, *Yeshua* taught from a boat. He sat down in the boat, which is typical of rabbinic teaching, and taught a little bit back from the shore.

Why does a rabbi travel around so much? The answer is simple. He wanted to be where the people were. *Yeshua* didn't have access to radio or television or Zoom. If He wanted people to hear his words, He had to travel to where they were.

#2 - Rabbis Were Poor

Rabbis depended upon the hospitality and generosity of others. Their lifestyles were rather trying even by first century standards. They would usually carry with them a bag of grain some nuts and maybe a few olives and dried figs and fruits. If they had money, it had come as a donation. Usually, it was not much, just enough to meet the needs for the day. In the *Mishna,* it is written that they carried water by measures and a handful of salt.

They were dressed in simple garments. The outer garment was called a *tallit*[89] or prayer shawl. The inner undergarment was called the *haluq*[90], but this garment was probably just wool, nothing fancy. He wore sandals and he lived very simply.

In fact, look what *Yeshua* said:

> And *Yeshua* said to him, "Foxes have holes and birds of the air have nests, but the Son of Man has nowhere to lay his head." (*Mattai* 8:20)

It was not an envied lifestyle. It was demanding and often hostile, relying heavily upon the hospitality of those who were interested in the rabbi's teachings.

The *Mishnah*[78], known as the oral law and meaning "Sayings of the Fathers," is a compilation of what many famous Jewish teachers have taught through the centuries. Compiled around 200 AD, following the loss of many Jewish teachers in the failed Great Revolt and *Bar-Kokhba*[91] rebellion, Rabbi *Yehudah Ha-Nasi* decided to secure Judaism's Oral Law by codifying it into 63 tractates called the *Mishnah*. The *Mishnah* is considered the first work of Rabbinic Judaism.

The *Mishnah* consists of six *sedarim*[92], which each contain 7-12 *masechtot*[93] each divided into *mishnayot*[94].

The *Shisha Sidrei Mishnah*[95] are as follows:

1. *Zeraim* (Seeds) – Agricultural laws and prayers
2. *Moed* (Festival) – Jewish holidays and Sabbath
3. *Nashim* (Women) – Marriage and divorce
4. *Nezikin* (Damages) – Civil and criminal law
5. *Kodashim* (Holy Things) – Sacrificial rites, the *Hayklo*, dietary laws
6. *Tohorot* (Purities) – Laws of purity and impurity

The *Mishnah* is the classic expression of Jewish wisdom. In the *Mishnah*, Rabbi *Yossi bar Yoezer* said, "Let your house be a meeting house for the sages and sit at the mid of the dust of their feet and drink in their words thirstily or with thirst." He lived one hundred fifty years before *Yeshua*. He is the one who made the statement about opening up your houses for rabbis. He was also crucified by the Romans.

Yossi bar Yoezer knew that if people would venerate rabbis in their own homes, then they would be much more willing to listen and perform duties consistent with those of disciples. It was more than letting one man into your home. You washed his feet, you fed him, you allowed others to come into your home to listen to him. It was a big deal, seeing as how the rabbi was dependent upon this gesture of goodwill.

Let's look at another interesting Scripture:

> Now it came to pass, afterward, that He went through every city and village, preaching and bringing the glad tidings of the kingdom of God. And the twelve were with Him, and certain women who had been healed of evil spirits and infirmities—*Miriam* called Magdalene, out of whom had come seven demons, and Joanna the wife of *Chuza*, Herod's steward, and Susanna, and many others who provided for him from their substance. (*Louko* 8:1-3)

These women helped to support *Yeshua* and the disciples out of their own means. This shows the poverty and simplicity of *Yeshua*.

#3 - Make Disciples

Reading from the *tractate* of *avot* in the *Mishna,* the division *nizikim*, we find one of the oldest statements in all the *Mishnah*:

> *Moshe* received the Law on Sinai and delivered it to Joshua; Joshua in turn handed it down to the Elders, from the Elders it descended to the prophets (beginning with Eli and *Samo'el*), and each of them delivered it to his successors until it reached the men of the Great Assembly. The last,

named originated three maxims: "Be not hasty in judgment; Bring up many disciples; and, Erect safeguards for the Law." (*Avot* 1:1)

The statement orders three things:

1. Be deliberate in judgment.
2. Raise up many disciples.
3. Make a fence around the Torah.

"Raise up many disciples," was the slogan on the doorpost of the great synagogue as you would enter. Doing this was at the very heart of the life of a rabbi. The word "disciple" is the Hebrew word *talmid,* meaning "student" or "learner."

The top priority of a rabbi was to train, equip, and raise up disciples and students. A famous rabbi is mentioned in the book of *Ma'aseh*[64] in the Bible: *Gamaliel*. The Scripture says he had over 500 disciples. The *Talmud*[113] (Jewish book on applying the law to everyday life) claims he had up to 1,000 disciples.

We know *Yeshua* had 12 disciples in his innermost circle, but we know also know that on the day of Pentecost, there were 120 disciples still hanging in there. And we know from other Scripture verses that there were a great number of disciples who followed him.

Yeshua taught not only the masses but also made a point of spending the majority of his time teaching the select disciples, the serious students, the learners. He invested in certain disciples, foregoing venues of speaking to greater masses. He spent time in building disciples. *Yeshua* was selective in choosing disciples. This is what rabbis do.

Being a disciple was not easy. You gave up everything to be with your rabbi every hour of every day. There was a cost to being a disciple, but it was these individuals that stood out that rabbis would invest in and build. These are the ones who would one day follow in the rabbi's footsteps, so it was important for rabbis to select dedicated disciples.

A wisdom story is given in the *Mishnah*[78] that advises a disciple on what to do if both his father and rabbi were taken hostage. The *Mishnah* advises to ransom the disciple's rabbi first and then ransom his father, unless of course, his father happens to be his rabbi and then he could ransom his father. The order is important, because the sages taught that your father brought you into this world, but the rabbi prepared you for the world to come. First priority was to your rabbi, not your own father.

There was enormous respect and love for the rabbis and it was accompanied by total respect, commitment, and dedication. The cost was high, and many turned away. This happened to *Yeshua*.

Making disciples is definitely the highest priority of *Yeshua's* ministry. Look what He commanded:

> Then the eleven disciples went to Galilee, to the mountain where *Yeshua* had told them to go. When they saw him, they worshiped him; but some doubted. Then *Yeshua* came to them and said, "All authority in heaven and on earth has been given to me. **Therefore, go and make disciples of all**

nations, baptizing them in the name of the Father and of the Son and of the *Roho-Kodsho*, and teaching them to obey everything I have commanded you. And surely, I am with you always, to the very end of the age." (*Mattai* 28:16-20)

The Great Commission requires us to make disciples everywhere. This is what mattered most to *Yeshua* and the last thing He said before ascending into Heaven. But we are removed from our Jewish roots, and we don't understand. There is no true evangelism apart from educating, teaching, and building disciples.

What did *Yeshua* want? He wanted us to make students of all the pagans in all the nations. How is this accomplished? By teaching them. You make disciples by teaching them.

> To the Jews who had believed him, *Yeshua* said, "If you hold to my teaching, you are really my disciples. Then you will know the truth, and the truth will set you free." (*Yohannon*[28] 8:31-32)

The verse presents a conditional statement. *If* you abide in, continue in, dwell in, and hold to my teachings, *then* you are my disciples and only then will the truth you learn set you free.

#4 - A Teacher of the Torah

Yeshua moves from *Natseret*[33] to *Kfar-Nahoum*[36] to teach as a rabbi. He teaches the *Torah*. He does not hang out with Gentiles because they are considered to be pagan.

There are exceptions, of course, but *Yeshua* says that He was sent to the lost sheep of *Yesrael*.

Why did *Yeshua* do this? Let's look at several Scriptures:

Now the LORD had said unto Abram, Get thee out of thy country, and from thy kindred, and from thy father's house, unto a land that I will shew thee. (*Bereshith*[96] 12:1)

Ob-Rohom[82] was chosen. With his selection came responsibility. We see this throughout Scripture. *Ob-Rohom* ends up being a teacher, blessing the nations of the world. The same principle applied to *Yeshua*. He was sent to *Yesrael*, the direct seed of *Ob-Rohom* and those with whom *Yahweh* made a covenant.

But *Yesrael* did repent. They did not turn to *Yeshua*:

> Then began He to upbraid the cities wherein most of his mighty works were done, because they repented not: "Woe unto thee, *Korazin*[34]! woe unto thee, Bethsaida! for if the mighty works, which were done in you, had been done in Tyre and Sidon, they would have repented long ago in sackcloth and ashes. But I say unto you, It shall be more tolerable for Tyre and Sidon at the day of judgment, than for you. And thou, *Kfar-Nahoum*, which art exalted unto heaven, shalt be brought down to hell: for if the mighty works, which have been done in thee, had been done in *Sodom*, it would have remained until this day. But I say unto you, that it shall be more tolerable for the land

of Sodom in the day of judgment, than for thee." (*Mattai*[4] 11:20-24)

Yeshua was sent to *Yesrael*, so He used the *Torah* to teach *Yahweh's* will. The *Torah* provided three things: direction, instruction, and guidance. *Yahweh* gave *Moshe* the *Torah* on *Mount Sinai*. The word *Torah* comes from three Hebrew root letters: *yud, resh, yud.* They indicated hitting the mark like an arrow striking a target. In essence, the Torah was how the people of *Yesrael* were to hit the mark of righteousness and life.

Sin, on the other hand, means to "miss the mark."

Yeshua constantly berated the Pharisees and Scribes because they had missed the mark. *Yeshua* was telling people that He had the correct view of the Torah so they could finally strike the target! There is the Good News in the Kingdom of Heaven. *Yahweh's* redemptive power is at work to bring life, guidance, direction, and instruction. *Yeshua* wanted this message to get out.

He used the *Torah* as the launching pad for his teaching. As Christians, we need to turn to the Bible more and more. We spend too much time on entertainment and other garbage. Being a disciple means we must study the Bible!

#5 – Rabbis Taught in Parables

It was common for rabbis to use parables, and *Yeshua* was no exception. *Yeshua* was the master storyteller. Almost one-third of all of *Yeshua's* teachings recorded in the Gospels are parables. As a first-century rabbi, *Yeshua* mastered commonly used techniques, one of which involved using parables.

There are a few principles that are absolutely fundamental to understanding the parabolic teaching method correctly. Scholars have studied 4000 parables in Jewish literature and tried to understand the truth from them. To do so, they dove into context and cultural customs. In truth, there are innumerable opinions about the meaning of *Yeshua*'s parables. To understand them correctly, we must follow a few principles.

Parables were simply aids to effective teaching. Their purpose was to clarify a point by using a story. Today, some of the parables seem obscure. In many cases, we are unfamiliar with the historical circumstances surrounding the parable. We are also removed from the Aramaic and Hebrew languages, culture, and specific circumstances that form the parable. If we know those things, the parables become easier to understand. If we go back to the Jewish roots of culture, context, and customs of the first-century, the parables begin to make more sense.

For the more advanced students, parables often had a deeper level of significance that a rabbi would only share with his inner circle. This was certainly the case for *Yeshua*. But when you give a sermon to a crowd, you simply deliver the story and the central meaning of the parable becomes abundantly clear because the parable conveyed a complex religious message very concisely.

It is important to understand that parables are not allegories.

They are not disguised messages. They are not symbolic. They are stories intended to illustrate a truth. Each parable has a specific function determined by the context of the teaching or current events. Without this knowledge, we can misinterpret parables.

There is a basic pattern that we see in *Yeshua's* ministry as a rabbi. First, there is an incident or a comment somebody makes. Then, *Yeshua* teaches. After the lesson, he illustrates his point, typically, with two parables.

The great rabbi *Hillel*[97], who lived just before *Yeshua*, established the school of discipleship that includes Judaism to this very day. He lays out for us seven principles of biblical interpretation and application. He was known by everyone in *Yeshua's* day. In fact, some have even speculated that *Yeshua* was a disciple of *Hillel* because *Yeshua's* teachings were so similar to *Hillel's*. This is only mentioned to point out that Jesus used well-established techniques.

Of these seven principles, one is very appropriate for our purposes. In Hebrew, it is called *Kol-Hakhomer*. It is the method of teaching the Scripture by going from the simple to the complex. Examine the following Scripture to illustrate.

> "Which of you, if your son asks for bread, will give him a stone? Or if he asks for a fish, will give him a snake? If you, then, though you are evil, know how to give good gifts to your children, how much more will your Father in heaven give

good gifts to those who ask him!" (*Mattai* 7:9-11).

Note the phrase "and how much more." That is *kol-hakhomer,* arguing from the simple to the complex. The first two verses are simple, but the last is complex.

Another example is found in (*Louko 23:26-31*). This is a fantastic Scripture, but the meaning is totally missed because we do not know the language, the context, or the culture. It is well worth the time to see the considerable sophistication of *Yeshua*'s teaching.

First, a little background about the passage. *Yeshua* is on the way to being crucified. He is carrying his cross when the soldiers tell *Simon of Cyrene*[98] to help. There was a large crowd following *Yeshua*, including women. Women are often emphasized as followers of *Yeshua*.

Note the passage from (*Louko*[13] *23:26-31*):

> As the soldiers led him away, they seized *Simon* from *Cyrene*, who was on his way in from the country, and put the cross on him and made him carry it behind *Yeshua*. A large number of people followed him, including women who mourned and wailed for him. *Yeshua* turned and said to them, "Daughters of *Or-Shlem*[5], do not weep for me; weep for yourselves and for your children. For the time will come when you will say, 'Blessed are childless women, the wombs that never bore and the breasts that have never nursed! Then they will say to the mountains, Fall on us! and to the hills, Cover us!' **For if people do these things**

when the tree is green, what will happen when it is dry?"

The last verse in the King James version mentions what will be done if the tree is dry instead of green. What is *Yeshua* saying here? He is suffering in agony, and He is still teaching? Indeed, He is doing so with great sophistication. The message is incredibly powerful, but you have to understand what He is saying.

First of all, *Yeshua* in this passage is hinting at or referring to two different texts in the Tanakh Old Testament Hebrew Scripture. The first one you should recognize in your Bible because it is probably marked: (*Hawshayah*[99] 10:8).

> The high places of wickedness will be destroyed
> it is the sin of *Yesrael*.
> Thorns and thistles will grow up
> and cover their altars.
> Then they will say to the mountains, "Cover us!"
> and to the hills, "Fall on us!"

Hawshayah is prophesying the destruction of *Or-Shlem*. A time of destruction and suffering is coming. The people will cry out to the mountains to fall on them. In other words, they will wish to die because the suffering will be so intense under the judgment of *Yahweh*. *Yeshua* is hinting that *Hawshayah*'s prophecy is about to happen.

Secondly, *Yeshua* is referring to a passage from *Khazkiel*[163]:

> The word of the Lord came to me: "Son of man,
> set your face toward the south; preach against the

south and prophesy against the forest of the southland. Say to the southern forest: 'Hear the word of the Lord. This is what the Sovereign Lord says: I am about to set fire to you, and it will consume all your trees, both green and dry. Everyone will see that I the Lord have kindled it; it will not be quenched.'" (*Khazkiel* 20:45-47)

Where is the south? That is *Yehudah* or *Or-Shlem*. *Yeshua* is wondering if the people crucifying Him are willing to do this when the tree is green, what will they be willing to do when it is dry or dead?

Now examine another passage from *Khazkiel*[163]:

"And when they ask you, Why are you groaning? You shall say, "Because of the news that is coming. Every heart will melt with fear and every hand go limp; every spirit will become faint and every leg will be wet with urine.' It is coming! It will surely take place, declares the Sovereign Lord." (*Khazkiel* 21:7)

The verse above is a continuing prophecy about the destruction of *Or-Shlem*. The green tree is the righteous and the dry tree refers to the wicked people. The dry trees bear no fruit, have no life in them and correspond to the unrighteous, the wicked, and the evil. *Khazkiel* is saying destruction is coming from *Yahweh* and it is going to consume everyone both the righteous and the unrighteous. They are all going to be consumed by the fire and fall under the sword of the Lord.

But to understand what *Yeshua* is saying completely, we must know that in rabbinic tradition during *Yeshua's* day, the term "green tree" was a term for the Messiah, He being the ultimate righteous one.

Yeshua is using the technique of *kol-hakhomer*. *Yeshua* speaks to these women mourning for him, saying, "Do not cry for me. The time is coming very soon when *Or-Shlem*[5] will be destroyed." Indeed, it came only 40 years later in 70 AD, and it was unbelievably horrible. In other words, if they treated *Yeshua*, the Messiah, this way, how much worse will it be for the unrighteous dry tree of *Or-Shlem*?

Even bleeding, His body broken, *Yeshua* manages to teach a truth moving from the simple to the complex with just a single statement. That is powerful!

Day Six: The Golan Heights Theme – The Roman Empire

- **Dado Observation point** – Overlooking the Lebanese border
- **Mount Bental** – Overlooking the Syrian border
- *Tel Dan* – The fortress and altar of the tribe of Dan
- **Caesarea Philippi** – The Roman temple dedicated to the god Pan
- **Dinner** and stay overnight in Kibbutz

Leaving the Hotel

After a healthy breakfast, the group should leave no later than 8:00 am. Much of the day will take place on the *Golan*[102] Heights including Mount Bental, *Tel Dan*, Caesarea Philippi, and the Dado Observation Point.

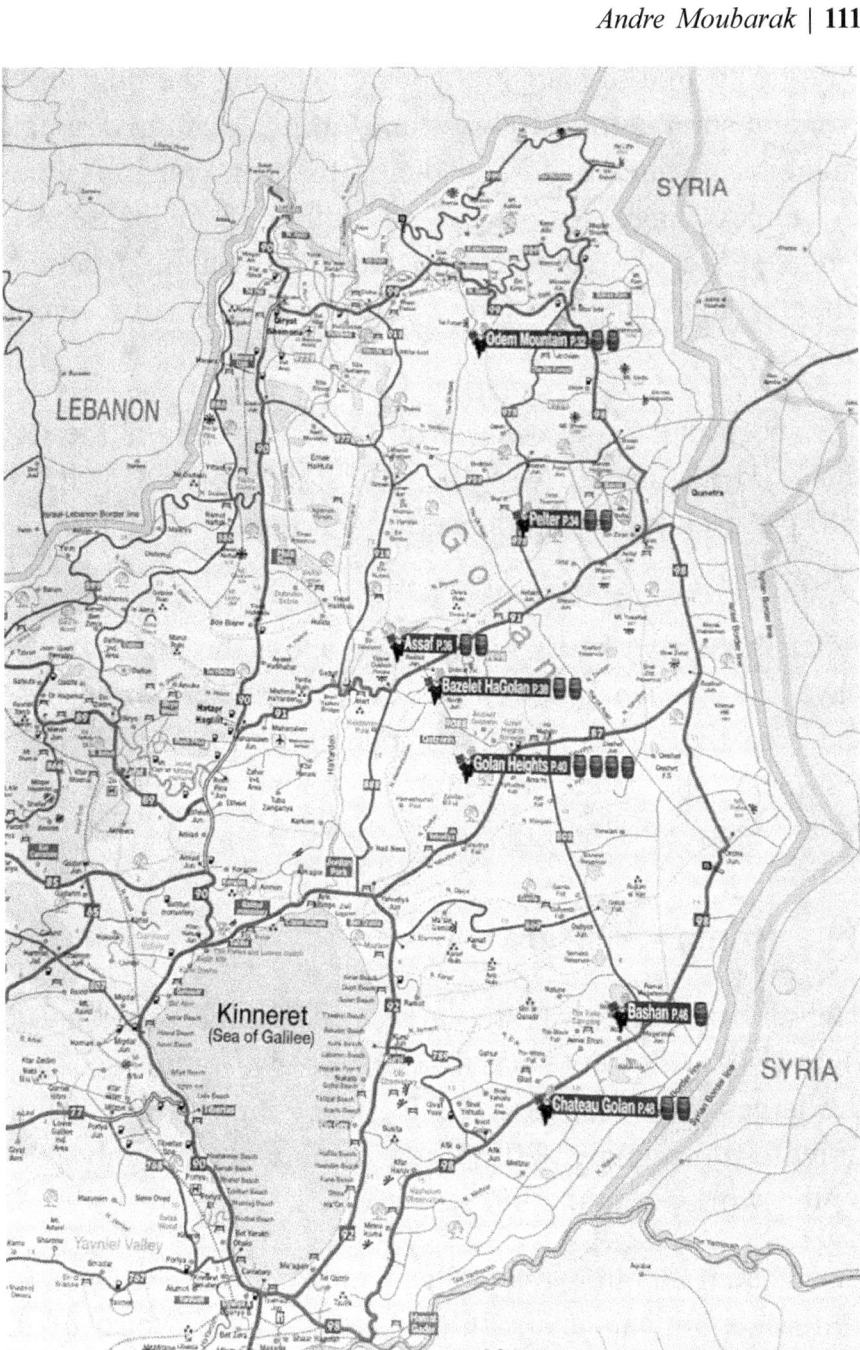

Map of the Golan

I typically like to start the day by teaching the pilgrims a worship song both in Hebrew and Arabic – and in Aramaic if they can handle it. This helps to hear worship songs in Semitic languages. There are around 15 major Semitic languages in the Middle East such as Swahili, Aramaic, Phoenician, Maltese, Hebrew, Arabic, and Amharic, among others.

We specifically sing *Mazmure*[101] 118:24, "This is the day the Lord has made; we will rejoice and be glad in it." It is a great cultural experience to sing the song in multiple languages.

After this time of worship, I teach about the theme of the day: The Roman Empire. The theme was chosen because the area the group visits was under the rule of Herodos Philipus, who ruled on behalf of Rome, which was part of the Decapolis.

The Roman Empire

The city of Rome was the largest city in the world c. 100 BC – c. 400 AD, with Constantinople (New Rome) becoming the largest city around 500 AD. The Empire's population grew to an estimated 70 million inhabitants (roughly 20% of the world's population at the time).

The Roman Empire was among the most powerful economic, cultural, political, and military forces in the world of its time. It was the largest empire of the ancient history era, and one of the largest empires in world history. At its height, under Emperor Trajan, who ruled from 98 to 117

AD, it covered 5 million square kilometres (3 million square miles) and was comprised of what are now 48 nations in the twenty-first century.

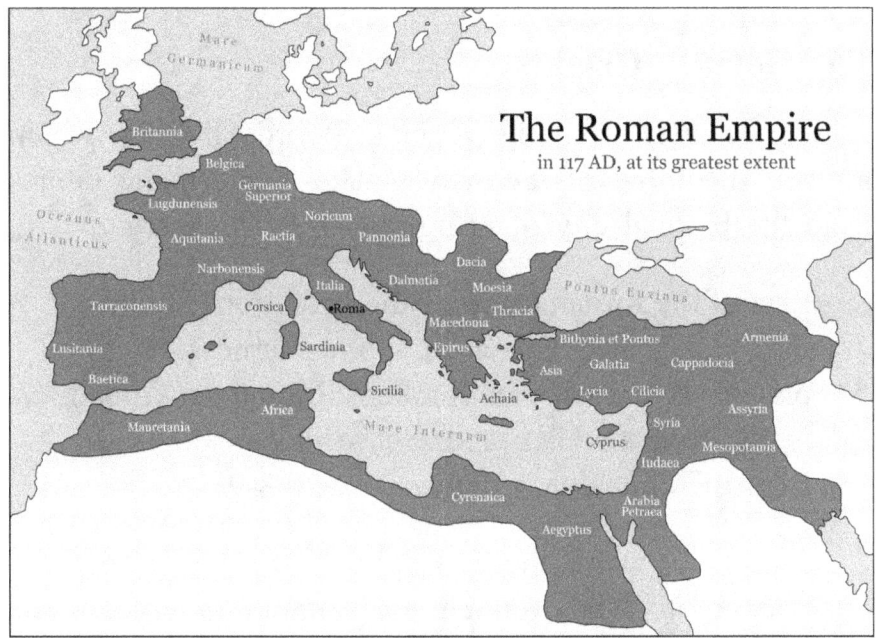

The Ancient Roman World

The vast extent of the Empire ensured the lasting influence of the Latin and Greek languages, culture, religion, inventions, architecture, philosophy, law, and forms of government on its descendants. Throughout the European medieval period, attempts were made to establish successors to the Roman Empire, including the Empire of Romania, a Crusader state.

By means of European colonialism following the Renaissance and their descendant states, Greco-Roman culture was exported on a worldwide scale, playing a crucial role in the development of the modern world, and especially in the United States of America. These nations inherited the Roman way of thinking, which affects the Western Church's mindset to this day.

The Golan[102] Heights

"Golan" comes from the Aramaic word (*Yajoul*), which means "the blow of the wind." The area's name comes from the biblical city of refuge of *Golan* in *Bashan*[103].

> East of the Jordan (on the other side from Jericho), they designated Bezer in the wilderness on the plateau in the tribe of Reuben, Ramoth in Gilead in the tribe of Gad, and *Golan* in *Bashan* in the tribe of Manasseh. (*Yehoshua*[104] 20:8-9)

> The cities were these: Bezer in the wilderness plateau, for the Reubenites; Ramoth in Gilead, for the Gadites; and *Golan* in *Bashan*, for the Manassites. (*Dbarim*[14] 4:43)

According to the Bible, an Amorite kingdom in *Bashan* was conquered by Israelites during the reign of *King Og*[105]. Throughout the Old Testament period, the *Golan* was "the focus of a power struggle between the kings of *Yesrael* and the *Aramaeans* who were based near modern-day *Damascus*.

> And they turned and went up by the way of *Bashan*: and *Og* the king of *Bashan* went out against them, he and all his people, to battle at *Edrei*.

The *Golan* is a rocky plateau, running north and south for 64 Km (40 miles). Its east to west width varies, but averages around 43 km (27 miles) in width. It covers 800 square km (500 square miles). The *Golan* Heights ranges in elevation from 2814 meters (9,232 feet) on *Mount Hermon*[110] in the north to about 396 meters (1,300 feet) high along the *Yarmouk*[107] River in the south.

A large area of volcanic basalt fields stretches north and east. In the north, there is the limestone bedrock of *Mount Hermon* that is separated from the basalt of the *Golan* by a valley called *Nahal Sa'ar*. It is bound on the west by the *Hula*[108] valley and the Sea of Galilee and on the east by the *Raqqad*[109] River. The south, which was known in the Bibly as the land of *Geshur*, is bounded by the *Yarmouk* River and the biblical lands of *Gilad*, part of *Yarden*[76].

The *Golan*[102] Heights is divided into three parts:

1. The Lower *Golan*
2. The Center *Golan*
3. The Upper *Golan*

The Lower Golan

This portion is made up of scenic valleys. Small Druze villages populate the area. It doesn't get much rain and is not good for agriculture. It is roughly 365 meters (1,200 feet) above sea level.

Katzrin[111] is the main city of this region and is famous for its wineries. *Katzrin* started as a Jewish settlement organized as a local council in the *Golan* Heights known as the "*capital of the Golan.*" It is the second largest town after *Majdal-Shams*[112] and has the largest Jewish population. In 2024, it had a population of 10,132. It is the seat of Golan Regional Council.

The Lower Golan

The Center Golan[102]

This region is marked by the *Hula*[111] Lake. It is roughly 76 meters (250 feet) above sea level and is about 193 square km (120 square miles) in size. It is home to the *Hula* Nature Reserve, which is one of the remaining areas of natural oasis in the north. It serves as a reminder of how much the *Golan* looked in the late 19th century. Marsh land and swamps. The Hula Nature Reserve was declared a protected area in 1964.

The Palestinian *Talmud*[113] and the Jerusalem *Talmud* refer to the same *Talmud*, and describes seven ancient seas that surround the land of *Yesrael*. Included among these is the Sea of *Hula*, a huge body of water that once occupied the *Hula* Valley roughly between the modern settlements of *Kiryat Shmona* and *Rosh Pina*. In the 1900s, this swamp and marshland covered somewhere around 6,000 hectares. Draining the swamps became a priority for the Jewish settlers who came to Palestine in the late 19th and early 20th centuries to farm the land.

Agriculture in the Hula Lake

The drainage program was highly successful. However, there was a high price to pay. Many migrating birds ceased nesting and feeding in the area, and some, such as the darter, have never returned. Several mammal species moved out altogether, while others invaded in high numbers.

Fearing the total disappearance of this unique wetland

ecosystem, the remaining area was declared a protected reserve in 1964, and a long-term management plan was devised. New pools connecting to a network of drainage channels were constructed, and constant monitoring of water levels and quality was introduced. To help finance the program, the reserve was opened to tourists in 1978. Attempts were made to bring life back again to the *Hula* Lake, but total recreation has not been achieved.

It is estimated that 500 million migrating birds now pass through the *Hula*[111] Valley every year. It is home to some 550 species of birds, including cranes, white storks, spotted eagles, and pelicans.

Hula Lake with Mount Hermon

The Upper Golan[102]

The Upper *Golan* is a key source of water. Rain runoff feeds the *Yarden*[32] River. It provides one-third of *Yesrael's* water supply. This region is 670 meters (2200 feet) above sea level and is good for agriculture. It features towering mountains and a rugged wilderness quite unlike the landscape of the rest of the country. Seasonal snows are visible on the southern slopes of *Mount Hermon*[114], attracting skiers during the winter months. Many of the Druze villages are surrounded by cherry and apple orchards and beautiful vineyards.

There are more than thirty Jewish settlements on the heights, with an estimated 20,000 settlers. There are some 20,000 Syrians in the area, most of whom are members of the Druze sect.

The Upper Golan

Kiryat Shmona

The town of *Kiryat Shmona* was established in 1949 on the site of the former Syriac village *Al-Khalisa*, whose inhabitants had fled after *Safed* was taken by the *Haganah* forces (Zionist military organization representing the majority of the Jews in Palestine from 1920 to 1948). During the 1948 *Arab–Yesraeli* War, an attempt by the village to come to an agreement with the Jewish authorities was rejected. *Shmona* means "eight" in Hebrew. *Kiryat Shmona* was named after eight Jewish militiamen, commanded by *Joseph Trumpeldor*, who had fallen in the 1920 Battle of *Tel Hai* during the Franco-Syrian War adjacent to the new town. It had originally been named *Kiryat Yosef* for *Trumpeldor*, but the name was changed to *Kiryat Shmona* in June 1950.

In 2024, it had a population of 25,625, the majority of whom are Jews, particularly of Moroccan origins. Located near the *Yesrael-Lebanon* border, *Kiryat Shmona* is border city. To have a virtual tour of the *Yesrael-Lebanon* borders check our virtual tours.

https://www.twinstours.com/virtual-tours

Kyriat Shmona near the Lebanese border

Metulla

Originally a Lebanese agricultural town named *Almtaleh*[115], this is *Yesrael's* most northern town. It is now called *Metulla* in Hebrew. It was one of the string of settlements that Jewish pioneers established in the upper Galilee. Like so many others, it owes its continued existence to the financial support of Baron Edmond de Rothschild. Nicknamed "*Yesrael's* Little Switzerland," it is still best known for "The Good Fence." A term referring to *Yesrael's* mountainous 80-mile northern border with *Lebanon*[116] during the period following the 1978 South *Lebanon* conflict.

When the baron bought his land, the local tenants who had been living on the property were furious. They made life miserable for the new farmers and, in 1920, bloody riots forced the pioneers to evacuate their homes.

But *Metulla*[115] residents were firmly resolved to settle the Upper Galilee, eventually returning to their little community. And it's lucky they did. When the land of *Yesrael* was divided between the English and the French in 1924, the British made sure that the thriving, ever-growing *Metulla* was to be placed inside the British Mandate. Thus, *Metulla's* position at the tip of the Galilee eventually determined the northern border of the State of *Yesrael*.

Metulla is best known for its Canada Center with its huge swimming pool and excellent ice rink. But what we like best about the town is its pastoral ambience and the welcome tranquility it offers to guests.

Beautiful *Ma'ayan* Park, situated at the entrance to *Metulla*, played an important part in the development of the settlement. In the late 19th and early 20th centuries, its spring supplied settlers with all of their water. When it had outlived its usefulness, the spring became covered with weeds and refuse. Fortunately, the Jewish National Fund stepped in and turned the entire area into an enchanting park full of canals, footbridges, and flowing water.

The Good Fence

The Good Fence

The Good Fence (*Fatima* Crossing) was a border crossing from *Metulla*[115] to *Lebanon*[116]; it opened in 1976, and was closed in 2000 after Israel's withdrawal from *Lebanon*. The border crossing had allowed Lebanese to find jobs in northern Israel, have access to health services, attend school, and transport goods.

On the afternoon of Sunday, March 10, 1985, a convoy of IDF (Israel Defence Forces) soldiers in Safari model trucks were driving from *Metulla* toward the Lebanese town of *Marj Ayoun*[117]. Dozens of soldiers, having just attended *Shabbat*, were on their way back to duty. In accordance with regulations, one armed jeep rode in the forefront and two were in the rear. Everyone was equipped with helmets and bulletproof vests. As they were crossing the narrow bridge over *Nahal Ayoun*[118], a red Chevrolet pickup truck drove toward them. The soldierofin the first jeep noticed that the driver had a friendly smile. They signalled for him to pull over and let the convoy pass. The first jeep and the first safari truck did so. The driver of the Chevrolet detonated an explosive device that shattered windows in town. Twelve soldiers were killed and 14 wounded.

During the 2006 *Lebanon* War, *Metulla* became a temporary ghost town when its populace fled *Hezbollah*[119] rocket fire. It was hit by 120 rockets during the war.

Israel–Hamas *War*

On October 7, 2023, the Palestinian Islamist group Hamas launched a surprise and large-scale assault from the Gaza Strip into southern Israel, involving thousands of rockets, armed infiltrations into Israeli communities, and the killing of approximately 1,200 people, including civilians and foreign nationals, and the taking of more than 250 hostages. Israel responded with a massive military offensive against Gaza, triggering what became the current full-scale war between Israel and Hamas. In the midst of the Israel–Hamas war, *Hezbollah*[119] targeted northern Israeli border communities with rockets and missiles, prompting the evacuation of several, including *Metulla*[115]. On October 07, 2023, a Hezbollah-launched anti-tank missile struck *Metulla*, resulting in the injury of one civilian and two IDF reservists. Sadly, wars are normal in this part of the world.

Our First Stop: Dado Observation Point

From here you can see the border crossing point between *Lebanon*[116] and *Yesrael* until the 2000 AD withdrawal of *Yesraeli* troops from southern *Lebanon*. In the past, Lebanese villagers were allowed to pass through in order to work on farms. These days, the border is all camouflage netting and a padlock. The Dado Observation Point gives an excellent perspective on the topography of *Hula* Lake, *Golan*[102], and *Lebanon*.

Dado Observation Point looking at Metula

Lebanon is home to two of the world's oldest cities, *Byblos* and *Sidon*. *Lebanon* is hemmed in by *Syria* and *Yesrael* on the coast of the Mediterranean Sea. Because of its strategic location, it has been part of many conflicts between *Syria* and *Yesrael*. One of the most populous nations in the Mediterranean, *Lebanon* is uniquely composed of both shiite and *Sunni* Muslims, as well as Christians and Druze. The official languages are Arabic, French, English, and Armenian. This diversity has made *Lebanon* a place of refuge for minorities throughout the region.

It is very important to understand the divide between *Shiite* and *Sunni* Muslims. It began in 632 A.D., when the Prophet Muhammad died and a debate emerged about who should be his successor.

Both sides agreed that Allah is the one true God and that Muhammad was his messenger, but one group (which eventually became the Shiites) felt Muhammad's successor should be someone in his bloodline, while the other (the Sunnis) felt a pious individual who would follow the Prophet's customs was acceptable.

The original schism between Islam's two largest sects was not over religious doctrine. It was over political leadership.

Their beliefs over who should have succeeded the Prophet Muhammad are the key theological difference between the two.

Sunnis also have a less elaborate religious hierarchy than *Shiites* have, and the two sects' interpretation of Islam's schools of law is different. *Shiites* give human beings the exalted status that is given only to prophets in the Quran, often venerating clerics as saints, whereas *Sunnis* do not.

The great majority – between 85 and 90 percent – of the world's more than 1.6 billion Muslims are *Sunnis*. *Shiites* constitute about 10 to 15 percent of all Muslims, and globally their population is estimated at less than 200 million.

Whereas *Sunnis* dominate the Muslim world, from West Africa to Indonesia, the *Shiites* are centrally located, with a vast majority in Iran, predominance in Iraq, and sizable populations in *Syria*, *Lebanon* and *Yemen*. When you understand the differences, you understand more the conflict between *Lebanon* and *Yesrael*.

Information about Lebanon[116]

Lebanon is a democratic republic of roughly 6.2 million people, and each major religion is represented in the parliamentary system. A civil war ravaged the nation from 1975 to 1990, and *Yesrael* and *Syria* became heavily involved. *Hezbollah*[119] was formed during this time and is credited with driving out the *Yesraeli* occupation of southern *Lebanon* in 2000. *Hezbollah* is widely viewed as a terrorist organization. It continues to have conflict with *Yesrael*, decimating parts of the country.

More recently, *Lebanon* has taken in roughly one million Syrian refugees, who now make up about thirty percent of the country's population. This refugee crisis has strained the economy. Many Lebanese suffer in poverty due to a lack of jobs and unemployment, and the numbers are increasing. Imagine living without electricity or water for many hours a day, governed by unthinkably corrupt politicians who often don't provide basic services like trash removal because they're too busy fighting about who gets the biggest position.

Map of Lebanon

Helpless people watch as the sectarian warlords enrich themselves while imposing taxes that make the cost of living practically unsustainable. They can only watch as their national institutions grow ever more dysfunctional and the economy hovers on the brink of collapse, all because a small group of very rich old men have long divided the spoils of power while allowing the state to crumble.

Lebanon is roughly 55% Muslim (evenly divided between *Shiite* and *Sunni*) and 40% Christian. This nation is home to the highest concentration of Christian believers in the Middle East. It is the only Arab nation that promotes religious freedom and legally allows for conversion, which provides an open door for the spread of the Gospel. By trying to provide for the physical needs of refugees, such as food, clothing, blankets and education, the Church is seizing opportunities to meet the spiritual needs of these hurting people. Both the size and influence of the Church in *Lebanon* have made it a unique and strategic center for Christian ministry throughout the entire Middle East.

Praying for Lebanon[116] and Learning about Hezbollah[119]

Hezbollah is a political and militant *Shiite* Muslim group based in *Lebanon*. *Hezbollah*, whose name means "Party of Allah" or the "League of Allah" was founded in 1982 following *Yesrael's* invasion of *Lebanon* in the First *Lebanon* War.

This group has close political and military ties with *Syria* and *Iran*. The political arm of *Hezbollah* is deeply involved in Lebanese politics, with seats in the government, and the group has a history of providing social programs, schools, and health care to the Lebanese *Shiite* community.

Hezbollah primarily operates in the *Shiite* dominated areas of southern Beirut, southern *Lebanon*[116], and the *Bakaa* Valley. The group's founding was inspired by the 1979

Islamic Revolution in *Iran*, and it received military assistance from Iran during the 1982 *Yesraeli* invasion of *Lebanon*. Soon after its establishment, *Hezbollah* replaced the *Amal* movement, the dominant *Shiite* military group at the time. Throughout the 1980s, *Hezbollah* carried out attacks against the *Yesraeli* army in *Lebanon* as well as targeting Western interests abroad. Along with Iran, it is the prime suspect in the 1994 bombing of a Jewish cultural center in Buenos Aires in which eighty five people were killed.

Yesrael's success in expelling militant Palestinian groups from southern Lebanon allowed *Hezbollah* to gain a stronger foothold in Lebanese politics. *Hezbollah* operatives were trained by Iranian forces, and the group became highly organized politically and militarily. After two decades of an *Yesraeli* presence in *Lebanon*, the IDF withdrew from the country in 2000 and *Hezbollah* assumed greater power in the war-torn south.

Yesrael's withdrawal from *Lebanon* did not end *Hezbollah's* war against the Jewish State. Although the group initially stated its primary goal was to "liberate" Lebanese soil, it also assumed the banner of fighting for the Palestinians and desiring to defeat *Yesrael* once and for all. With close cooperation from *Syria* and *Iran*, *Hezbollah* continues to confront *Yesrael* over disputed territories.

In the aftermath of the war with *Yesrael*, *Hezbollah* quickly moved toward demanding greater inclusion in *Lebanon's* political decision making. In May 2008, the group successfully received veto power over any cabinet decisions.

Another conflict began on October 8, 2023, when *Hezbollah* launched rockets toward Israeli positions in Shebaa Farms in solidarity with Hamas' October 7th assault. *Yesrael* responded immediately with drone strikes, artillery, and air campaigns deep into southern Lebanon.

Over the next year, peaking in September and November of 2024, *Hezbollah* and *Yesrael* engaged in intense exchanges: rocket barrages and drone strikes by *Hezbollah* contrasted by *Yesraeli* air raids, assassinations of *Hezbollah* leadership (including Hassan Nasrallah and successor Hashem Safieddine), and a covert "pager bomb" operation that left scores dead and injured.

Ceasefire & Aftershocks

A U.S.-brokered ceasefire began on November 27, 2024, requiring *Hezbollah*[119] to withdraw its forces north of the *Litani* River and *Yesrael* to withdraw from southern *Lebanon*[116], with Lebanese Army deployment under UNIFIL supervision. It was extended into early 2025.

Despite the ceasefire, *Yesrael* has carried out neardaily strikes in southern *Lebanon*, including a strike on a *Hezbollah* missile depot in Beirut's Hadath neighborhood in late April 2025.

Hezbollah & Yesrael: Current State in Mid-2025 – Hezbollah's Position

As of August 5, 2025, *Hezbollah* leader Naim Qassem claimed the war had killed 5,000 fighters and wounded

13,000, including leadership losses. Still, he stated the group remains operationally capable and threatened missile attacks if *Yesrael* renews hostilities.

Hezbollah strongly rejected a Lebanese government plan to disarm the group by year's end, dismissing it as U.S. coercion and calling it a "grave sin."

Lebanese Government's Stance

On August 6, 2025, Lebanese authorities directed the army to draft a national disarmament plan aimed at monopolizing weapons under state control by late 2025. *Hezbollah* ministers walked out in protest.

President *Joseph Aoun* has reiterated calls for *Hezbollah's* full disarmament, insisting it be contingent on *Yesrael's* full withdrawal and cessation of air strikes. He also proposed international reconstruction aid tied to the plan.

Hezbollah remains a strong opposition force with representatives in *Lebanon's* parliament, and it still enjoys large support from the country's *Shiite* population as well as backing from *Syria* and *Iran*.

This is a good opportunity to stop and pray for peace and protection while overlooking *Lebanon*. This is a powerful opportunity to build on all the prayers that many pilgrims have given over the years for this part of the world.

From here, the group gets back to the bus and you go to *Tel Dan*.

Tel Dan National Park

Tel Dan is a nature reserve and a major source of water to the *Dan* and *Yarden*[32] Rivers. It is an impressive archaeological site with unique remains of the Canaanite and Israelite cities and of a biblical high place.

The *Tel Dan* Preserve, covering a total area of 120 acres, has four nature trails that cross or follow the brooks and water channels amid the dense plantation that grows in this wonderland. There is also an ancient water-powered flour mill located in the center of the nature preserve. It was built 150 years ago and operated until 1948.

The hike takes about one hour, and it is beautiful. I always like to take the longer hikes that lead us to see more things. I encourage visiting the altar that was built during the reign of the corrupt king *Yerba'am*[126]. We will also see the Israelite city gate and then the Canaanite city gate, also knowns as the *Ob-Rohom*[82] gate.

Tel Dan **National Park**

Biblical Period: The Relocation of Dan

A large number of families from the Israelite tribe of *Dan* relocated during the 12th century BC from the central region near the Mediterranean Sea the coastal plain of *Yesrael* to the area around the Canaanite city of *Laish-Leshem*[120]. They were forced out of the coastal plain by the Philistines. The area on the foothills of *Mount Hermon*[114] was a perfect place, since it is located in the heart of a fertile valley with plenty of water coming down from *Mount Hermon* and the hills around it. The tribe of *Dan* changed its destiny for a better life. The clan members refused what *Yehoshua*[104] allotted for them when he divided the land.

The Bible tells how six hundred families of the tribe of *Dan* looked for a substitute for their location by sending five spies to the Canaanite city named *Laish*. The story is found in (*Shophetim*[121] 18 1-2).

> In those days *Yesrael* had no king. And in those days, the tribe of the Danites was seeking a place of their own where they might settle, because they had not yet come into an inheritance among the tribes of *Yesrael*. So, the Danites sent five of their leading men from Zorah and Eshtaol to spy out the land and explore it. These men represented all the Danites. They told them, "Go, explore the land." So, they entered the hill country of Ephraim and came to the house of Micah, where they spent the night.

The spies returned and praised the fertile area (*Shophetim*[121] 18:9):

> We have seen the land, and behold, it is very good.

They later captured the city (*Shophetim* 18:27):

> And came unto *Laish*, unto a people that were at quiet and secure: and they smote them with the edge of the sword, and burnt the city with fire.

The Israelites renamed the city to *Dan* (*Yehoshua*[104] 19:47):

> And the coast of the children of *Dan* went out too little for them: therefore, the children of *Dan* went up to fight against *Leshem*, and took it, and smote it with the edge of the sword, and possessed it, and dwelt therein, and called *Leshem*, *Dan*, after the name of *Dan* their father.

The Israelite city walls

The High Place

On the north side of the mound, above the spring and overlooking the valley with beautiful views of *Mount Hermon*[114], is the area that is the remains of a high place. The excavation team unearthed and reconstructed the remains of a unique Israelite ritual place. It was in use since the times of King *Yeroba'am*[124], son of *Nebat* (930 BC), and reused during the Hellenistic period (3rd century BC) until the end of the Roman period.

The altar of Tel Dan

The above photo shows a reconstruction of the altar in the center (the metal frame), the houses of the priests (behind the altar), and a large, raised platform: *Bemah*[122] to the right of the great oak tree, with an 8-meter (26 foot) staircase leading up from the altar.

High places consisted of a platform with various cult objects and an altar that provided a place for the sacrificial offerings in places other than *Or-Shlem*. Some of these high places were set aside for *Yahweh* and some were used for foreign gods. The use of high places to worship foreign gods is universally condemned in the Bible. (*Dbarim*[14] 12:1-7) makes it clear that once the *Hayklo*[3] is built, people should worship the Lord there:

> These are the decrees and laws you must be careful to follow in the land that the Lord, the *Yahweh* of your ancestors, has given you to possess as long as you live in the land. Destroy completely all the places on the high mountains, on the hills and under every spreading tree, where the nations you are dispossessing worship their gods. Break down their altars, smash their sacred stones and burn their Asherah poles in the fire; cut down the idols of their gods and wipe out their names from those places.
>
> You must not worship the Lord your *Yahweh* in their way. But you are to seek the place the Lord your *Yahweh* will choose from among all your tribes to put his Name there for his dwelling. To that place you must go; there bring your burnt offerings and sacrifices, your tithes and special gifts, what you have vowed to give and your freewill offerings, and the firstborn of your herds and flocks. There, in the presence of the Lord your *Yahweh*, you and your families shall eat and shall rejoice in everything you have put your hand to, because the Lord your *Yahweh* has blessed you.

King *Hizkiyyah*[123] successfully removes the high places dedicated to *Yahweh* in (2 *Malachim* 18:4):

> He removed the high places, smashed the sacred stones and cut down the *Asherah* poles. He broke into pieces the bronze snake *Moshe* had made, for up to that time the Israelites had been burning incense to it.

The purpose was so that people might worship at the *Hayklo*³ in *Or-Shlem* (2 *Malachim*⁹⁰ 18:22):

> But if you say to me, "We are depending on the Lord our *Yahweh*"—isn't he the one whose high places and altars Hezekiah removed, saying to *Yehudea* and *Or-Shlem*, "You must worship before this altar in *Or-Shlem*"?

Manasseh rebuilt the high places, but it wasn't until *Josiah* became king that there was a systematic removal of high places read (2 *Malachim*⁹⁰ 23:1-29).

Scholars have determined that this archaeological find in Dan is not only a high place but an actual *Hayklo*³ complex in which the golden calf was located. Let me set the stage for you and give you the background of the story. In (1 *Malachim* 11:34-39), *Yahweh* is furious with *King Solomon* for his lack of faithfulness and tells *Yarba'am*[124] that He will give him a dynasty as great as *Dawood's*[125] if he will just obey Him:

> But I will not take the whole kingdom out of *Shelmo's* hand; I have made him ruler all the days

of his life for the sake of my servant, whom I chose and who obeyed my commands and decrees. I will take the kingdom from his son's hands and give you ten tribes. I will give one tribe to his son so that *Dawood* my servant may always have a lamp before me in *Or-Shlem*, the city where I chose to put my Name. However, as for you, I will take you, and you will rule over all that your heart desires; you will be king over *Yesrael*. If you do whatever I command you and walk in obedience to me and do what is right in my eyes by obeying my decrees and commands, as *Dawood* my servant did, I will be with you. I will build you a dynasty as enduring as the one I built for *Dawoo*d and will give *Yesrael* to you. I will humble *Dawood's* descendants because of this, but not forever.'"

(1 *Malachim*[90] 12:25-31):

But *Yarba'am*[83] refuses to obey *Yahweh* and thinks he knows better how to establish his kingdom, so the Bible describes *Yarba'am*, son of *Nebat*, erecting a golden calf and building an altar in *Dan*. The purpose of the ritual place was to serve as an alternative worship site in place of *Or-Shlem*. After *Yarba'am* divided the kingdom, he didn't want his people to return to *Or-Shlem* to worship *Yahweh*, so he built two places as alternatives: one in *Beth-El* and the other in *Dan*. This marked the start of the civil war between *Yehuda* and *Yesrael*.

Then *Yarba'am* fortified *Shechem*[169] in the hill

country of *Ephraim* and lived there. From there he went out and built up *Peniel*.

Yarba'am thought to himself, "The kingdom will now likely revert to the house of *Dawood*. If these people go up to offer sacrifices at the *Hayklo* of the Lord in *Or-Shlem,* they will again give their allegiance to their lord, *Rehav'am*[126] king of *Yehudea*. They will kill me and return to King *Rehoboam*."

After seeking advice, the king made two golden calves. He said to the people, "It is too much for you to go up to *Or-Shlem*. Here are your gods, *Yesrael*, who brought you up out of *Metsrayin*[24]." One he set up in *Beth-El*, and the other in *Dan*. And this thing became a sin; the people came to worship the one at *Beth-El* and went as far as *Dan* to worship the other.

Yarba'am built shrines on high places and appointed priests from all sorts of people, even though they were not Levites. He instituted a festival on the fifteenth day of the eighth month, like the festival held in Judah, and offered sacrifices on the altar. This he did in *Beth-El*, sacrificing the calves he had made. And at *Beth-El* he also installed priests at the high places he had made. On the fifteenth day of the eighth month, a month of his own choosing, he offered sacrifices on the altar he had built at *Beth-El*. So, he instituted the festival for the Israelites and went up to the altar to make offerings.

Why did *Yarba'am* pick these two sites? *Dan* is in the opposite direction of *Or-Shlem* and *Beth-El*, 16 km (10 miles) north of *Or-Shlem*. The King is imitating the real *Or-Shlem* and thus causes *Yesrael* to sin. He is hoping to get pilgrims to stop at *Beth-El* and not to travel the few more miles to *Or-Shlem*. This is another trick of *Shaitan*[54] to set up camp just off where *Yahweh* wants us to be or send us in the opposite direction away from *Yahweh*, to distract the nation from worshiping in the real *Hayklo*[3].

The Golden Calf

Yarba'am set up golden calves in *Dan* and *Beth-El*. There is an interesting history here. Here's a similar story from (*Shemoth*[22] 32:1-8).

> When the people saw that *Moshe* was so long in coming down from the mountain, they gathered around *Ahron*[126] and said, "Come, make us gods who will go before us. As for this fellow *Moshe* who brought us up out of *Metsrayin*[24], we don't know what has happened to him."
>
> *Ahron* answered them, "Take off the gold earrings that your wives, your sons and your daughters are wearing, and bring them to me." So, all the people took off their earrings and brought them to *Ahron*. He took what they handed him and made it into an idol cast in the shape of a calf, fashioning it with a tool. Then they said, "These are your gods, *Yesrael*, who brought you up out of *Metsrayin*."

> When *Ahron* saw this, he built an altar in front of the calf and announced, "Tomorrow there will be a festival to the Lord." So, the next day the people rose early and sacrificed burnt offerings and presented fellowship offerings. Afterward, they sat down to eat and drink and got up to indulge in revelry.
>
> Then the Lord said to *Moshe*, "Go down, because your people, whom you brought up out of *Metsrayin*[24], have become corrupt. They have been quick to turn away from what I commanded them and have made themselves an idol cast in the shape of a calf. They have bowed down to it and sacrificed to it and have said, 'These are your gods, *Yesrael*, who brought you up out of *Metsrayin*.'"

What was the problem at the beginning of this story? Impatience! The people did not like how long it was taking for *Moshe* to commune with *Yahweh*. Why does *Ahron* tell the people to remove their earrings because they represent slavery in *Metsrayin*? These earrings should have represented their allegiance to *Yahweh* as master, but these rings are the very things they use to build an idol.

The people were saying that they were their own masters. Notice that *Aharon* only asked for the earrings from the women and children. But whatever his reasons for this, all the people, men included, throw their earrings into the fire.

(*Shemoth*[22] 32:5-6):

> When *Ahron* saw this, he built an altar in front

of the calf and announced, "Tomorrow there will be a festival to the Lord." So, the next day the people rose early and sacrificed burnt offerings and presented fellowship offerings. Afterward, they sat down to eat and drink and got up to indulge in revelry.

Ahron creates a festival that *Yahweh* has not ordained, all in an effort to please the people. He even claims it as a festival to the *Yahweh*, but on the eve of the festival, he points to the calf and proclaims that it is the God responsible for bringing the Children of *Yesrael* out of *Metsrayin*[24]. Everyone involved breaks the First Commandment: "I am the Lord thy *Yahweh*, thou shalt not have any strange gods before Me." In fact, *Ahron* makes the people into idols in his desire to please them. Notice the result of these actions: the people go wild.

He builds an altar in front of the golden calf. This is the normal position for an altar so *Yahweh* can see the sacrifice. But where does *Shemoth*[22] say the altar of burnt offerings is supposed to go? Outside the holy of holies, beyond the curtain. This was so that the people of *Yesrael* could exercise their faith and believe that *Yahweh* sees their sacrifices. Again, *Ahron* is attempting to remove the need for faith.

What is *Yahweh's* response? He gives them what they want. They desire to be their own masters, so He sends them to the Promised Land without his presence. In *Shemoth* Chapter 32, humans seek to control their experiences of *Yahweh* and religion. Their impatience, the desire for no master, their lack of faith, and the longing to mold and create their own beliefs are an affront to *Yahweh*. *Ahron* is dragged into their sin even as he tries to rescue them.

Yarba'am Changes *Sukkot*[128]

(*1 Malachim*[90] 12:31-33) reads:

> *Yarba'am* built shrines on high places and appointed priests from all sorts of people, even though they were not Levites. He instituted a festival on the fifteenth day of the eighth month, like the festival held in *Yehudah,* and offered sacrifices on the altar. This he did in *Beth-El,* sacrificing to the calves he had made. And at *Beth-El* he also installed priests at the high places he had made. On the fifteenth day of the eighth month, a month of his own choosing, he offered sacrifices on the altar he had built at *Beth-El.* So, he instituted the **festival** for the Israelites and went up to the altar to make offerings.

The festival being talked about is the Feast of *Sukkot. Yahweh* instituted the Feast of *Sukkot* on the fifteenth day of the seventh month. *Yarba'am* moves the festival to the fifteenth day of the eighth month. Why does he make it later? Crops ripen later for people in the north, so this made the Feast of *Sukkot* more convenient.

What is *Yarba'am* doing? The same thing *Ahron* did. He is trying to please the people to hold their allegiance. He invents something that looks like what *Yahweh* wants but is not what *Yahweh* has commanded. It is an imitation just to please the people.

Let's look at the result of *Yarba'am* actions in (2 *Malachim*[90] 10:29-32).

However, he did not turn away from the sins of *Yarba'am* son of *Nebat,* which he had caused *Yesrael* to commit—the worship of the golden calves at *Beth-El* and *Dan.*

The Lord said to *Jehu,* "Because you have done well in accomplishing what is right in my eyes and have done to the house of *Ahab*[49] all I had in mind to do, your descendants will sit on the throne of *Yesrael* to the fourth generation." Yet *Jehu* was not careful to keep the law of the Lord, the *Yahweh* of *Yesrael,* with all his heart. He did not turn away from the sins of Jeroboam, which he had caused *Yesrael* to commit.

In those days, the Lord began to reduce the size of *Yesrael*. Hazael overpowered the Israelites throughout their territory.

Yesrael begins to shrink. This is what happens when we try and cut *Yahweh* out of our lives. The more we minimize *Yahweh's* presence in our lives and start to depend on ourselves, the more the influence of the *Roho-Kodsho*[8] begins to retreat.

This is clearly the handiwork of *Shaitan*. He sets up rival systems of religion to compete against what *Yahweh* is doing. He wants people to move in the opposite direction. The same is true for those who only come to church looking for what they can get out of it instead of what they can contribute.

There is also a danger here of pastors becoming like *Ahron* and *Yarba'am*, using technology and money in such ways that it removes the need for faith. Pastors might do this because they want to please the people and not lose them.

The difference between what *Yarba'am* does and what happened in *Shemoth* 32 is that *Moshe* moves quickly to put an end to the idolatry. This doesn't happen with *Yarba'am*. *Yarba'am* never repents of his actions and never removes the golden calves from *Dan* and *Beth-El*.

The ultimate result of what *Yarba'am* does is the enslavement of *Yesrael*. In 721 BC, the Assyrian army captured the Israelite capital of Samaria and carried away the citizens of the northern Kingdom of *Yesrael* into captivity. *Beth-El* and *Dan* were destroyed completely. But the kingdom of the south, *Yehuda,* with its capital, *Or-Shlem*, survives. After the fall of the Northern Kingdom, the kings of *Yehuda* try to extend their influence, protection, and authority to those inhabitants who yet remain. The latter part of the reigns of *King Ahaz* and *King Hizkiyyah*[126] are periods of stability during which *Yehuda* consolidates both politically and economically. When you are with *Yahweh*, you are always protected.

This is a great time to rest and take pictures.

The Canaanite City Gate – Ob-Rohom's[82] Gate

Tel Dan was settled first settled during the Neolithic period nine thousand years ago. It became a city in the early Bronze Age (2700-2400 BC). The city expanded and transformed into a large Canaanite city (18th Century BC). The ancient city—named *Leshem*[120] or *Laish* covers a large area. Then the Israelites captured it (12th century BC).

The Canaanite Gate – Ob-Rohom Gate

The abundant source of water, its strategic location on major ancient crossroads, the *Via Maris*[31], the road of the sea, and the fertile valley around it were the reasons why a mighty Canaanite city was established here almost 5,000 years ago. The 18th century BC Canaanite city had an impressive brick gate on its southeast side that was (7 meters /275 inches high), which was unearthed by archaeologists. A stepped path approaches the gate from the east. The gate is built of three arches, which were constructed from sun-baked bricks.

The outer arch (2.4m /94 inches wide) is visible on the sides of the entrance. The arch-shaped lintel is one of the earliest complete standing arches found in the world, and the archway is the earliest intact structure in the world. To help preserve this find, a modern arched construction was built over it to protect it from the elements.

This was the gate *Ob-Rohom*[82] passed through during his pursuit of the northern kings. *Bereshith*[72] 14:14): "And when Abram heard that his brother was taken captive, he armed his trained servants, born in his own house, three hundred and eighteen, and pursued them unto Dan."

The Israelite Gate

The large Israelite gate, dating back to the Kingdom of *Ahab*[49] (9th century BC), was reconstructed by archaeologists. A large, paved space (400 m2/15,7748 inches) is located in front of the gate. The main gate was composed of three pairs of beams surrounding a paved road that entered the city. This design created four guard rooms, which is typical of Iron Age gates from the time of *Shelmon*[148] and *Dawood*[125].

Israelite city gate chambers

The Israelite gate is based on an outer gate and an inner gate, which is located on the left of the wall in the center. The road winds its way to the left, passing through the inner gate, moving between two pairs of chambers on both sides, then continues into the city.

Opposite the gate's opening is the base of a canopy, which is modelled on the flower-shaped stones with top grooves that hold the poles. The raised platform may have been the sitting place of the king or judge. Second (*Malachim*[90] 23:8): "Then the king arose, and sat in the gate."

The seat of the king

The city gate was very important in biblical times. It was the central location for many activities. Important business transactions were conducted there, courts were convened, and public announcements were often heralded at the city gate.

The city gate was an important cultural hub of society, and the Bible speaks about it often. (*Mishley*[149] *1:21*) says, "She cry in the chief place of concourse, in the openings of the gates: in the city she utters her words." In order to speak wisdom to the masses, words were spoken loudly at the city gate.

- The Bible first discusses the city gate in (*Bereshith*[99] 19:1). At the gate of *Sodom, Lot, Ob-Rohom*'s nephew, greeted the angelic visitors to his city.

- In (*Ruth* 4:1-11), *Boaz* officially claims the position of kinsman-redeemer by meeting with the city elders at the gate of *Beth-Lhem*[63]. It was at the city gate that the legal matters concerning his marriage to Ruth were resolved.

- Likewise, in (*Dbarim*[14] 21:18-12), the Bible speaks of the parents of a rebellious son who were told to bring the boy to the city gate, where the elders of the city would examine the evidence and pass judgment on him.

- (1 *Samo'el*[131] 4:18) says that when *Yesrael* battled with the Philistines, the priest *Eli* waited at the city gate for news about the ark and to hear how his sons fared in battle.

- King *Dawood*, as the ruler of *Yesrael*, stood before his troops and gave instructions from the city gate (2 *Samo'el* 18:1-5). When *Dawood's* son *Ab-Shalom*[132] died, *Dawood* returned to the city gate along with his people (2 *Samo'el* 19:1-8). King *Dawood's* appearance at the gate signalled that the time of mourning was over and that the king was once again back to governing.

- Controlling the gates of a conquered enemy was a symbol of defeating that enemy. Part of *Oh-Rohom's*[82] blessing from the Lord was the promise that "your offspring shall possess the gate of his enemies" (*Bereshith*[99] 22:17).

- In (*Mattai* 16:18), *Yeshua* declared, "And I say also unto thee, that thou art *Kepha*[2], and upon this rock I

- will build my church; and the gates of hell shall not prevail against it." *Yeshua's* statement made clear that the evil plans of *Shaitan,* which would take place at the gates, would not destroy the church that *Yahweh* ordained.

In essence, the city gate was the "town square" of culture in biblical times. Behind it, along the wall, is a stone bench on which the elders of the city sat. This custom is referred to in several biblical passages.

The House of Dawood Inscription

Fragments of a basalt stone with an Aramaic inscription, dated to the 9th century BC, were found in the wall. This unique stele includes a reference to the "House of *Dawood,*" and parallels to the biblical description in (*2 Malachim*[90]), of the murders of Kings *Yoram* and *Ahaziah.*

An Aramaean king, most likely *Hazael of Damascus,* occupied the Israelite city of *Dan* ~840 BC after which he evidently erected this inscription in a public place to indicate his reign over the city. After his hold on the city ended, the Israelites seem to have torn down the inscription, broken it up, and reused its fragments in the construction of a new outer gate.

Why is this inscription so important historically? In this text, the Aramaean king claims to have killed the kings of both *Yesrael* (*Yoram*) and *Yehuda* (*Ahaziah*) in the course of his southern conquests. Interestingly, this parallels an account of the murders of *Yoram* and *Ahaziah* in (*2 Malachim*[90] 9), but in the Hebrew Bible's account, it is *Jehu* who kills the two kings in a bloody coup and seizes the throne of *Yesrael* for himself!

So, we have a strange, complicated set of parallel texts, in which each names a different murderer. More importantly, perhaps, is the fact that the Aramaean king refers to the kingdom of *Yehuda* by its dynastic name, a name frequently used in the Hebrew Bible as well: The House of *Dawood*. This not only indicates that the family of *Dawood*[125] still sat on the throne of *Or-Shlem*, but this inscription represents the oldest textual reference to the historical King *Dawood* ever discovered!

House of David inscription in Aramaic

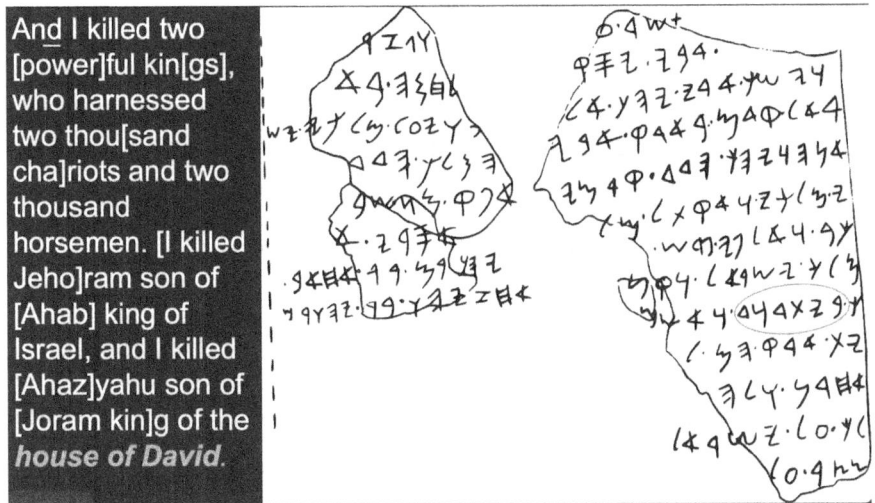

And I killed two [power]ful kin[gs], who harnessed two thou[sand cha]riots and two thousand horsemen. [I killed Jeho]ram son of [Ahab] king of Israel, and I killed [Ahaz]yahu son of [Joram kin]g of the *house of David*.

Translation of the inscription

Tel Dan - The Modern Period

The city was in ruins since the Roman period, and its location was lost. The site was examined in the PEF (Palestine Exploration Fund) survey (1866-1877) by Wilson, Conder, and Kitchener. They correctly identified it as the site of Dan, based on *Josephus* and other writings.

The site was excavated by an *Yesraeli* team headed by *Aharon Birun* (1968-1970) and a new team (since 2005). Some of the archaeological findings are on display in the regional nature and archaeological museum of Beit-Ussishkin, located nearby in Kibbutz *Dan*.

Tel Dan was a front military post until 1967, when the border with *Lebanon*[116] and Syria passed at this location. A great panorama of *Mount Hermon*[114] and the bordering villages in *Lebanon* can be seen from this abandoned trench located near the high place.

The nature reserve of *Tel Dan* is open to the public with a choice of various trails and interests and is one of the most fascinating sites in the area. It combines both natural attractions, pools, streams, plantations, and historic cities with unique findings, so come and visit this place, a few groups include *Tel Dan* in their itineraries.

The Bus Drive to Caesarea Philippi – Panias

Before leaving, try the apples. The *Golan*[102] Heights apples are among the best in the world, and everyone enjoys them. Caesarea Philippi is on the border between *Yesrael* and *Lebanon*[116], and you'll be able to see Lebanese villages, such as *Ghajar* village on the drive.

Ghajar is an Alawite-Arab village on the *Hasbani* River on the border between Lebanon and the *Yesraeli*-occupied portion of the *Golan* Heights, internationally considered to be part of Syria. In 2024, it had a population of 3,607.

In 1967, *Yesrael* captured the *Golan* Heights from Syria and those *Ghajar* residents who remained later chose to accept *Yesraeli* citizenship when the territory was annexed in 1981. In 1982, when *Yesrael* occupied southern *Lebanon*, the village expanded into Lebanese territory. When *Yesrael* pulled out of southern *Lebanon* in 2000, the residents in northern *Ghajar* suddenly found themselves living in *Lebanon*, while their relatives and neighbors who previously lived just across the street now lived in a separate country and in an enemy state.

Ghajar Village

The division of the village (one-half in *Yesrael*, the other in *Lebanon*) lasted until 2006 when *Yesrael* invaded north *Ghajar* during the Second *Lebanon* War.

In November 2005, *Hezbollah* launched an assault on the village, firing mortars and *Katyusha* rockets on IDF positions and civilian houses. Nine months later, an all-out war erupted, triggered by a cross-border kidnapping of two *Yesraeli* soldiers not far from *Ghajar*. The second *Lebanon* war resulted in the deaths of over one thousand four hundred Lebanese and one hundred sixty-three *Yesraelis*.

But while the residents of *Ghajar* have endured wars and terrorism, their concern is the future of the village. The UN and *Beirut* insist that the northern half of the village should be returned to *Lebanon*[116], despite the fact that the

Blue Line border runs directly through *Ghajar's* center and several nearby houses. In 2010, the *Yesraeli* cabinet came close to an agreement to withdraw but the matter remains to be settled. The residents are opposed to the division.

Caesarea Philippi – The Roman Temple of Pan

Pan was the god of shepherds and flocks, of mountain wilds, of hunting, and of rustic music. He wandered the hills and mountains of Arkadia in Greece, playing his panpipes and chasing Nymphs, a female Greek deity. This Greek legend tells us that Pan's unseen presence aroused feelings of panic in men passing through the remote, lonely places of the wilds in Greece.

Pan is depicted as a man with the horns, legs, and tail of a goat, with a thick beard, snub nose, and pointed ears. He often appears in the entourage of Dionysus alongside the other rustic gods. Greeks in the classical age associated his name with the word "pan"—meaning "all." In short, the Temple of Pan was the main place of worship, while the Court of Pan was an outdoor area for rituals and celebrations. How was he honored?

Sacrifices: Revelers threw goats into the water inside the cave. If the animal disappeared into the depths, it meant Pan had accepted the offering. If blood appeared, it meant the sacrifice was rejected.

Dancing and Music: After offering the sacrifice, the people stayed and enjoyed themselves. They played flutes, drums, and lyres, creating wild, lively music. Men and women danced in a circle, moving their feet quickly, clapping, and sometimes even leaping like playful goats just like Pan himself!

The dancing wasn't just for fun; it was a way to connect with nature and to show respect to Pan's wild energy.

Pan

People sometimes wore wreaths made of leaves or animal skins to feel closer to him. They believed their dancing connected them to Pan. The dancing often continued for hours, sometimes even all night, filled with laughter, song, and celebration. It was a way to thank Pan for his blessings and to ask for his protection in the future.

Many pagan gods, including Pan, were connected to fertility. People believed that by engaging in certain sexual acts near the temple, they would gain blessings for good crops, healthy animals, and strong children.

Prayers for Protection: Since Pan was associated with nature and animals, people prayed to him for protection over their flocks, crops, and even themselves when they were in the wilderness.

There is no record of *Yeshua* entering the city, but the Great Confession and the Transfiguration both occurred in the vicinity of what was known as *Caesarea Philippi* (*Mattai* 16:13).

The Sacred Niches

Adjacent to the sacred cave is a rocky cliff with a series of hewn niches. We know that statues of the deity were placed in these niches by depictions of such on coins of the city. Inscriptions in the niches mention those who gave large donations. *Caesarea Philippi* was more than a city. It was a pantheon carved into the cliffs.

Canaanites worshipped *Ba'al*, the storm god of fertility. *Ba'al* means "master," and his cult was rooted in controlling nature.

Greeks introduced Pan, the half-goat god of wild places and sexual chaos. The cave in Caesarea Philippi was known as the Gates of Hades, a portal to the underworld.

Hermes, messenger of the gods, and guardian of travelers and commerce and trade, was also venerated here.

Under Roman rule, Zeus and Nemesis were honored with temples. (2nd Temple Period).

Augustus Caesar was deified here. The Imperial Cult built temples proclaiming, "Caesar is Lord."

The river Banias with the niches

Andre waiting for his group

Read (*Mattai* 16:13-18):

When *Yeshua* came to the region of Caesarea Philippi, he asked his disciples, "Who do people say the Son of Man is?" They replied, "Some say *Yohannon Hamatbil*; others say *Elyahu*; and still others, *Yermyahu*[86] or one of the prophets." But what about you? he asked. "Who do you say I am?" *Kepha* answered, "You are the *Mshiho*[10], the Son of the living *Yahweh*." *Yeshua* replied, "Blessed are you, *Kepha bar Yonnon*, for this was not revealed to you by flesh and blood, but by my Father in heaven. And I tell you that you are *Kepha,* and on this rock I will build my church, and the gates of Hades will not overcome it. I will give you the keys of the kingdom of heaven; whatever you bind on earth will be bound in heaven, and whatever you loose on earth will be loosed in heaven." Then he ordered his disciples not to tell anyone that he was the Messiah.

Why Did Yeshua Bring His Disciples to Caesarea Philippi?

It is at least a two-day walk from Galilee to *Caesarea Philippi*. But *Yeshua* had something He needed to teach his disciples. In a way, it was like a graduation lesson for them. *Yeshua* was with the Apostles for almost three years, teaching them about the Kingdom of Heaven, but *Yeshua's* time was almost up. Soon, He would go up to *Or-Shlem*[5] to be crucified, and his disciples would need to take up what He had started.

So, *Yeshua* brought his disciples to this Roman pagan temple and asked them the famous question found in (*Mattai*[4] 16:13): "Who do people say the Son of Man is?"

Yeshua wanted to know if his disciples understood who He was, but first, He asked them who other people thought He was. The disciples gave four answers about people who were dead by that time.

1. *Yohannon Hamatbil*[74]: Herodos's son (Herodos Antipas) was responsible for *Yohannon* death, but some people thought he had been reborn or resurrected.

2. *Elyahu*[87]: He was a prophet from the Old Testament thought by Jews to return to Earth to welcome and prepare for the Messiah.
3. *Yermyahu*[86]: This is another Old Testament prophet who suffered for delivering *Yahweh's* message and spoke of the need for a new covenant between *Yahweh* and His people.
4. One of the other prophets.

But what did the disciples think?

Kepha, often the spokesperson for the disciples, answered, "You are the *Mshiho*[10], the Son of the living *Yahweh*." The disciples had spent time listening to *Yeshua* and witnessing his miracles. However, *Yeshua* said that it was *Yahweh,* through the *Roho-Kodsho,* who brought *Kepha* to his understanding. *Yeshua* praised *Kepha* for speaking out and made important promises concerning *Kepha* and the Church.

Early Jewish tradition says that the word "rock" does not literally refer to *Kepha* but to his words when he declared that *Yeshua* was the *Mshiho*[10], *Yahweh's* Son. *Yeshua* meant that the foundation of the Church was to be this faith.

- *Kepha* is the stone in *Yahweh's* building. *Yeshua* is the foundation and *Yahweh's* building is the Church. *Kepha* was the first person to declare a belief in *Yeshua* and he became an important leader and teacher in the Early Church. On the day of *El-khamsin*[133], he was the first to start preaching, and over 3,000 people were converted.

- The Roman Catholic Church teaches that at Caesarea Philippi, *Kepha* was made the first Pope and the keys are a symbol of the authority he was given. This authority, Catholics believe, has been passed down through generation after generation of pontiffs, right down to the present day. The Pope, as *Yahweh's* representative on Earth, has the power to forgive sin and permit or prohibit things on Earth.

The Temple of Pan Was Built on a Rock

The *Hayklo* of Pan was built upon a large rock. *Yeshua* brings his disciples to this place and tells them, "On the rock of revelation that *Yeshua* the *Mshiho*[10], I will build my church." In an Aramaic mindset, the disciples knew his words were a metaphor. They could see the rock upon which the Temple of Pan was built. To them, *Yeshua* was saying that his church would overshadow the *Hayklo* of Pan. The name of *Yeshua* would spread throughout the Roman world. *Yeshua* assured the Apostles that his name would prevail against everything they could see.

This is exactly what happened after 400 years. The entire Roman world followed the message of *Yeshua*. The word "church" (*Kehila* in Hebrew, *Beth-Edtho* in Aramaic) means "a congregation or community." *Yeshua* told *Kepha* that he and the other disciples would carry the Lord's vision and conquer the pagan Roman world. This certainly happened when Rome upheld the name of *Yeshua* over every god they once worshiped! The *Kehila* of *Yeshua* was built and became a community of believers all over the world.

Caesarea Philippi Was Located in Enemy Territory

In the Old Testament, *Yahweh* stood in the middle of *Yesrael* and drew followers to himself. In *Yeshua, Yahweh* invaded enemy territory to redeem humanity. *Caesarea Philippi* was under Roman control. *Yeshua* brought his disciples to enemy territory to make this claim of his Church. He proclaimed that He was above all gods, even the god of Pan. The keys *Yeshua* mentioned represent power and authority of the Kingdom of Heaven over Roman gods on earth.

Caesarea Philippi: The Gateway to Hades

At the time of *Yeshua,* the hole in the rock upon which the *Hayklo*[3] of Pan stood was part of a larger cave system. The spring water flowing out from under the rocks once flowed out of the cave in *Yeshua's* day.

Josephus in his *Jewish Wars (1.21.3),* tells us:

> Where is a top of a mountain that is raised to an immense height, and at its side, beneath, or at its bottom, a dark cave opens itself, within which there is a horrible precipice that descends abruptly to a vast depth. It contains a mighty quantity of water, which is immovable, and when anybody lets down anything to measure the depth of the earth beneath the water, no length of cord is sufficient to reach it.

As was mentioned, sacrifices to Pan were thrown into the water to be sucked down into the realm where Pan lived, to be accepted or not. For many, this may have suggested an early Jewish tradition that the river was a pathway to Hades, given that the river marked the boundary of Hades in Roman mythology. This is why *Yeshua* says the "gates of hell" will not prevail.

Honor and Shame: What the West Misses

In the West, we often think in terms of guilt and innocence. "Did I break a rule?" "Am I forgiven?" But in the Middle East, where I'm from, and where the Bible was born, the real question involves honor and shame.

Honor is your reputation, your name, your place in the community. It's how your father is remembered at the city gate. It's how your family is greeted in the marketplace. It's what opens doors for marriage, trust, and blessings.

To lose your honor is to lose your name. It's to be cast out, silenced, forgotten.It's not just painful, it constitutes social death.

In our Aramaic culture, when someone sins, we don't say, "I made a mistake."We say, "I brought shame on my house."

We don't just ask, "Am I guilty?" We ask, "Can I be restored? Will my name be remembered?"

Yeshua Knew This.

That's why *Caesarea Philippi* matters so much.

He didn't just walk into just any pagan city. He walked into a theater of shame, a place where gods mocked, where identity was lost, where Jewish honor was violated.

And in that place, He didn't perform a miracle. He didn't preach a sermon. He asked a simple question: "Who do you say that I am?"

And *Kepha* answered. Not with theology. But with honor.

"You are the *Mshiho*[10] the Son of the Living *Yahweh*."

At that moment, *Yeshua* gave *Kepha* a new identity:

"You are *Kepha* the Rock. And on this rock, I will build my *Kehila*. I will restore my community, etc."

This wasn't just about *Kepha*. It was about every disciple who's ever felt ashamed, cast out, or unworthy. It was about every one of us who wondered:

- Can my past be redeemed?
- Can my name be lifted again?
- Can I belong?

And *Yeshua's* answer?

"Yes. Even here. Even in the most shameful place. I will restore your name. I will give you a place in My Kingdom. And the gates of Hades cannot take that from you."

Today's Conflicts in Israel: Echoes of the Past

Caesarea Philippi was once Rome's way of saying, "This land is ours." They planted idols in our soil. They built power on top of fear. They mixed religion with control, and people suffered.

Today, the names are different. Not Zeus or Pan, but power still hides behind holy language. Still, this land bears the scars of empire not just from tanks and treaties, but from the deeper war: the one for honor, belonging, and truth.

And yet… in that same place of darkness, *Yeshua* spoke words of light.

He didn't draw borders.
He didn't curse His enemies.
He didn't build walls of stone.

He built a Kingdom of the heart.

"On this rock I will build my community…and the gates of Hades will not overcome it."

Israel is not just a battlefield. It is a meeting place of faith and fire, of struggle and story, of family.

The same ground where gods once demanded blood is the same ground where our *Mshiho*[10] offered peace.

So, when I walk with people through the ruins of *Caesarea Philippi*, I don't just teach about Pan or Rome.

I tell them how hope came to the most hopeless place. How *Yeshua* didn't wait for peace to arrive. He declared it into the chaos.

And always remind my guests, Peace doesn't come when

power wins. Peace comes when shame is healed, and when hearts are restored to God and each other.

From Caesarea Philippi to the Transfiguration

It is worth noting that from this hub city of paganism, *Yeshua* took his disciples to the mount where He was transfigured before them. Let's examine this in more detail.

Read (*Mattai* 17:1-9).

> After six days *Yeshua* took with him *Kepha*, *Ya'coub*[39] and *Yohannon*[28] the brother of *Ya'coub*, and led them up a high mountain by themselves. There he was transfigured before them. His face shone like the sun, and his clothes became as white as the light. Just then there appeared before them *Moshe* and *Elyahu*, talking with *Yeshua*.
>
> *Kepha* said to *Yeshua*, "*Morio*[25], it is good for us to be here. If you wish, I will put up three shelters—one for you, one for *Moshe* and one for *Elyahu*."
>
> While he was still speaking, a bright cloud covered them, and a voice from the cloud said, "This is my Son, whom I love; with him I am well pleased. Listen to him!"
>
> When the disciples heard this, they fell facedown to the ground, terrified. But *Yeshua* came and touched them. "Get up," he said. "Don't be afraid." When they looked up, they saw no one except *Yeshua*. As they were coming down the mountain, *Yeshua*

instructed them, "Don't tell anyone what you have seen, until the Son of Man has been raised from the dead."

The mountain of transfiguration took place on *Mount Hermon*[114]. The *Hayklo*[3] of Pan and *Caesarea Philippi* were built at the base of this mountain.

Background to the Transfiguration

Moshe and *Elyahu*[87] are two key figures from the Old Testament. *Moshe* led *Yahweh's* people, the Israelites, out of slavery from *Metsrayin*[24]. He met with *Yahweh* on *Mount Sinai* and gave the people *Yahweh's* laws, the Ten Commandments. *Moshe's* face was radiant after such close contact with *Yahweh*. *Elyahu* was a prophet, one of *Yahweh's* messengers. He also went to *Mount Sinai* where *Yahweh* revealed himself in a gentle whisper.

The roles of these two men can be summarized as follows:

- *Moshe* = The Law
- *Elyahu* = The Prophets

In the Bible, *Yahweh's* presence is often shown by cloud or fire. Mountaintops were often the location for appearances from *Yahweh*. This special cloud or fire was called *shekinah*[134]. The presence of *Yahweh* is also the revealing of His glory and represented moments of revelation.

The word "transfiguration" means a change of form or appearance. In this passage, *Yeshua's* appearance changes so that a glimpse is given of His full heavenly glory: "His face shone like the sun and his clothes became as white as the light."

In (*Mattai*[4] 16:13-20), *Kepha* has shown understanding of *Yeshua's* identity, that He is the Christ the *Mshiho*[10]. This *Galyono* experience is to help deepen this understanding. It is so special that only *Yeshua's* three closest followers, *Kepha, Ya'coub*[39], and *Yohannon*[28], are chosen to witness it. *Yeshua* wants them to understand that his role as *Mshiho* will involve suffering and death, but this will not be the final outcome of his mission. *Yeshua* has come from Heaven, and He will return there when He has completed his task on Earth.

This story is filled with Old Testament references, which *Mattai's* readers would easily understand. It takes place six days after *Kepha's* declaration of faith. This may be a link to *Moshe,* who spent six days in preparation before he was called to approach *Yahweh* in a cloud on *Mount Sinai*. This incident also takes place up a mountain with a cloud; this latter symbolizes the presence of *Yahweh*.

Moshe and *Elyahu* appear and stand beside *Yeshua*. This symbolizes that *Yeshua* is their successor and has fulfilled both purposes. He is now bringing a new covenant from *Yahweh* for all people.

When *Yahweh's* voice is heard, He is reassuring the disciples that even though *Yeshua* must suffer, they must listen to and obey him. *Yeshua* again commands the disciples not to tell others of the experience. The time for this will be later, after his death and resurrection.

Mount Tabor is the traditional spot of the transfiguration. It stands just east of *Natseret*[33], making it a place *Yeshua* and his disciples were certainly familiar with, and it has the benefit of tradition on its side. Origen, an Early Church Father (AD 231-254), said, *"Tabor* is the mountain of Galilee on which *Yeshua* was transfigured." In the fourth century, Cyril and Saint Jerome added their voices to this tradition.

Several churches have been built on *Mount Tabor* to mark the supposed location of the Transfiguration. The earliest of these dates back to the fifth century, but the most recent was a modern church built in 1924.

Such is the long-standing tradition; we can get closer to an answer by looking at the scriptural account.

Mount Tabor the traditional Church of Transfiguration

An Alternative Location in Morqos's Gospel

The account takes up only six verses (*Morqos*[12] 9:2-8).

> Now, after six days, *Yeshua* took *Kepha, Ya'coub*[39], and *Yohannon*, and led them up on a high mountain apart by themselves; and He was transfigured before them. His clothes became shining, exceedingly white, like snow, such as no launderer on earth can whiten them. And *Elyahu* appeared to them with *Moshe*, and they were talking with *Yeshua*. Then *Kepha* answered and said to *Yeshua*, "Rabbi, it is good for us to be here; and let us make three tabernacles: one for You, one for *Moshe*, and one for *Elyahu*" because he did not know what to say, for they were greatly afraid.
>
> And a cloud came and overshadowed them; and a voice came out of the cloud, saying, "This is My beloved Son. Hear Him!" Suddenly, when they had looked around, they saw no one anymore, but only *Yeshua* with themselves.

The text from *Morqos* doesn't give us much to go on, beyond the identification of a "high mountain." (*Mattai* 17:1-8) and (*Louko*[13] 9:28-36) aren't much help either. However, backtracking in the Gospel of *Morqos* provides some additional clues:

- In (*Morqos*[12] 8:22-26), a blind man is healed at *Beth-Saida*[35], a town directly northeast of the Sea of Galilee.

- In (*Morqos* 8:27-30), *Kepha* makes his great confession of *Yeshua* as the *Mshiho*[10] at *Caesarea Philippi*, a town at the southern base of *Mount Hermon*[114] and roughly 30 miles north of *Beth-Saida*.

So, we see *Yeshua* traveling north from *Beth-Saida* to *Caesarea Philippi*. And what about after the Transfiguration? Where does *Yeshua* go then? In (*Morqos* 9:33), *Yeshua* and his disciples come to the city of *Kfar-Nahoum*[36] located on the northern coast of the Sea of Galilee. The next geographical marker comes in 10:1 when *Yeshua* arrives in the region of *Yehuda* as He begins the final journey to the cross.

This geography points to a location of the Transfiguration in the far north. Otherwise, there is little reason for *Yeshua* to travel north to *Caesarea Philippi* just to turn around and begin a journey to *Or-Shlem*. It makes even less sense for *Yeshua* to change his direction significantly out of the clear path laid out in chapters 8-10 in order to reach *Mount Tabor*.

Mount-Hermon[114] as the Site of the Transfiguration

Tor Hermon stands just to the north of *Caesarea Philippi*, making it a likely candidate for the location of the transfiguration. It certainly meets the criteria of a "high mountain," with an elevation of 2813 meters (9,232 feet) compared to 574 meters (1,886 feet) of Mount Tabor. *Tor Hermon* seems to fit the geographical context of the Gospel account.

Mount Hermon

On the Bus to Mount Bental

On the way to Mount *Bental*, we pass by several Druze villages in the Upper *Golan*[102]. At some point, the group will see a yellow square sign with a red triangle warning of landmines.

Land mines

Around 1.2 million landmines were laid during the 1950s and 1960s, contaminating a combined area of 50,000 acres in the *Golan* Heights, the Arava Valley, and along the Jordan River. This includes more than 300,000 landmines contaminating 5,000 acres of agricultural and residential land. A State Comptroller audit conducted in the late 1990s found that hundreds of minefields no longer contributed to *Yesrael's* security and that no government agency had presented a plan to clear them. Three unsuccessful attempts to offer a legal solution to the landmine problem were proposed in the early 2000s.

In 2009, Jerry White, an American who survived a landmine incident in the *Golan* Heights, drafted a call to action and a legal framework for humanitarian demining in *Yesrael*. In February 2010, an eleven-year-old *Yesraeli* boy, Daniel Yuval, lost his leg to a landmine while walking in the snow in the *Golan* Heights. Following this incident, Yuval joined the Mine-Free *Yesrael* and petitioned the Prime Minister and Members of the parliament to support the drafted bill. The campaign secured the support of seventy-three members and became a law on March 14, 2011.

Mount Bental – Overlooking the Borders of *Syria*

The drive to the top is steep. It is actually an extinct volcano 1,165 meters (3,822 feet) above sea level. It looks more like a cone-shaped hill. The hike takes you to a lookout where we can see *Syria*. In one day, you have seen three countries: *Lebanon*[116], *Syria*, and *Yesrael*.

The hike takes you by some interesting recycled-metal art.

These are all the work of Johannes (Joop) de Jong, a Dutch artist who lived and worked in the nearby Kibbutz Merom Golan. Johannes de Jong used recycled and reclaimed metal scraps found in the area to create these beautiful statues. Take the time to enjoy them and take some pictures on the way to the view.

Mount Bental Artifacts

The Coffee Annan Café can be seen along the way. *Annan*, in Hebrew, means "clouds," so this is the coffee shop in the clouds. The hike takes you to a large signpost, showing distances to various cities around the world from that spot.

Coffee Annan Café

Signpost on Mount Bental

View from Mount Bental

From the top of *Mount Bental*, there are magnificent views in all directions. To the north is *Mount Hermon*[114] (*Yesrael's* highest peak) and beyond that *Syria*. *Mount Hermon* is part of a narrow mountain ridge that forms the *Lebanon-Syria* border along its spine. The ridge is about 70km (45 miles) long), but only 11% of its southern area is inside the land of *Yesrael*. The highest peak is (2814m / 9,235 feet) tall, and it is in *Syria*.

Though *Mount Hermon* is the highest peak in the area, the highest elevation under *Yesrael* control is *Mizpe Shlagim*, the "Snow Observatory," at 2,224 meters (7,300 feet). UN observers have a base on the mountain, and both *Yesrael* and *Syria* have observation posts. You can try skiing on *Mount Hermon* during the winter months (roughly December-February).

From *Mount Bental*, there is a bird's eye view of many of the Druze villages below. In the distance, the crests of the mountain ranges of the Upper Galilee can be seen. In front of the group is the Syrian village of *Quneitra*[135]. The ruins of the flattened houses of the city, which once had a population of 20,000, provide an eerie atmosphere, because of all the destruction reminiscent of post-apocalyptic films. After the 1974 ceasefire, *Yesraeli* troops withdrew from *Quneitra*. Before handing *Quneitra* back to *Syria*, the *Yesraeli's* evacuated the population and then systematically destroyed the buildings of the city, selling anything movable to *Yesraeli* contractors. These actions were heavily condemned by the UN.

The destroyed town of Quneitra

The Syrian President of that time ordered that the city would not be rebuilt. Since then, the ruins have become something of an exhibit. The area is under Syrian control within the UN-patrolled demilitarized zone between *Syria* and the *Yesraeli*-occupied *Golan*[102] Heights.

To the south is *Mount Avital*. To the east is a hill split from the center. If you look carefully, you will see a road in the center of the hill that leads to Damascus around 64 km (40 miles) away. We cannot see Damascus from *Mount Bental* because it is over the last ridge on the far horizon. The peak of *Mount Bental*, gives travelers an appreciation for the strategic importance of the *Golan* Heights by observing the proximity of *Syria*. The *Golan* Heights give *Yesrael* an excellent vantage point for monitoring *Syrian* movements. The topography provides a natural buffer against any military thrust from *Syria*.

The group is likely to see UN observers. The white buildings in the center once housed the UN forces. The area is no longer safe, so they have moved into *Yesrael* and are now making use of the observation posts here. The UN forces often come and set an observation point at the top of *Mount Bental* to monitor activity in the area.

The *Syrian* Civil War began in March 2011 and the end is not in sight. It is ongoing. The border between *Yesrael* and *Syria* has switched hands a few times between Assad's regime and different rebel groups. Although *Yesrael* has taken no position in the conflict, *Syrian* rebel shells have mistakenly fallen in *Yesrael* on a couple of occasions, and a few retaliatory attacks in *Syria* have been attributed to *Yesrael*. Injured *Syrians* who come to the *Yesraeli* border crossing can expect to receive treatment regardless of which side they represent.

Back in the 1940s and early 1950s, my father told me that his grandfather used to be able to take a bus from *Or-Shlem* to *Yarden*[76] and then to *Syria*. If he wanted to have nice dinner, he could go with his friends to *Syria* for a weekend and come back. Things were more open than today.

Modern Historical Divisions of the Middle East

The Sykes Picot Agreement was a 1916 secret treaty between the United Kingdom and France, with assent from the Russian Empire and Italy, to define their mutually agreed spheres of influence and control in an eventual partition of the Ottoman Empire. The agreement effectively divided the Ottoman provinces outside the Arabian Peninsula into areas of British and French control and influence. The British and French controlled countries were divided by the Sykes–Picot line.

The agreement granted British control of what is today southern *Yesrael* and *Palestine*, *Yarden*[76], and southern *Iraq*, and an additional small area that included the ports of *Haifa* and *A'cco*[168] to allow access to the Mediterranean.

France received control of south-eastern Turkey, northern *Iraq*, *Syria*, and *Lebanon*. Because of the mandate, the Middle East was divided, which started the conflict that continues to this day. As soon as things were developed, every Arab nation wanted its independence during the Arab nationalist movement. One of the primary goals of Arab nationalism is the end of Western influence in the Arab world and the removal of those Arab governments considered to be dependent upon Western power. It rose to prominence with the weakening and defeat of the Ottoman Empire in the early 20th century and declined after the defeat of the Arab armies in the Six-Day War.

The Six Day War

War broke out in June 1967. *Syria's* shelling greatly intensified, and the *Yesraeli* army captured the *Golan*[102] Heights on June 10, 1967. The area that came under *Yesraeli* control as a result of the war consists of two geologically distinct areas: the *Golan* Heights proper, with a surface of 1,070 square km (410 sq miles), and the slopes of the *Mount Hermon*[114] range with a surface of 100 square kilometres (40 sq miles). This is what we see from *Mount Bental.*

During the war, between 80,000 and 131,000 Syrians fled or were driven from the Heights. Around 7,000 remained in the *Yesraeli*-occupied territory. The Committee for Refugees and Immigrants reported that much of the local population of 100,000 fled as a result of the war, whereas the Syrian government stated that a large proportion of it was expelled. *Yesrael* has not allowed former residents to return for security reasons. The remaining villages were *Majdal Shams*[115], *Shayta* (later destroyed), *Ein Qiniyye, Mas'ade,* and *Buq'ata*. These are the five Druze towns along with, outside the *Golan* proper, *Ghajar* village.

Yom Kippur War

The *Yom Kippur* War took place in 1973. It was one of the largest tank battles in history. Despite having only 160 tanks, *Yesrael* prevailed. The *Syrians* attacked with 1,500 tanks and 1,000 artillery pieces. But they were slowly cut down by the determined *Yesraeli* force. The *Yesraeli* army suffered significant casualties as well. By the end of the battle, only seven *Yesraeli* tanks were operational. After nine hundred *Syrian* tanks were destroyed, the *Syrians* fled. Today, the area below the mountain, reaching *Mount Hermon*, is called "The Valley of Tears."

Psalm 133

Read (*Mazmure*[101] 133) to the group:

> Behold how good and pleasant it is when brothers dwell in unity! It is like the precious oil on the head, running down on the beard, on the beard of Ahron, running down on the collar of his robes! It is like the dew of Hermon, which falls on the mountains of Zion! For there the LORD has commanded the blessing, life forevermore.

Mazmure[101]133 is a Song of Ascent—a song for going up to a high place. For the Jewish people in ancient times, that high place was the *Hayklo* in *Or-Shlem*. One literally "goes up" to *Or-Shlem*. The city crowns the hill and its *Hayklo* stood on a mount. In this exalted place, the highest act was to worship *Yahweh*.

The Jewish people sang *Mazmure* 133 to express their joy in coming together for worship at the *Hayklo*, where *Yahweh* promised to meet them. The Psalm imparts blessing and life to *Yahweh's* people. And it proclaims oneness in faith. These themes—abundance and unity—flow from *Mazmure* 133.

As the *Hayklo* in *Or-Shlem* was the high place for the Jewish people, so Easter is the high point of the Gospel. From that moment, the Gospel spread around the world. *Yeshua* went from the Mount of Transfiguration, *Mount*

Hermon, all the way to *Or-Shlem* to be crucified. He died during *Phischa*[55]. He rose from the tomb, just as He raises us up from unbelief to faith, from death to everlasting life. This is exactly what we are doing at our next location tomorrow. We will go up to *Or-Shlem*.

Two liquids are mentioned in *Mazmure* 133. Oil is the first, but the second is the "dew of *Hermon*" (verse 3).

Mount Hermon is far to the north of *Or-Shlem*. *Mount Hermon* rises above the upper *Yarden*[32] Valley. It has its share of heavy rainfall and snow. The melting snow, or dew, flows down into the valley. It feeds the *Yarden* River and reaches as far as the Oasis of *Hieriho*[137]. In a dry country, where the rain is scarce and the rivers dry up, the land and the people depend on water that comes from a distant source. *Yeshua's* life and resurrection do the same thing. He will leave the Mount of Transfiguration like the *Yarden*[32] River's water to be crucified in *Or-Shlem*. But the "dew" of his resurrection continues to bring life to those who follow him.

I often ask two or three people to pray over the borders between *Syria* and *Yesrael*, for ISIS, for the Aramaic Christians, and Muslims in Syria to see and recognize the real *Mshiho*[10], the source of life who died to bring us life and peace – and to end war and bloodshed.

But, for now, the carnage continues.

On June 22, 2025, a suicide bombing and mass shooting at the Greek Orthodox Prophet Elias (*Mar Elias*) Church in Damascus killed 22 Christians and injured over 50 more.

It was carried out by the Islamic State (*Saraya Ansar al-Sunnah* also claimed involvement).

In July 2025, the Suwayda region: At least 12–20 Christians, including Pastor Khaled Mazher of the Church of Jesus the Good Shepherd (a former Druze convert), were slain by *Sunni* Islamist militia members amid escalating sectarian conflict between Druze, Bedouin, and jihadist factions.

The IDF Bunker

Mount Bental has an abandoned army post. Until it is reoccupied, the government allows people to wander around inside. It is dark, so take your own source of light.

IDF bunker on Mount Bental

In a small room within the bunker, the tale of the battle can be read from signs on the wall. Maps help to understand the planning and geography of the battle. When emerging from the bunker, a coin-operated binocular allows you to see the *Yesraeli-Syrian* frontier and the old battlefield now covered over with fields of grain and produce.

Wine Tasting in the Golan[102] Heights

The *Golan* is covered in vineyards, and the *Golan* Heights is considered "the Napa Valley of the Middle East." Six of the main wineries have combined to produce a wine route. Each contributes something different to the mosaic of *Golan* wine.

Tasting wine in the place it is made is always a special experience. However, you can do better if you can drink wine in the vineyard where its grapes are grown. It is always worthwhile visiting a vineyard or two because it adds context and allows you to understand and appreciate *Golan* wine to the fullest.

As recently as the mid-1990s, there were just seven wineries in *Yesrael*. Today, the nation boasts nearly three hundred. Every winery has its distinctive qualities, but the *Golan* Heights Winery is one of the best known, exporting its celebrated bottles to over twenty-five different countries.

After the difficult stories of war and destruction, a visit to the Golan Heights Winery will help everyone wind down. The staff does a great job of making everyone feel at home. The winery has one of the most comprehensive visitor centers and is the best touring option of any winery in *Yesrael,* hands down.

The *Golan* Heights Winery offers four standard tour options, ranging from one to four hours in length. I recommend the one-hour-long "Classic Visit." If you're a bit of a wine connoisseur and would enjoy a more extensive tasting session with a greater variety of wine options, allow two hours for the fuller "Professional Wine Tasting Visit."

Even if you're not much of a wine drinker, you'll certainly enjoy the striking scenery and the pastoral atmosphere that surrounds the *Golan* Heights Winery.

From here, we return to the bus in a great mood and travel back to the hotel.

Vineyards of the Golan Heights

Day Seven: Light to the Nations
Theme – The Gentile Pentecost

- **Tel Megiddo** – The mountain fortress and the site of Revelation's Armageddon
- **Har Kerem-El**[142] – Eliyahu[89] versus the priests of Baal
- Lunch – Druze Village
- **Caesarea Maritima** – Home of Cornelius, the *Yahweh*-fearing Gentile, and *Kepha's* message
- **Aqueduct** along the beach of the Mediterranean
- *Yuffi*[158]
- **Or-Shlem** – Ascending to the Holy City

Leaving the Sea of Galilee to Tel Megiddo

We will be leaving the lovely Sea of Galilee and heading up to *Or-Shlem*[5] to stay for three nights. Make sure you have all your possessions. Remember to check your room's safe before you close the door for the final time.

The theme of the day is "Light to the Nations – The Gentile Pentecost."

Driving Through the Jezreel[143] Valley

The Bible, geography, and history in the *Jezreel* Valley are perhaps more closely entwined and visible in this area than anywhere else in the country. The central *Jezreel* Valley is roughly (233 km²/145 miles²). It is bounded on the north by the *Natseret*[33] Mountains and *Mount Tabor*. *Deborah* and *Barak* camped on *Mount Tabor* with the Israelite army before attacking and defeating Sisera's Canaanite force (*Shophetim*[121] 4:1-16). I will often read the story to the group.

The Canaanites had iron chariots (verse 3), so *Deborah* advised *Barak* to take the militias of *Naphtali* and *Zebulun* and go to Mount *Tabor*. On Mount *Tabor*, the Israelites would have had the better defensive position, given the elevation and the wooded mountain. However, *Deborah* was obedient to *Yahweh* to fight the battle in the open fields in the valleys, which seems contrary to military doctrine. But *Yahweh* sent rain, and the chariots became stuck in the mud, allowing the Israelites the victory over a much stronger enemy.

"From heaven they fought" is probably referring to a rainstorm. Anyone who lives in the *Jezreel* Valley knows that during the dry months, the valley is rock solid, but after a couple of rainy days, the thick, rich, black soil turns to mud, and sections become total swamps. Not even a jeep, let alone a chariot, can maneuver during a rainstorm where the *Ka'ine* Stream by *Megiddo* and the *Kishon* Brook through the valley overflow and wash away everything in their path. The only way through the muddy swamp would be on foot, hence Sisera's abandoning of his chariots. (*Shophetim*[121] 4:13-16)

> *Barak* descended from Mount Tabor with the ten thousand men behind him. The Lord panicked Sisera and all the chariots and the entire camp by the edge of the sword before Barak; Sisera dismounted from his chariot and fled on his feet. *Barak* chased after the chariots and after the camp until *Haroshet-goiim* and the entire camp of *Sisera* fell by the edge of the sword; not even one was left.

Mount Tabor

Another mountain visible from the *Jezreel* Valley is Mount *Gilbo'a*[138], referring to a freshwater spring located there. King *Shawol*[16] committed suicide on those slopes while

while facing certain defeat by the Philistines. *Yonathon*[139], *Dawood's* bosom companion, and King *Shawol's* two other sons, *Abi-Nadab* and *Malchi-Shua*, were killed here during the battle (1 *Samo'el*[131] 31:1-6). In light of *Shawol* and *Yonathan's*[139] deaths, *Dawood*[85] cursed the mountain: "O mountains of *Gilbo'a*, may you have neither dew nor rain, nor fields that yield offerings" (2 *Samo'el* 1:21).

Mount Gilbo'a

Also, at the foot of Mount *Gilbo'a,* is the location of another famous story: *Jado'an's*[140] victory over the Midianites (*Shophetim*[121] 6:3) with only 300 men. He succeeded in routing the entire enemy force with *Yahweh's* help. According to (2 *Malachim*[90] 9:1–9:10*),* after *Jehu* killed King *Yehoram,* he confronted *Yezabeel*[141] in the *Jezreel* Valley and urged her eunuchs to kill her by throwing her out of a window.

And when *Jehu* came to *Jezreel*, *Yezabeel* heard of it; and she painted her eyelids with kohl, and adorned her head, and looked out a window. And as *Jehu* entered in at the gate, she said, "Is it peace, you *Zimri*, murderer of his master?" And he lifted up his face to the window, and said, "Who is on my side?" And there looked out at him two or three eunuchs. And he said, "Throw her down." So, they threw her down; and some of her blood was sprinkled on the wall, and the horses entered and trod her under foot. Then he went in to eat and drink, and he said, "See now to this cursed woman, and bury her; for she is a king's daughter." And they went to bury her, but they found no more of her than her skull and her feet and the palms of her hands. And when they returned, they told him, and he said, "This is the word of the Lord which he spoke by his servant *Elyahu* the Tishbite, saying, "In the field of *Jezreel* shall dogs eat the flesh of *Yezabeel*; And the corpse of her shall be as refuse upon the face of the field of *Yezabeel*; and there will be none to bury her, so that they shall not say, 'This is *Yezabeel*.'" (2 *Malachim*[90] 9:30-37)

Mount *Kerem-El*,[142] also visible from the *Jezreel*[143] Valley, is the site of the *Morio's*[25] victory over the prophets of *Baal* when *Eliyahu* called down fire from heaven to consume his sacrifice, the altar, and all the water surrounding it. *Eliyahu* had the prophets of *Baal* slaughtered at the *Kishon* Brook.

These mountain passes have played a significant role in world history for thousands of years, emphasizing *Yesrael's* role as a bridge linking Africa, Asia, and Europe. Ancient caravans bearing merchandise and the innovations of far-off cultures, and the armies of antiquity have all marched into this large area of the *Jezreel* Valley.

Jezreel[143] had been fertile but during the Ottoman Empire, neglect had turned most of it into swamps. Beginning in 1911, pioneers drained the swamps, making the valley bloom again. Today, this valley is *Yesrael's* breadbasket, growing wheat, cotton, sunflowers, and harboring fishponds. Among the many attractions that make *Jezreel* one of *Yesrael's* most inviting destinations are its historical and biblical treasures.

Tel Megiddo – The Mountain Fortress

The land of Canaan connects *Metsrayin*[24] to *Ashour*[144]. Over 4,000 years ago, *Ob-Rohom*[82] believed in one *Yahweh* though his father was an idol maker by profession. *Ob-Rohom* came from *Ur* of the Chaldeans. Where was it located?

1. *Sumerian Ur* (Tel el-Muqayyar, Iraq)

This is a famous city with a ziggurat and royal tombs. It was excavated by Sir Leonard Woolley in the 1920s. Because it is far south, *Ob-Rohom* would've taken a strange detour through Haran. The town was Sumerian, not Semitic. The term "Chaldees" (*Kasdim*) doesn't fit that time or place (it appears much later).

2. *Urfa* (Orhay in modern Turkey)

This is a traditional site in the Jewish, Christian, and Islamic traditions. It features a cave linked to *Ob-Rohom*. It is close to *Haran*, in the region of *Aram-Naharaim*[145] (Northern Mesopotamia). Its importance only began in the Hellenistic period. There is no strong archaeological evidence from *Ob-Rohom's* time.

3. *Urkesh* (Tel Mozan, Syria)

This was a Hurrian city active during *Ob-Rohom's* time (Middle Bronze Age). Located near *Haran*, it lies east of the Euphrates, which matches the biblical route. Archaeology shows it was a big religious and political center. A tablet mentions a man named *Terru*, possibly *Ob-Rohom's* father *Terah*. Culturally, it aligns with the Aramean world that *Ob-Rohom* came from. The name *Urkesh* even sounds like *Ur Kasdim*.

Urkesh fits the Bible's geography, culture, and timeline better than the southern *Ur* or *Urfa*. It likely was the real "Ur of the Chaldees" where *Ob-Rohom* began his journey.

Because of the terrain and desert, any empire that wanted to control the region or move down to or up from *Metsrayin*[24] had to pass through the land of *Canaan*, which meant passing through the *Jezreel* Valley. This is true of the Assyrian Empire, the Babylonian Empire, Alexander the Great, the Romans, and even the Crusaders Turks and British.

Read (*Dbarim*[14] 26:5):

Then you shall declare before the Lord your *Yahweh:* **My father was a wandering Aramean**, and he went down into *Metsrayin* with a few people and lived there and became a great nation, powerful and numerous.

Who is my father? He was a wandering Aramean? This was *Ob-Rohom*. Have you paid attention before to this verse? If *Ob-Rohom* was from the area of *Paddan-Aram*, he was under the Aramean Kingdom. What do you think was the language of *Ob-Rohom*? Many will think it is Hebrew! He said he was a wandering Aramean? Some will tell me it is Aramaic! It is neither Hebrew nor Aramaic!

Historically, *Ob-Rohom* lived around 1800 BC. The Old Testament was written later, between 1500 BC and 400 BC. In 1800 BC, the language of that area and time was *Akkadian.* Aramaic first appeared during the late 11th century BC. This is why the writer of *Dbarim*[14], when he wrote the *Torah* at a later time in history, the language was Aramaic, and he said *Ob-Rohom* was a wandering Aramean.

Back on track. *Megiddo* is key to controlling the region. In a way, it was the center of the ancient world, like New York or any other important city in the modern world. Travelers coming from the east had to travel around a great desert road by what is known as the *Via Maris*[31]. This is what *Ob-Rohom* did when he came with his flocks. He needed water, so he went up and around, not across the desert. He came first to *Haran*, an important city on the *Via Maris*[31] route. *Yahweh* called *Ob-Rohom* in *Haran* and said, "Go, walk through the length and breadth of the land, for I am am giving it to you." And *Ob-Rohom* obeyed *Yahweh*. (*Bereshith*[72] 13:17)

There is a smaller topographical map of *Megiddo* in the museum, showing the controlled narrow canyon between the mountains from the valley to the plains beyond. This makes *Megiddo* a strategic location. *Phero Thutmose III* described the journey through the pass. The canyon was so narrow that he could not put one chariot with two horses together. The fortress was a crossroads and a source of water.

The map inside the museum at Megiddo

The ancient Egyptian account gives the date of a battle as the twenty-first day of the first month of the third season of Year 23 of the reign of *Thutmose III*. The Egyptians routed the Canaanite forces, which fled to safety in the city of *Megiddo*. Their action resulted in the lengthy siege of *Megiddo*. *Thutmose III* finally succeeded in conquering it after seven or eight months. This is the earliest war documented in the *Jezreel*[143] Valley. The last major battle there took place in 1917. General Allenby of the British captured the area and was called the "Lord of Armageddon" because he fought against the Turks.

The Seal of *Megiddo*

The seal was discovered in 1904 during the earliest excavation of *Megiddo*, led by Gottlieb Schumacher. The German archaeologist excavated the area from 1903 to 1905. The seal belonged to a royal minister in the 8th century BC. It is engraved with the figure of a roaring lion (symbol of the Kingdom of Judah) with a beautifully curved tail. It was skilfully executed. The inscription reads *"Shema"* at the top and *"Servant of Yeroba'am*[126]*"* at the bottom.

The Seal of Megiddo

The inscription likely proclaims the name and rank of its owner, one of the ministers of King *Yeroba'am II* who reigned from 787-747 BC. The word "servant" is the Hebrew word (*e'bed*) and is mentioned in the Bible as one of high dignitaries in the government. Many seals have been discovered with similar inscriptions, such as "the servant of the king."

King *Yeroba'am*[126] – Historical Background

> In the fifteenth year of *Amaziah*, the son of *Joash*, king of Judah, Jeroboam the son of Joash, king of Yesrael, became king in Samaria, and reigned forty-one years. And he did evil in the sight of the LORD; he did not depart from all the sins of Jeroboam the son of Nebat, who had made *Yesrael* sin. (2 *Melachim*[88] 14:23-25)

Yeroba'am means "may the people grow numerous." He was *Yeroba'am II*, the son of *Joash*, king of *Yesrael*. The Lord had pity on *Yesrael* in the north, according to the prophet *Yonnon*[146] and allowed *Ashure* to weaken Damascus and *Hamath* to relieve *Yesrael* of the Syrian yoke. *Yeroba'am II* came in and conquered the territory (2 *Melachim* 14). This made the Northern Kingdom powerful and wealthy, although the prophet *A'mos* protested against their boasting.

It is interesting that the monarch was given the name of *Yeroba'am* since *Yeroba'am I* was the first ruler of the Northern Kingdom in the early 10th century BC, someone *Shelmon*[148] sought to kill.*mYeroba'am*Ifled to *Metsrayin*[24] for refuge with King *Shishak* until *Shelmon* died. *Yeroba'am* was in constant conflict with the House of *Dawood* in the south. He is specifically mentioned as the one who led *Yesrael* into idolatry. According to the Bible, every king of the Northern Kingdom of *Yesrael* was evil and followed *Yeroba'am*'s sins.

Maps of the Chariots

King *Shelmon* had 450 chariots that kept the peace in his day. There was no war for 40 years, unheard of in ancient times. *Shelmon* formed relationships and made connections with so many kingdoms that he was able to keep the peace. "Peace" is *Shlama* in Aramaic, *Shalom* in Hebrew. Consequently, *"Shelmon"* means "making peace."

The Israelite City Gate

Besides being part of a city's protection against invaders, city gates were places of central activity in biblical times. Important business transactions were made there; the court was convened; public announcements were heard. Accordingly, it is natural that the Bible frequently speaks of "sitting in the gate" or of the activities that took place at the gate. In (*Mishley*[149] 1:21), wisdom is personified: "At the head of the noisy streets she cries out, in the gateways of the city she makes her speech." To spread her words to the maximum number of people, Wisdom took speeches that took place at the city gates.

The gate of the city was also a podium for the *Yesraelite* prophets of old, the feisty social reformers of their day. "Hate evil and love good," declared *A'mos,* "and establish justice in the gate." Not only must justice be done but it must also be seen. For the ancient *Yesraelites,* the one place in the city where transparency was guaranteed was the city gate.

It was an extraordinarily progressive judicial system for its day but apparently could not entirely prevent official corruption. "They hate the one who reproves in the gate," *A'mos* scathingly noted, presumably referring to himself. He raged against those "who afflict the righteous, who take a bribe, and push aside the needy in the gate" (*A'mos* 5).

Megiddo, in its day, was similar to the White House in the U.S. It had power over much of the ancient world as it literally became the gateway between nations.

Megiddo's city gate

The View at the Top of the Fortress

Tel is an Aramaic word that means "an archaeological mountain." In *Megiddo*, you can see the layers between each period of history. There are 29 layers of history here, meaning there are 29 civilizations that once lived on this exact spot. Each civilization was built upon the ruins of the previous one. This effectively raised the elevation, which became an important part of the defences of the new civilization.

Overview of the excavations

Haar Megiddo

Haar Megiddo is mentioned 18 times in the Old Testament.

- *Haar* is a "mountain" in Hebrew.
- *Megiddo* in Aramaic is the word *Al-Majd*. It means "the glory."
- *Haar Megiddo* means "the mountain fortress that holds the glory."

Because of its strategic location, one could easily say that the glory of any nation is held in *Megiddo*. Whoever controlled the fortress controlled the region. The glory of the end of days will come on the battlefield before *Megiddo*. It will be not only between *Yesrael*, the world, and neighboring countries, but also against all her enemies at once, and *Yahweh* will show His glory. This is the typical understanding of the battle of *Armageddon* (*Haar Megiddo*).

In the Aramaic mindset, it is more inward thinking; you and I are like *Haar Megiddo* in our hearts. There is a personal battle between the forces of light and darkness inside our lives. You must be ready to fight this battle, much like *Yesrael* prepares its army against any invasion. *Haar Megiddo* is a symbol of being ready and alert for the final battle that so many people do not even know is coming. Prepare yourself spiritually. Be ready, clean, and healthy to face the battle when it comes, even every day, the battle of glory. This mountain fortress is a symbol of holding the glory!

Are you holding the glory of *Yahweh* in your life? Are you alert? Are you ready?

Some references from the Bible to *Megiddo:*

1. (*Yehosuhea*[75] 17:11):

    And *Manasseh* had opposite *Issachar* and *Asher*, *Beth-shean* and its towns, and *Neb-leam* and its towns, and *En-dor* and its towns, and *Taanach* and its towns, and *Megiddo* and its towns, three districts.

2. (*1 Melachim*[88] 9:15):

And this is the portion of tribute which King *Shelmon* levied to build the house of the Lord and his own house. And he also built the wall of *Or-Shlem* and *Millo* and *Hazor* and *Megiddo* and *Gezer*.

3. (*1 Melachim* 4:26):

   And *Shelmon* had forty thousand stalls of horses for his chariots and twelve thousand horsemen.

4. (*2 Melachim* 15:29):

   In the days of *Pekah* king of *Yesrael*, *Tiglath-pileser* king of *Assyria* came and took *Ijon, Abel, Mehola,* and all *Beth-maachah,* and *Niah, Kedesh, Hazor, Gilead,* and *Galilee,* and all the land of *Naphtali,* and carried the people captive to *Assyria.*

5. (*2 Melachim* 23:29):

   In his days Pharaoh the Lame, king of *Metsrayin*, went up against *Mabog* which is by the river Euphrates; and King Josiah went to meet him, to fight against him; and Pharaoh said to him, I have not come against you, turn aside from me; but Josiah did not listen to him; so Pharaoh smote him at *Megiddo*, when he saw him there.

The Silo Lookout

There is a huge circular silo, dug 7 meters (22 feet) into the ground and 11 meters (36 feet) in diameter, located at *Megiddo*. It is capable of storing 1000 tons of grain. Two staircases around the sides lead to the bottom. A domed roof probably covered the structure, which dates from 700 BC. The silo was most likely constructed by *Yeroba'am II.*

The silo

The Megiddo Water System

At the bottom of the vertical shaft, the workers of *Megiddo* dug a horizontal tunnel nearly 67 meters (220 feet) long to the cave where the spring was located. Apparently, one crew began in the cave and another one at the bottom of the shaft. The chisel marks in the walls, still visible today, indicate that the workers came from either end to meet in the middle. How they knew the exact direction to dig and the depth at which to begin is unknown. But when they finished, they had accomplished one of the engineering wonders of the world.

The shaft was sealed from the outside, securing *Megiddo's* water supply from enemy attack. The city had the convenience of a freshwater source inside its walls. Every day, the women descended the shaft and walked through the horizontal tunnel to the spring. Though the tunnel shown here has electric lights and a modern walk for visitors, the people of *Megiddo* walked through it in near darkness. Later, the tunnel was deepened so that the water flowed to the base of the vertical shaft, so water could be drawn from above.

The shaft and tunnel system of *Megiddo* is one of the largest and most famous of the great water systems of biblical times. There are 183 steps down and then 80 steps up.

The entrance to the shaft

Inside the shaft

The Spring of Megiddo

The shaft and spring are connected to the aquifer and the underground lake. To keep the enemy from discovering their fresh water supply, the entrance was camouflaged. There was always the possibility of having the water fouled or poisoned, so the rulers took great care to keep it secure.

There are two things we must remember about every site in *Yesrael*. First, they were always built near a water source. The second is security. Was the site easy to defend? This is much the same today.

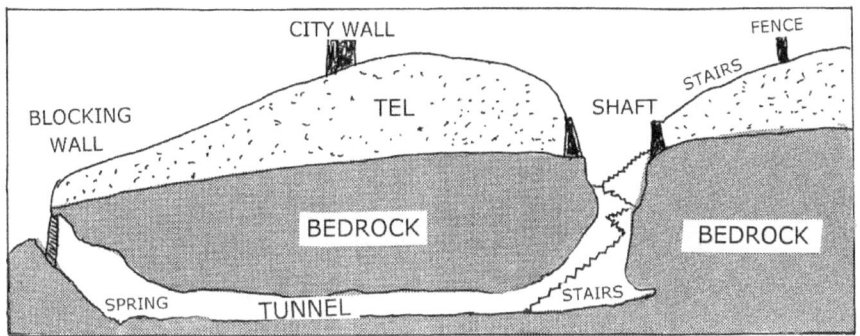

The Megiddo water system

Mount Kerem-El

Mount *Kerem-El*[142] is a mixture of limestone and flint, containing many caves, and covered in volcanic rocks. The sloped side of the mountain is covered with lush vegetation, including oak trees, pine, olive, Atlantic pistachio, and other laurel trees.

The mountain range is approximately 6.5-8 km (4-5 miles) wide and 40 km (25 miles) long, sloping gradually toward the southwest, but forming a steep ridge on the north-eastern side where the bus is heading. The mount is 546 meters (1,791 feet) high with views to the *Jezreel*[143] Valley lying to the northeast. The range forms a natural barrier in the landscape, just as the Valley forms a natural passageway. As a result, the mountain range and valley have had a large impact on migration and invasions through the Fertile Crescent. Many battles and Bible stories took place in these two locations.

Elyahu[87] and the Two Bears

> Then he went up from there to *Beth-El*; and as he was going up by the way, young lads came out from the city and mocked him and said to him, "Go up, you baldhead; go up, you baldhead!" When he looked behind him and saw them, he cursed them in the name of the *Morio*[25]. Then two female bears came out of the woods and tore up forty-two lads of their number. And he went from there to Mount *Kerem-El*, and from there he returned to Samaria (2 *Melachim*[88] 2:23-25)

This region was part of the Northern Kingdom, and Samaria was the capital. *Elyahu*[87] traveled to Mount *Kerem-El*[142] after cursing a group of young men because they had mocked him, by saying, "Go on up, bald man!" After this, bears came out of the forest and wounded 42 of them. *Yahweh* once again was at work for his children.

Bible teachers of the Gospel, pastors, and other believers involved in the ministry of the Word can expect opposition. It simply goes with the territory. This is clearly evident in this short passage.

The King James Version reads "little children" instead of "young lads," which really misses the meaning here. These were not children, but young men. The word "lads" is *naar*[151] in Hebrew. This was a crowd of men in their youth, already mature not little children, perhaps students of the false prophets, who were opposed to *Elyahu's*[87] prophetic ministry and authority. If not students, they might have been sent by the false prophets or idolatrous priests of *Beth-El* to stop *Elyahu*[87] from entering the city.

Elyahu[87] "cursed them in the name of the Lord." He was trusting in the Lord and leaving it in *Yahweh's* hands. The key here is in the word "curse." It does not mean to swear with vile words. Rather, this is the Hebrew word, g*alal*[152] meaning "roll away, be swift, slight, trifling, or of little account." The primary meaning is "to be light or slight." Both verb and noun forms seem to represent a formula that expresses a removal or lowering from the place of blessing; this is how we understand scripture in my Near Eastern culture.

Let me try to put it in my own words. *Elyahu*, as a prophet, saw their hardened and rebellious condition, unresponsive to correction. In the name of the *Morio*[25] (i.e., by his authority), *Elyahu* turned them over to the *Morio* and to their own devices, which had the effect of removing them from the common protection of *Yahweh*. He probably said something like, "May *Yahweh* deal with you according to what you deserve," or "May you be cursed for your sins of rebellion."

This would demonstrate to the city and to people all around a vital truth: without the *Morio*, there was no protection and that blasphemy of *Yahweh's* servants and His Word in order to hinder *Yahweh's* message was serious business. Note that *Elyahu* did not call out the bears; *Yahweh* did. Two female bears came out and tore up forty-two young men.

History of Mount Kerem-El[142]

According to *Yosef Ben Metatyahu*, the Jewish historian, Mount *Kerem-El* had been the stronghold of the Essenes. They came from *Natseret*[33] but should not be confused with the "Nazarene" sect, which followed the teachings of *Yeshua*, although they associated with the Pharisees.

According to Epiphanius, the bishop of *Salamis,* Cyprus, at the end of the 4th century, Mount *Kerem-El* was also a refuge place for the Early Church Fathers. Later in history, the Crusaders took shelter there and founded the Carmelite order in the 12th century. They based it on a cave they believed to be the grotto where *Eliyahu*[66] stayed, and although there is no evidence for it, a monastery was later founded at this location called The Carmelite Monastery, named after Mount *Kerem-El,* and the Carmelite Crusader order was founded.

Since the 12th century, the site on Mount *Kerem-El* has been visited by Christian, Jewish and Muslim pilgrims as the site of *Eliyahu's* altar. For over 100 years, the site has been owned by the Carmelite Order, and their monastery is named after the Prophet E*liyahu*. The present chapel was built in 1883. The chapel altar is made with twelve stones in reference to the twelve stones used by *Eliyahu*. These stones were brought from the mountain itself.

During World War I, Mount *Kerem-El* played a significant strategic role. The 20th century Battle of *Megiddo* took place at the head of a pass through the Carmel Ridge, which overlooks the Valley of *Jezreel*[143] from the south. General Allenby led the British in the battle, which was the turning point in the war against the Ottoman Empire.

All Jewish, Christian, and Islamic followers believe that *Eliyahu* is associated with the mountain, and it is held that he sometimes resided in a cave on the mountain.

Also, the mountain is a place of refuge, and this is why a Druze community is established on this mountain.

Mount Kerem-El Monastery

The Druze

Worldwide, there are probably about one million Druze living mainly in *Syria* and *Lebanon*[116], with around one hundred thousand in *Yesrael*, including about 20,000 in the

Golan (which came under *Yesraeli* rule in 1967) and several thousands who emigrated to Europe and North and South America.

The Druze community in *Yesrael* has a special standing among the country's minority groups, and members of the community serve in the IDF (Israel Defence Forces), and they have attained high-level positions in the political, public, and military spheres. During the British Mandate over *Palestine*, they refrained from taking part in the Arab-Jewish conflict, but during *Yesrael*'s War of Independence (1948), they became active participants on *Yesrael's* side.

The Druze religion has its roots in Islam. It is a religious philosophical movement founded by the Fatimid Caliphate in *Metsrayin*[24] in the tenth century. During the reign of *Al-Hakim* (996 - 1021), the Druze religion came into being, blending Islamic monotheism with Greek philosophy and Hindu influences. Since about 1050 AD, the community has been closed to outsiders.

The first Druze settled in southern *Lebanon*. By the time of the Ottoman conquest of *Syria* (1516), Druze also lived in the hill country near *Aleppo*. The civil war between the Lebanese Druze and the Maronite Christians ended in 1860 with the autonomous administration of Mount *Lebanon*, which was imposed by the Great Powers. During the revolt of the peasants, the Maronites were freed from Turkish rulers, and the Druze never regained power in the region. The center of the Druze community moved to Mount *Hauran* in Syria, which became known as *Jebel-el-Druze*[153], the name was formerly synonymous with Mount *Lebanon*.

Until the end of Ottoman rule (1918), the Druze were governed as a semi-autonomous community. In 1921, the French tried to set up a Druze state under the French Mandate, but the attempt failed.

The Druze in Galilee and on Mount *Kerem-El*[142] have always kept in contact with the other branches of the community, especially with those of *Syria* and *Lebanon*.

The Druze community

Beliefs and Traditions of the Druze

The Druze consider their faith to be a new interpretation of the three monotheistic religions: Judaism, Christianity, and Islam. For them, the traditional story of the Creation is a parable, which describes *Adam* not as the first human being, but as the first person to believe in one *Yahweh*. Since then, the idea of monotheism has been spread by prophets, guided by "mentors" who embody the spirit of monotheism.

The mentors and prophets come from all three religions, and include *Jethro* and *Moshe, Yohannon Hamatbil*[74] and *Yeshua* of *Natseret*[33], and *Mohammed,* all reincarnations of the same monotheistic idea. In addition, the Druze hold other influential people regardless of their religion as advocates of justice and belief in one *Allah*[154]. These include the Egyptian Akhenaton, the Greek philosophers Socrates, Plato, and Aristotle, and Alexander the Great.

Although the Druze recognize all three monotheistic religions, they believe that rituals and ceremonies have caused Jews, Christians, and Muslims to turn aside from "pure faith." The Druze thus eliminated all elements of ritual and ceremony; there are no fixed daily liturgies, no defined holy days, and no pilgrimage obligations. The Druze perform their prayers with *Allah*[154] at all times and, consequently, need no special days of fasting or atonement.

The Druze religion is secret and closed to converts. From a theological perspective, the secrecy arises from the tenet that the gates of the religion were open to new believers for the space of a generation when it was first revealed, and everyone was invited to join. Since, in their belief, everyone alive today is the reincarnation of someone who lived at that time, there is no reason to allow anyone new to join today. Therefore, the Druze refrain from missionizing, and no member of another religion can become Druze.

Druze religious books are accessible only to the *Uqqal* ("Knowers"). The *Juhal* ("ignorant ones") accept the faith on the basis of the tradition handed down from generation to generation. The Druze do not believe in polygamy; they have only one wife. They are very hospitable people. In a way, they compare to the Amish in the West, who are isolated in their own communities.

Mount Kerem-El **Overlooking the** Jezreel[143] **Valley**

Once you arrive at the monastery, there is a 15-minute hike to a lookout over the *Jezreel* Valley. The trek is often preferable to visiting the very crowded church. The trail can be a bit confusing and rugged if you go this way, so everyone should stay together.

Mount *Kerem-El* means "The Vineyards of *Yahweh.*" It is known for its fertile and lush vineyards.

The Jezreel Valley View from Mount Kerem-El

The Prophet Eliyahu and Mount Kerem-El[142]

Read (1 *Melachim*[88] 18:16-19):

> So *O'badyah*[156] went to meet *Ahab*[49] and told him, and *Ahab* went to meet *Elyahu*[87]. When he saw *Elyahu*, he said to him, "Is that you, you troubler of *Yesrael*?"
>
> "I have not made trouble for *Yesrael*," *Elyahu* replied. "But you and your father's family have.

> You have abandoned the Lord's commands and have followed the *Baals*. Now summon the people from all over *Yesrael* to meet me on Mount *Kerem-El*. And bring the four hundred and fifty prophets of *Baal* and the four hundred prophets of *Asherah*, who eat at *Yezabeel's* table."

O'badyah[114] was in charge of *Ahab's* palace, but he was a follower of *Yahweh*. He hid a hundred prophets of *Yahweh* in two caves, fifty in each, to protect them from *Yezabeel*[141], *Ahab's* wife:

> While *Yezabeel* was killing off the Lord's prophets, *O'badyah* had taken a hundred prophets and hidden them in two caves, fifty in each, and had supplied them with food and water.

Ahab was the son and successor of *O'mri*, his father. King *O'mri* was a successful military campaigner who extended the northern kingdom of *Yesrael*. *Ahab* was one of *Yesrael*'s worst kings. The Bible presents him as the seventh king of *Yesrael* since the beginning of the divided monarchy following *Shelmon's*[148] death. The first of those seven kings was *Yeroboam* remember, he had raised two false altars one in *Beth-El* and one in *Dan*, and all the kings of *Yesrael* followed his sin.

Ahab reigned over the Northern Kingdom of *Yesrael* from 871 to 852 BC.

Again in 922 BC, the nation of *Yesrael* was torn into two nations: *Yesrael* to the north and *Yehuda* to the south. *Yesrael* was full of internal tribal differences, and as a result, became vulnerable to frequent invasions. It was, however, following the beliefs of *Yahweh*, the "one and true" *Yahweh*, according to the Bible. Phoenicia (now known as *Lebanon*), located to *Yesrael's* north, was just the opposite: cosmopolitan, populous, and religiously diverse.

At the beginning of the 9th century, a Phoenician princess named *Yezabeel* was born. She was the daughter of the king of *Tyre*, named King *Eth-Baal*. The Bible does not describe *Yezabeel's* childhood, but it is assumed that she lived in a fine home and was educated. Her family worshipped many gods, the most important being *Baal*.

While *Yezabeel* was growing into a woman, *Yesrael* crowned a new king. To create an alliance with their neighbors to the north, King *O'mri* arranged for his son *Ahab* to marry *Yezabeel*. Their marriage cemented a political alliance. The two worked together to spread idol worship of *Baal* and fought against the prophets of *Yahweh*, including *Eliyahu*. Eventually, they ruled as king and queen. *Yezabeel* continued worshiping *Baal*. *Eliyahu* despised her actions.

In the 860s BC, King *Ahab* of *Yesrael* called *Eliyahu* a troublemaker. You can see his point. At *Eliyahu's* word, a great drought had come upon the land. After nearly three years, the situation had become desperate. Mount *Kerem-El* is typically a very wet place, so if it is dry here, it is dry everywhere.

Eliyahu wanted to get *Yesrael's* attention, and he succeeded. The daily tide of evil rose higher and higher, until it had swept practically everything before it. Scripture tells us that

Eliyahu was "very jealous for the Lord *Yahweh* of hosts" *(1 Melachim*[88]*19:10)*

The prophet was deeply disturbed by the horrible insults against *Yahweh*. Consequently, "… it rained not on the earth for the space of three years and six months."

Eliyahu[89] laid the blame back at *Ahab's*[49] feet for it was under the King's rule that worship of the deity *Baal* had entered the land, and *Yesrael* had abandoned the commands of *Yahweh*. The Lord had sent *Eliyahu* to return the nation to righteousness. The process started with the drought, for only by bringing the people and the king to their knees would they repent. *Eliyahu* was *Yahweh's* agent, working for his people's long-term recovery; *Ahab* was the real troublemaker, responsible for the nation's decline.

Mount *Kerem-El*[142] in Upper Galilee receives the most rain today. The same was probably true in ancient times, too. It gets somewhere between 76-100 cm (30-40 40 inches) of rain per year. *Baal*, the storm god, would be strongest on a mount such as this. But it had not rained for three years and six months. Even *Baal* could not break the drought. *Baal* was supposed to be strong on the mount, so *Eliyahu* calls for a confrontation on the pagan god's "home court."

> *Baal* means "lord, master, or husband." His mate was the fertility goddess/sister/wife *Asherah*. *Baal* was the god of storms, rain, and lightning, perfect for a farmer to worship, but it was a strange religion. *Baal* worship involved offering animal sacrifices. Some of the priests of *Baal* made their

sons pass through fire as sacrifices. Male and female prostitutes were available to worshipers to inspire the fertility of both the land and the people. *Baal* was usually associated with a bull and depicted with a threatening lightning bolt in hand. His whole presence shouted, "I am the one who gives life (fertility) through rain!"

Baal stood in direct opposition to the *Yahweh* of *Yesrael*. The Jewish people had been wanderers, not farmers. They were primarily shepherds. They were used to a harsh, arid environment. Coming to a fertile land with *Baal* worship forced an identity crisis for them. Who was the true *Yahweh* of life that deserved their worship? They became confused. *Elyahu* forced a decision.

> Now summon the people from all over *Yesrael* to meet me on Mount *Kerem-El*. And bring the four hundred and fifty prophets of *Baal* and the four hundred prophets of *Asherah*, who eat at *Yezebeel's* table.

So, we have *Ahab's* gods and *Eliyahu's Yahweh* in a classic showdown on Mount *Kerem-El* to determine which is true. One prophet of *Yahweh* against eight hundred fifty prophets of false gods. Seems a bit one sided, doesn't it?

Eliyahu's name means "m*y Yahweh* is the Lord." *Yahweh* is the past, present, and future.

The Prophets were the voice of *Yahweh*, calling His people to faithfulness. They were men of truth who called people to repent when they went astray lest *Yahweh* send judgment to the nation. Even today, we must honor the prophets among us. They lead difficult lives. They also lead lives of confidence and faith in the Word of *Yahweh*.

Eliyahu refused to compromise, and *Yahweh* used him to expose the fertility and foolishness of the *Baal* worship. *Elyahu's*[87] dependence was on *Yahweh*, not man. He did not need *Ahab* and *Yezabeel's*[141] approval, financial aid, or protection. He was a man of *Yahweh* on a mission to declare to them, and to all of *Yesrael,* their sins. He was a man of prayer and intercession; he was courageous against the tide of defection sweeping the land.

(1 *Melachim*[88] 18:20-29):

> So, *Ahab* sent word throughout all *Yesrael* and assembled the prophets on Mount *Kerem-El*. *Elyahu* went before the people and said, "How long will you waver between two opinions? If the Lord *Yahweh*, follow him; but if *Baal* is God, follow him."
>
> But the people said nothing.
>
> Then *Elyahu* said to them, "I am the only one of the Lord's prophets left, but *Baal* has four hundred and fifty prophets. Get two bulls for us. Let *Baal's* prophets choose one for themselves, and let them cut it into pieces and put it on the wood but not set fire to it. I will prepare the other bull and put it on the wood but not set fire to it. Then you call on the name of your god, and I will call on the

name of the Lord. The *Yahweh* who answers by fire—he is *Yahweh.*

Then all the people said, "What you say is good."

Elyahu said to the prophets of *Baal,* "Choose one of the bulls and prepare it first, since there are so many of you. Call on the name of your god, but do not light the fire." So, they took the bull given them and prepared it. Then they called on the name of *Baal* from morning till noon. "*Baal,* answer us!" they shouted. But there was no response; no one answered. And they danced around the altar they had made.

At noon *Elyahu* began to taunt them. "Shout louder!" he said. "Surely, he is a god! Perhaps he is deep in thought, or busy, or traveling. Maybe he is sleeping and must be awakened." So, they shouted louder and slashed themselves with swords and spears, as was their custom, until their blood flowed. Midday passed, and they continued their frantic prophesying until the time for the evening sacrifice. But there was no response, no one answered, no one paid attention.

The stage was now set. The huge audience was assembled, and one of the most dramatic stories in the whole history of *Yesrael* was about to happen. There was to be a public contest between the forces of good and evil. On the one side was *Baal* with his 850 of his prophets, and on the other *Yahweh* and His lone servant *Eliyahu.*

From morning to evening, the false prophets of false gods prayed, cried, begged, and even began cutting themselves with stones until the blood gushed out all in an effort to get *Baal's* attention. But it was to no avail. He never answered, and they were exhausted from their unsuccessful efforts.

Eliyahu even mocked them. "So, they shouted louder and slashed themselves with swords and spears, as was their custom, until their blood flowed" (1 *Melachim* 18:28). What a concept they must have held of their deity who required such cruel failure. The service of *Shaitan*[54], whether in the observance of idolatrous worship or in the practice of immoralities, is cruel and tends to torment. *Yahweh* desires only our happiness and never requires one thing that is not for our benefit, for there cannot be any real happiness apart from holiness.

This failure of the false prophets' part exposed the powerlessness of their false gods! Such gods are impotent creatures, unable to help their fans or followers in the hour of need. They are useless for this life; how much more so for the life to come!

Even determined worship will make utter fools of its victims, as was manifest in Mount *Kerem-El*. The prophets of *Baal* raised their altar and placed upon it the sacrifice, and then called upon their God for the space of six hours all in vain. Their urging met with no response: the heavens were closed as a locked door. No tongues of fire leapt from the sky to lick up the flesh of the slain bullock. The only sounds were the cries of anguish from the lips of the frantic priests as they oppressed themselves until their blood gushed forth.

Compare these words to our culture today. Do you worship the false gods such as your iPhone, your car, your house, your bank account? What is the priority in your life? *Yahweh* or the false gods? Again, you can name hundreds of these false gods, like the internet, food obsession, your possessions, whatever. What is your priority in this world?

Read (1 *Melachim*[88] 18:30 -40):

> Then *Elyahu* said to all the people, "Come here to me." They came to him, and he repaired the altar of the Lord, which had been torn down. *Elyahu* took twelve stones, one for each of the tribes descended from *Ya'coub*, to whom the word of the Lord had come, saying, "Your name shall be *Yesrael*." With the stones he built an altar in the name of the Lord, and he dug a trench around it large enough to hold two seahs of seed. He arranged the wood, cut the bull into pieces and laid it on the wood. Then he said to them, "Fill four large jars with water and pour it on the offering and on the wood."
>
> "Do it again," he said, and they did it again.
>
> Do it a third time," he ordered, and they did it the third time. The water ran down around the altar and even filled the trench.
>
> At the time of sacrifice, the prophet *Elyahu* stepped forward and prayed: "Lord, the *Yahweh* of *Ob-Rohom*, *Eshhak*, and *Yesrael*, let it be known today that you are *Yahweh* in *Yesrael* and that I am your servant and have done all these things at

at your command. Answer me, Lord, answer me, so these people will know that you, Lord, are *Yahweh*, and that you are turning their hearts back again."

Then the fire of the Lord fell and burned up the sacrifice, the wood, the stones and the soil, and also licked up the water in the trench.

When all the people saw this, they prostrated and cried, "The Lord—he is *Yahweh*! The Lord—he is *Yahweh*!"

The*n Elyahu* commanded them, "Seize the prophets of *Baal*. Don't let anyone get away!" They seized them, and *Elyahu* had them brought down to the Kishon Valley and slaughtered there.

Remember there is a drought, and every tiny bit of water is needed, and here is *Eliyahu*, wasting the water on the altar. Then he prayed the prayer in verses 36 – 37:

> Lord *Yahweh* of *Ob-Rohom*, *Eshhak*, and *Yesrael*, let it be known this day that you are the *Yahweh* in *Yesrael*, and that I am your servant, and that I have done all these things at your word. Hear me, O *Morio*[25], hear me, that this people may know that you are the *Morio Yahweh*, and that you has turned their hearts back again.

Then fire fell from heaven and consumed the sacrifice, and the wood, the stones, the dust, and licked up the water that was in the trench. And when the people saw it, they fell on their faces and said, "The Lord, he is the *Yahweh;* the Lord, he is the *Yahweh*!"

This was the high point of *Eliyahu's* life. He commanded all the false prophets to be slain. Then, with the offenders and false worshipers removed from the nation, *Eliyahu* could call for blessings to be restored. He went to the top of the mountain to pray for rain. *Yahweh* opened the heavens and poured out rain upon the thirsty land, ending a devastating drought.

Whenever there is evil, sin, and injustice in a nation, blessings are cut off. *Eliyahu* challenged the nation to condemn *Baal* and declare *Yahweh* to be God. He prayed that *Yahweh* would turn the people's hearts back to him. The prophet lived up to his name and submitted himself to the Lord in the face of wicked leaders who threatened him with death. When the people saw the power of *Yahweh*, they turned away from their useless, deaf, and dumb idols and to the living *Yahweh* who answers by fire.

Yahweh sent fire from Heaven. *Yahweh* wins!

The Prophet Eliyahu's statute

It would be very meaningful for the group to sing the following worship song together:

"Days of Elijah"

These are the days of Elijah,
Declaring the word of the Lord
And these are the days of Your servant Moses,
Righteousness being restored.
And though these are days of great trial,
Of famine and darkness and sword,
Still, we are the voice in the desert crying
"Prepare ye the way of the Lord!"

Behold He comes riding on the clouds,
Shining like the sun at the trumpet call,
Lift your voice, it's the year of jubilee,
And out of Zion's hill salvation comes.

These are the days of Ezekiel,
The dry bones becoming as flesh,
And these are the days of Your servant David,
Rebuilding a temple of praise.

These are the days of the harvest,
The fields are as white in Your world,
And we are the labourers in Your vineyard,
Declaring the word of the Lord!

Behold He comes riding on the clouds,
Shining like the sun at the trumpet call,
Lift your voice, it's the year of jubilee,
And out of Zion's hill salvation comes.

There's no God like Jehovah.

There's no God like Jehovah!
There's no God like Jehovah, hey!

Behold He comes riding on the clouds,
Shining like the sun at the trumpet call,
Lift your voice, it's the year of jubilee,
And out of Zion's hill salvation comes.

Behold He comes riding on the clouds,
Shining like the sun at the trumpet call,
Lift your voice, it's the year of jubilee,
And out of Zion's hill salvation comes.

Behold He comes riding on the clouds,
Shining like the sun at the trumpet call,
Lift your voice, it's the year of jubilee,
And out of Zion's hill salvation comes.

Behold He comes riding on the clouds,
Shining like the sun at the trumpet call,
Lift your voice, it's the year of jubilee,
And out of Zion's hill salvation comes.
Lift your voice, it's the year of jubilee,
And out of Zion's hill salvation comes.

After fifteen minutes or so for reflection and pictures, it's time to head back to the bus. I love taking the groups to a Druze house to sample the local Druze food instead of going to one of the major restaurants. Usually, it is a simple sandwich that consists of falafel or shawarma and a lot of tasty salads.

Druze food

Caesarea Maritima

After Mount *Kerem-El*[142], the group will head to Caesarea by the sea. It is a great idea to pre-arrange to watch a ten-minute documentary at the national park about the history of *Caesarea*. It's a wonderful introduction to the site. There is a large national park with lots to see. You will spend at least 90 minutes.

(Remember to bring water, hats, sunscreen, headsets, and Bibles.)

Brief History of Caesarea

There is a model of *Caesarea* located adjacent to the southern main entrance. This will give everyone a general idea of the site and the route during the tour.

The model in Caesarea

The Roman Emperor, *Caesar Augustus*, gave the site to *Herodos* the Great. Between 25 and 13 BC, *Herodos* constructed his most extensive building project, a city designed on the Roman model. He wanted to make a mini-Rome in the land of Palestine, and he named the city in honor of the Emperor *Augustus Caesar*.

As the commercial and cultural capital of the region, *Caesarea* attracted not only pagans but also Samaritans and Jews. Despite *Herodos's* grand scheme, tensions between Jews and non-Jews always ran high at *Caesarea*. Some thirty-three years after the time of *Yeshua,* the desecration of the city's synagogue, and the slaughter of 20,000 Jews (nearly all the Jewish community) was one of the contributing causes of the First Jewish Revolt (66-70 AD). When the Roman general *Vespasian* arrived to crush the revolt, he set up his headquarters in the city and directed military operations from there until he was proclaimed emperor in 69 AD.

Emperor *Vespasian* granted the city the status of a Roman colony, making the towns people full Roman citizens. He then gave the task of repressing the revolt to his son *Titus*, who in 70 AD destroyed *Or-Shlem*[5] and the second *Hayklo*[3]. Following the Roman victory, *Titus* celebrated his brother *Domitian's* birthday at *Caesarea* with a display of animal fights and gladiatorial contests in which 2,500 Jewish prisoners of war died.

Herodos managed to build the first artificial seaport ever in the history of the ancient world. In most cases, builders searched under the surface for a strong base upon which to build. But *Herodos* created his own foundation under the water by placing large slabs of rock on the bottom after which he built the harbor.

Marina archaeologists are amazed how *Herodos* built below water without the invention of cement. Marina archaeologists found that all the foundation stones under the water were chiselled from each corner to absorb the current of the waves of the sea. *Herodos* wanted to become a god, conquer nature, and do the impossible.

Herodos the Great built the second largest seaport in the Roman Empire though some scholars say Caesarea's harbor was as large as that of *Piraeus*, Athens' port. It brought status and revenue to *Herodos's* kingdom. He used the port to import materials for his numerous building projects. The harbor also made Palestine easily accessible to the ancient Roman world, only a ten-day voyage away from Rome.

Caesarea Harbor

Herodos was a businessman first and foremost and this explains much of what he did in *Caesarea*. The city encompassed 250 acres, boasting a theatre, an amphitheater, a hippodrome, palaces, public buildings, storerooms, residential areas, public toilets, and a sewer systems.

Archaeological excavations of the site began in 1951. In 1968 its 250 acres of ruins became a national park. Major excavations conducted by numerous expeditions from *Yesrael* and abroad have exposed impressive reminders of this forgotten large city. Excavations and restorations are still ongoing till today, especially in the crusader part, which the group will visit later.

The Caesarea Theatre

The most ancient of all the theaters found in *Yesrael*, it was built at the southern end of the city by *Herodos* during the first stages of the city's construction. The theater was intentionally aligned so it faced directly toward *Herodos's* palace with two seating areas accommodating around 4,000 spectators. It was intended to introduce a chiefly Hellenistic concept of drama and public performances to this part of the world.

Caesarea's Theatre

The floor of the orchestra (the semicircular space in front of the stage where the important people sat in Roman times) was colorfully painted stone in *Herodos's* time and later paved with marble. The front of the stage (orchestra wall) was painted stones. There are six wedges of seats. The square place for the governor's seat can be seen midway in the center wedge.

The floor of the arena itself was made of marble imported from Greece. We do not have marble in the *Ar'o-Kdosho*[157]. On this stage, the Romans re-enacted many of their victorious battles.

The Bible records the death of *Herodos Agrippa I*, which *Josephus* recorded taking place in this theater:

(*Ma'aseh*[64] 12:19-23):

> After *Herodos* had a thorough search made for him and did not find him, he cross-examined the guards and ordered that they be executed.
>
> Then *Herodos* went from Judea to *Caesarea* and stayed there. He had been quarreling with the people of Tyre and Sidon; they now joined together and sought an audience with him. After securing the support of Blastus, a trusted personal servant of the king, they asked for peace, because they depended on the king's country for their food supply.
>
> On the appointed day *Herodos*, wearing his royal robes, sat on his throne and delivered a public address to the people. They shouted, "This is the voice of a *Yahweh*, not of a man." Immediately, because *Herodos* did not give praise to *Yahweh*, an angel of the Lord struck him down, and he was eaten by worms and died.

The death of *Herodos Agrippa I* is one of the few events that is reported by both the book of *Ma'aseh* and Josephus Flavius. The Bible teaches us that *Agrippa* was struck down by an angel of the Lord while delivering a public address in *Caesarea*. What we just read was brief, but the immediate cause of his illness is clearly given in the text: the crowd hailed *Herodos* as a God and the king passively accepted their praise.

Despite the miraculous elements, most scholars believe that the account in *Ma'aseh*[50] is generally accurate because of a parallel record in the book of *Josephus* (*Antiquities*. 19.8.2). Most scholars believe that the two reports had independent sources, and though they agree in several respects, Josephus's longer account contains more details including the incident's occasion, location, and aftermath.

The book of *Ma'aseh*[64] records that *Herodos* gave the address in Caesarea. *Josephus* precisely places it in the theater of Caesarea. *Ma'aseh* does not say anything about the time of day, but Josephus writes that it occurred early in the morning. *Ma'aseh*[64] connects the episode with the resolution of a quarrel with the people of Tyre and Sidon, but says of the public address itself only that it occurred "on the appointed day."

Josephus relates that King *Agrippa I* appeared to the crowd on the second day of a festival intended to honor Caesar. Both sources speak of *Herodos's* clothing, but whereas *Ma'aseh* says simply that he was "wearing his royal robes," Josephus describes the garments as made "wholly of silver" and when "illuminated by the fresh reflection of the sun's rays...was so resplendent as to spread a horror over those that looked intently upon him." Josephus indicates that the crowd hailed King *Agrippa* as a god because of his radiant clothing, but *Louko's* brief account implies that they did so in response to the sound of *Agrippa's* voice. Both agree that *Agrippa* accepted the crowd's enthusiastic praise and consequently died shortly thereafter.

Excavations at *Caesarea* are helpful in reconstructing this event. It is likely that as successor to most of the vast holdings of his grandfather King *Herodos, Agrippa I* took up residence in the promontory palace on the south side of the city. About a decade later, *Agrippa's* successor, the Roman governor Felix, occupied the same palace (*Ma'aseh*[64] 24:35).

Roman power is evident in *Caesarea*, but even Rome was built around Greek culture. This dual culture influences the Christian Church to this very day. Hellenism started with Alexander the Great. Alexander's empire and the empires that succeeded his, known as the Hellenistic empires, lasted for hundreds of years, and spread Greek culture over huge territories.

Jewish culture and civilization during the Hellenistic period were intense and evident against the Hellenistic culture and civilization, but still, we can see its effect in the translation of Hebrew Scriptures into Greek, a translation we know as *The Septuagint*. That's certainly an example of the way in which Greek literary forms and Greek language impacted Jewish civilization and literary traditions.

That impact extends far beyond Scripture. And during the Hellenistic period, Jews adopted literary forms of the Greek tradition and the writing of plays, epic poems and lyric poems, all in the Greek language. Much of this activity would have been centred in Alexandria, the capital of *Metsrayin*[24], but there was similar activity going on in Palestine, and some of these literary products that survived in some cases only in fragments were probably written in Palestine by Jews who had adopted Hellenistic culture.

Even in philosophy and art, there is an influence that is still felt in the linguistic, intellectual, and artistic foundations of Western civilization today. Importantly, these ideas were spread in part through the commercial connections between Europe, the Middle East, and Asia formed during Alexander's reign.

The Hellenistic perspective is inherently selfish. It is all about me. You can see it in *Herodos* Agrippa's address in the theatre where the people focused solely on him to the point where they claimed he was a god.

The Jewish culture, *Yeshua's* culture, and the church culture are centered on *Yahweh*. It does not depend on my feelings; it depends on the moment or the reality of the situation. Emotions are important, no doubt, but we cannot build our lives on feelings. Instead, we should build our lives according to the Word of *Yahweh*, according to the truth of Scripture. It should be about serving, others not me.

Romans have a history of pleasure seeking. Being entertained and having fun is one of the ultimate goals in life in their culture. But life is not all about having fun. Sex, gay marriages, even in churches. However, the church begins to blur these lines because of this culture of self-appeasement. But sin cannot be blurred in *Yahweh's* eyes. Instead of life, liberty, and the pursuit of happiness, we should have life, liberty, and the pursuit of holiness.

We must be careful not to amuse ourselves, even with death-entertainment culture, like what happened in the theater.

The American Dream is all about the individual. Let me give you a personal example. One of my dreams as a kid was to watch an NBA basketball game live. This came true while visiting Texas. There was a game in San Antonio between the San Antonio Spurs and the Phoenix Suns. I bought the ticket online and drove the car to the AT&T Center Stadium. As soon as I arrived, I had a culture shock! The size of the parking lots was so huge that I could easily get lost just parking the car!

You have to understand. I come from the tiny city of Old *Or-Shlem*. I think the size of the stadium and parking lots were larger than the old city itself. And the tickets were expensive, around $250 each. I realized later that it is all about money when it comes to these games. It all reminded me of what the Roman culture sought back in the first century in Caesarea.

We parked the car and walked for 20 minutes to the stadium and got our seats. I was so disappointed. I was far away from the floor. Everything looked so tiny. There was some entertainment, cheerleaders dancing, a few announcements, and then the introduction of the players. At last, the game started. I was so excited, but I grew even more disappointed, because I could not see much. The players looked tiny from so far away.

My small TV screen in my home in the old city in *Or-*

Shlem[5] would've given me a better view. The game stopped every fifteen minutes. I was not able to enjoy it with all the distractions, the commercials, vendors selling drinks and food, and t-shirt cannons firing objects into the crowd.

That is the Roman-Greek cultural influence at its best and worst: selfish!

But what was *Yeshua's* culture? What did He tell his disciples, even though they lived in the midst of the peak of Roman Hellenism? *Yeshua* grew up in Galilee under *Herodos Antipas's* rule. And *Herodos*, more than anyone, wanted to be Roman.

Yeshua told us the last shall be first and the first last. He taught us to put others ahead of ourselves, contrary to the Roman and Greek way of thinking. *Yeshua* wants us to serve others and to connect to family and community. He never advocates an individualistic approach. There is a reason why *Yeshua* used the Greek word "hypocrite" 17 times in teaching his disciples.

A hypocrite is an actor, someone who pretends to be something they are not. The Romans, of course, were famous for their plays and theater. Today, too many people put on a mask and hide behind a false front. You can see this the world over, particularly in American culture with its emphasis on celebrities. Nothing, it seems, has changed over the centuries.

Statues at the entrance of the theater

In the theater area, archaeologists unearthed a statue of Diana of Ephesus, several statues of clothed women, a female mask, and fragments of statues, reliefs, and inscriptions that all pointed to the emphasis on hypocrisy, exactly the opposite of what *Yeshua* taught. *Yeshua* taught that life comes by dying to self. Notice *Yeshua's* reaction to the Pharisees in (*Mattai*[4] 23:13-29):

> "Woe to you, teachers of the law and Pharisees, you hypocrites! You shut the door of the kingdom of heaven in people's faces. You yourselves do not enter, nor will you let those enter who are trying to.

> "Woe to you, teachers of the law and Pharisees, you hypocrites! You travel over land and sea to win a single convert, and when you have succeeded, you make them twice as much a child of hell as you are.

"Woe to you, blind guides! You say, 'If anyone swears by th*e Hayklo*, it means nothing; but anyone who swears by the gold of the *Hayklo* is bound by that oath.' You blind fools! Which is greater: the gold, or the *Hayklo* that makes the gold sacred? You also say, 'If anyone swears by the altar, it means nothing; but anyone who swears by the gift on the altar is bound by that oath.' You blind men! Which is greater: the gift, or the altar that makes the gift sacred? Therefore, anyone who swears by the altar swears by it and by everything on it. And anyone who swears by the swears by it and by the one who dwells in it. And anyone who swears by heaven swears by *Yahweh*'s throne and by the one who sits on it.

Woe to you, teachers of the law and Pharisees, you hypocrites! You give a tenth of your spices—mint, dill and cumin. But you have neglected the more important matters of the law—justice, mercy and faithfulness. You should have practiced the latter, without neglecting the former. You blind guides! You strain out a gnat but swallow a camel.

"Woe to you, teachers of the law and Pharisees, you hypocrites! You clean the outside of the cup and dish, but inside, they are full of greed and self-indulgence. Blind Pharisee! First clean the inside of the cup and dish, and then the outside also will be clean.

"Woe to you, teachers of the law and Pharisees, you

hypocrites! You are like whitewashed tombs, which look beautiful on the outside but on the inside are full of the bones of the dead and everything unclean[28]. In the same way, on the outside you appear to people as righteous but on the inside, you are full of hypocrisy and wickedness.

"Woe to you, teachers of the law and Pharisees, you hypocrites! You build tombs for the prophets and decorate the graves of the righteous. And you say, 'If we had lived in the days of our ancestors, we would not have taken part with them in shedding the blood of the prophets.' So, you testify against yourselves that you are the descendants of those who murdered the prophets. Go ahead, then, and complete what your ancestors started!"

How do we compromise our values with the secular culture? How do we affect our culture as we participate in it but resist its effect on us? We need to wrestle with the culture every single day and live like *Yeshua* and not like the Romans.

Here are some questions to consider:

- What are you building your life on?
- What do you depend on more? *Yahweh* or your bank account?
- What will your life show for this short time on earth?

Herodos depended on his money, business, and projects. Look around you. Look at everything he created. It is all destroyed. What will remain in the test of time from your life? *Yeshua* taught us to focus on the Kingdom of

Heaven, on eternal things. *Yeshua* told us to die so that we might live.

(*Louko*[13] 9:23-24):

> Then he said to them all: "Whoever wants to be my disciple must deny themselves and take up their cross daily and follow me. For whoever wants to save their life will lose it, but whoever loses their life for me will save it.

(*Mattai* 6:19-20):

> "Do not store up for yourselves treasures on earth, where moths and vermin destroy, and where thieves break in and steal. But store up for yourselves treasures in heaven, where moths and vermin do not destroy, and where thieves do not break in and steal.

I always tell my groups to take some time to absorb the teaching and to take pictures. If you have someone with a good voice, have them go to the center of the theatre and sing a worship song. The voices will echo throughout the theatre.

Groups in the Theater

Archaeology of Caesarea

Where the pillars stand is the upper palace of *Augustus*, housing the public wings. Adjacent is the lower palace, which is comprised of private wings and a swimming pool. The pool in the center was nearly Olympic in size and was filled with fresh water. A statue once stood in the center. *Caesarea* has the largest Roman praetorium. From here, *Vespasian* went to suppress the first revolt and so with *Hadrian* during the second revolt. Josephus called this a "most magnificent palace" that *Herodos* the Great built.

Herodos's Palace

To the north is the hippodrome, capable of seating 38,000 people. It was 457 meters (1,500 feet) long and 76 meters (250 feet) wide. Some of the stones used to build the harbor's breakwater were 15 meters (50 feet) long, 2.4 meters (8 feet) wide, and 2.7 meters (9 feet) thick. The word *Hippodrome* in Latin means a "horse racetrack."

The Hippodrome

Herodos built a gigantic U-shaped entertainment complex on the south quarter behind the port. Originally, it was used as a racetrack for horses and chariots. A big ceremony took place in 9 BC at this hippodrome when *Herodos* established the Olympiads in *Caesarea* that continued every 4 years. This place was mainly for sports activities.

Herodos also built a lighthouse in the seaport area. This tower was three times higher than what we see today. It is also home to a seaport and the crusader fortress.

The Crusader fortress

The Biblical Story of Cornelius

The Bible tells of a story that took place in *Caesarea*. Read it in the book of (*Ma'aseh*[64] 10:24-48).

Being a light to the nations is a very important theme in the New Testament. *Kepha*, a loyal Jew kept kosher law. So why did he have a vision of unclean meats while in *Yuffi*[158]? This was the city to which *Yonnon*[147] fled to catch a ship to get away from *Yahweh's* command to preach in *Nineveh*. In a similar set of circumstances, *Kepha* is told to give the Gospel to the Gentiles.

Here we have two men of negative attitudes toward Gentiles, *Kepha* and *Yonnon*. Both are law abiding Jews chosen by *Yahweh* for the same mission. *Yonnon* was to preach to the Ninevites and *Kepha* to the Gentiles. After *Yeshua's* resurrection, He commanded his disciples to take the Gospel message to all the world. However, the Early Church did not comply quickly. The *Roho-Kodsho*[8] fell on the Romans: "While *Kepha* was still speaking these words, the *Roho-Kodsho* fell upon all those who heard the word" (*Ma'aseh*[64] 10:44). Who were these people? They were Gentiles searching for the truth. Then look in verse 45: "And those of the circumcision who believed were astonished." Who? The Jews. They were shocked that this happened. This is the first time they saw the *Roho-Kodsho* falling on someone who was not a Jew!

This is where the Gentile Church was born in *Caesarea* and represents the first reconciliation in history between a Jew and a Gentile. It transpired because of the *Roho-Kodsho*. We read in *Roma'yeh*[57] that it was always *Yahweh's* plan to include the Gentiles.

Shawol Comes to Caesarea

Yahweh was not going to cancel his own law. In fact, *Shawol*[16] was not against the *Torah* in his letters. He was against Jews requiring the *Torah* be kept for non-Jewish believers. It makes sense that *Shawol* would work well with Gentiles. After all, he grew up outside of the Jewish homeland. He was just a kid in the Diaspora. And though he had a Jewish education, he was also exposed to the Greco-Roman way of life and would have had contact with non-Jews throughout his life.

So, when S*hawol* saw that the Jews aren't exactly welcoming *Yeshua* with open arms, he came up with other plans. *Shawol* believed that, while *Yahweh* originally planned to bring salvation to the Jewish people through *Yeshua,* the Lord had decided to expand his reach to the Gentiles.

Read (*Ma'aseh*[64] 23:23-27):

> Then he called two of his centurions and ordered them, "Get ready a detachment of two hundred soldiers, seventy horsemen and two hundred spearmen to go to Caesarea at nine tonight. Provide horses for *Boulos*[7] so that he may be taken safely to Governor Felix."
>
> He wrote a letter as follows:
>
> Claudius Lysias, To His Excellency, Governor Felix: Greetings. This man was seized by the Jews and they were about to kill him, but I came with my troops and rescued him, for I had learned that he is a Roman citizen.

It is not hard to imagine *Shawol* during his two-year imprisonment in *Caesarea*, confined in one of the basement storage areas of *Augustus's* palace. The palace lasted for centuries. It was ruined by a huge earthquake in 749 AD that shook the fault line running right through the harbor. The palace complex was the praetorium of *Caesarea*. Most scholars believe that is the location where *Shawol* appealed to the governor Festus.

Shawol remains under heavy guard in *Caesarea*. When he sees that he may yet fall into the hands of the Jews, he tells Roman Governor Festus: "I appeal to Caesar!" (*Ma'aseh*[64] 25:11)

We need a little background about why *Shawol* appealed to Caesar.

Roman Procurator Porcius Festus

Our only firsthand information about Porcius Festus comes from the book of *Ma'aseh*[64] and the writings of *Josephus*. Festus succeeded Felix as procurator of Judea in about 58 AD and evidently died in office after governing just two or three years.

For the most part, Festus appears to have been a prudent and capable procurator, in contrast with his predecessor, Felix. At the beginning of Festus's time in office, Judea was plagued by bandits. According to Josephus, "Festus made it his business to correct those that made disturbances in the country. So, he caught the greatest part of the robbers, and destroyed a great many of them." During his tenure, the Jews built a wall to prevent King Agrippa from observing what took place in the *Hayklo*[3] area. Festus initially ordered them to dismantle it. At the Jews' request, however, he later allowed them to present the matter to the Roman Emperor Nero.

Festus appears to have taken a firm stand against criminals and insurgents. But in his desire to maintain good relations with the Jews, he was willing to set aside justice at least in his dealings with the Apostle *Boulos*[7].

King Herodos Agrippa II

The *Agrippa* referred to in *Ma'aseh* chapter 25 is King *Herodos Agrippa II*, great-grandson of *Herodos* the Great and son of the *Herodos* who had attacked the *Or-Shlem*⁵ congregation 14 years earlier (*Ma'aseh*⁶⁴ 12:1). Agrippa was the last of the Herodian emperors.

Upon the death of his father in 44 AD, 17-year-old *Agrippa* was in Rome, where he was being educated at the court of Roman Emperor Claudius. The emperor's advisers considered *Agrippa* too young to inherit his father's domain; thus, a Roman governor was appointed instead. Even so, according to Josephus, while Agrippa was still in Rome, he intervened for the Jews and represented their interests.

In about 50 AD, Claudius assigned Agrippa kingship over Chalcis and in 53 AD, over Ituraea, Trachonitis, and Abilene. Agrippa was also given oversight of *Or-Shlem's Hayklo* with authority to appoint the Jewish high priests. Claudius's successor Nero extended *Agrippa's* realm to include parts of Galilee and Paerea. At the time of his meeting *Shawol*, Agrippa was in *Caesarea* with his sister Bernice, who had left her husband, the King of Cilicia (*Ma'aseh*⁶⁴ 25:13).

In 66 AD, when *Agrippa's* efforts failed to calm the Jewish rebellion against Rome, he himself became a target of the rebels, and he was left no choice but to join the Romans. After the Jewish revolt was crushed, a new emperor, Vespasian, gave Agrippa further territories as a reward.

Shawol's Appeal

After being arrested, *Shawol* was transported to *Caesarea* where he would go before Festus, the Roman governor. *Shawol*¹⁶ pleaded his case to Festus. Remember, Pontius

Pilate once privately declared *Yeshua* innocent but then handed him over to be crucified. In a similar fashion, Festus declared *Shawol* innocent, but he did not set him free.

Instead, he kept *Shawol* until *Agrippa*, the Jewish king, could come down and hear the case. When given the opportunity, *Shawol* did not plead his case legally. He did not argue his innocence, though he did make it clear that he was innocent. He did not try to argue the law at all. Instead, *Shawol* gave full testimony to why he followed *Yeshua* and why everyone else in the court should as well.

The most natural thing for *Shawol* to do would have been to try to save his own life. Instead, he tried to save the souls of everyone present. Agrippa even scoffed at *Shawol*, asking if he really thought he could convince Agrippa to believe in such a short time.

Shawol's response? "I absolutely hope so!"

Shawol was drawing on the promise that *Yahweh* does not forget his saints. *Shawol* believed *Yahweh* gives power to his people in their moment of need. He trusted in this, and he declared it. He did not fear or cower or try to manipulate.

In the end, *Shawol* was sent to Rome to face Caesar. It was legal, but it was not right. He was innocent but he was condemned. A Roman governor conspired with a Jewish king to kill an innocent man for honoring *Yahweh*. And the innocent man went willingly. *Shawol* did not wonder what *Yeshua* might have done. He did precisely what *Yeshua* had done: he let them take him.

In a culture where we demand our rights, *Shawol's* humble obedience to *Yahweh* in the face of a personal injustice gives us something to think about. *Yahweh* works through our seasons of ease as well as hardship, which means whatever season we're in, *Yahweh* is with us, no matter how unfair things seem.

Read (*Ma'aseh*[64] 25:1-12):

> Three days after arriving in the province, Festus went up from *Caesarea* to *Or-Shlem*, where the chief priests and the Jewish leaders appeared before him and presented the charges against *Boulos*[7]. They requested Festus, as a favor to them, to have *Boulos* transferred to *Or-Shlem*, for they were preparing an ambush to kill him along the way. Festus answered, "*Shawol*[16] is being held at *Caesarea*, and I myself am going there soon. Let some of your leaders come with me, and if the man has done anything wrong, they can press charges against him there."
>
> After spending eight or ten days with them, Festus went down to Caesarea. The next day he convened the court and ordered that *Boulos*[7] be brought before him. When *Shawol* came in, the Jews who had come down from *Or-Shlem*[5] stood around him. They brought many serious charges against him, but they could not prove them.
>
> Then *Boulos* made his defense: "I have done nothing wrong against the Jewish law or against

the *Hayklo* or against Caesar."

Festus, wishing to do the Jews a favor, said to *Boulos*, "Are you willing to go up to *Or-Shlem* and stand trial before me there on these charges?"

Shawol answered: "I am now standing before Caesar's court, where I ought to be tried. I have not done any wrong to the Jews, as you yourself know very well. If, however, I am guilty of doing anything deserving death, I do not refuse to die. But if the charges brought against me by these Jews are not true, no one has the right to hand me over to them. I appeal to Caesar!"

After Festus had conferred with his council, he declared: "You have appealed to Caesar. To Caesar you will go!"

The Pontius Pilate Inscription

During renovations in 1961, a stone tablet was uncovered with a four-line Latin inscription, the left part of which had been chipped away. A possible reconstruction in Latin reads:

> **DIS AUGUSTI|S TIBERIEUM**
> **[PO] NTIUS PILATUS**
> **[PRAEF] ECTUS JUDA [EA] E**
> **[DEDIT DEDICAVIT]**

It translates: "Pontius Pilate, prefect of Judea, gave and dedicated a temple of Tiberias."

Originally, it had been placed in a temple dedicated to the Roman Emperor Tiberius (successor to Augustus) by Pontius Pilate (26-36 AD), the fifth Roman prefect of Judea.

The stone was salvaged from the building and reused in the theatre's steps during the 2nd century AD renovation.

The actual stone is now in the Israel Museum in *Or-Shlem*. It is one of the few pieces of extra-biblical evidence of the life of a man whose name is often repeated each Sunday in the Apostles Creed: "suffered under Pontius Pilate." Pontius Pilate was a full-time resident of *Caesarea* and only made the 60-mile journey to *Or-Shlem* at times of potential unrest, like the *Phischa*[55]. Thus, he was present during the trial of *Yeshua*.

Pilate inscription

Now is a good time for a picture break. Nice selfies with the background of Augustus Palace and the Mediterranean Sea.

Crusader Fortress of Caesarea

In 1101, the Crusader army under King Baldwin I conquered *Caesarea*. *Caesarea* became the seat of an archbishop and eastern Christians and then Muslims settled there.

Caesarea was captured by Saladin in 1187 after only a short siege. It was retaken in 1191 by Richard the Lionheart, King of England, who exiled the Muslim inhabitants.

Because of the growing Muslim threat, Louis IX, King of France, restored and fortified *Caesarea* in 1251-52. A magnificent 4 meter (13 foot) thick wall, some 1.6 km (1 mile) long, surrounded the city, which covered an area of about 40 acres. It was also protected by glacis, towers, and a 10 meter (32 foot) deep and 15 meter (49 foot) wide moat.

The cathedral of the Crusader city was built on the podium raised by King *Herodos* to serve as his city's acropolis. The 12th century cathedral, the eastern part of which was added in the middle of the 13th century, was a modest structure measuring 55 x 2 meters (180 x 6 feet). The hall was divided into a central nave and two aisles that ended in the east in three apses; the floor was paved in mosaics. The vaulting was supported by rectangular piers and pilasters.

The end of Crusader *Caesarea* came in 1265, when the Mamluk Sultan *Baybars* attacked the city. After a short siege, the Crusader defenders gave up hope and evacuated the city. The conquering Mamluks, fearing a return of the Crusaders, razed the city's fortifications to the ground.

Open Promenade and Crusader Marketplace

On June 10, 2020, a newly opened promenade and Crusader marketplace were unveiled in *Caesarea*. It dates back to the 13th century. The ancient sites are now accessible to the public for the first time in hundreds of years, the latest development in one of the largest archaeological projects ever undertaken in *Yesrael*.

There is a movie inside the newly renovated Crusader fortress – highly recommended.

Access to the Crusader city was via gates, the main one located in the eastern wall, which you will exit through later. There was also access through a bridge built on arches. These were supported by piers at the bottom of the moat.

The square gatehouse had a cross-vaulted ceiling supported by consoles decorated with floral motifs. The doors were closed on the inside with wooden bars and were protected on the outside by an iron grill, which was lowered through a slot from the ceiling. These most impressive fortifications were described in great detail by contemporary Crusader chroniclers.

You will exit the city gate and return to the bus to drive to the Roman aqueduct of *Caesarea*.

Crusader walls

The Roman Aqueduct

Since *Caesarea* had no rivers or springs, drinking water for the prospering Roman and Byzantine city was brought via a water aqueduct. The aqueduct consisted of three canals. The first aqueduct was built by *Herodos* (37 BC to 4 BC) at the time the new city was founded and dedicated to the Roman Caesar, Augustus. It brought the water from the southern side of Mount *Kerem-El* at *Shummi* about 10 km (6 miles) to the northeast of the city. The water flowed on a single raised canal.

Since even this was not sufficient, a second aqueduct was built by the legions of the Emperor Hadrian (2nd century AD). It brought water from the *Tanninim* (crocodiles) River, farther from *Shummi*. This section, with a tunnel of about

6 km (3.7 miles) long, was tapped into the older aqueduct and doubled its capacity. This new source of water was added to the right of the first canal, and the aqueduct was thus doubled in width. The builders used the same building materials and style, so it is hard to see that the pair of tunnels were built in different ages.

These twin parallel aqueducts, termed today as the high-level aqueducts, continued to supply water for 1200 years. During the ages, they were repaired several times. Eventually, however, they were beyond fixing. In the Crusaders period (12th century AD), a third, smaller canal was built to replace the first two. At that time, the city was smaller and required less water, so the third smallest canal was sufficient.

The aqueduct of Caesarea

After a brief break, it will be time to head to *Yuffi*[158]. Here is a summary of the most important things that happened in *Caesarea* that you can share on the Bus.

- *Caesarea* was the site of many conflicts between the Jewish and Gentile populations. Demonstrations against the Roman control of Palestine were frequent, culminating in the Jewish Revolt of AD 66.
- Pontius Pilate, prefect of *Yehudea*, lived in the governor's residence in *Caesarea*. An inscription on a stone found recently in the theater reads: "Pontius Pilate, the Prefect of Judea, has dedicated to the people of *Caesarea* a temple in honor of Tiberius."
- After baptizing the Ethiopian eunuch, Philip was "transported" to *Azotus* (Ashkelon) and from there continued to *Caesarea*, evangelizing as he travelled. (*Ma'aseh*[64] 8:40)
- As a result of *Shawol's* boldly proclaiming *Yeshua* in *Or-Shlem*, the Hellenistic Jews there plotted to put him to death. Believers who were concerned for his life brought him from *Or-Shlem* to *Caesarea* to return him to his hometown of Tarsus. (*Ma'aseh*[64] 9:28, 29).
- An angel of the Lord visited Cornelius, a God-fearing Roman centurion at *Caesarea*, instructing him to send for *Kepha* who was in *Yuffi*[158]. (*Ma'aseh*[64] 10:1-8).
- Immediately after *Kepha's* vision of various animals lowered from heaven in a white sheet, messengers arrived, summoning him to the centurion's residence in *Caesarea*, a two-day journey up the coast. There, *Kepha* first preached the Gospel to the Gentiles.

- Cornelius and his Gentile household. They believed in *Yeshua* and received the gift of the *Roho-Kodsho*[8], validating the fact that salvation of *Yeshua* was for all people. (*Ma'aseh*[64] 10:24-48).

- *Herodos Agrippa I* died in *Caesarea* after "being eaten by worms" as God's judgment on him for receiving praise due only to *Yahweh*. (*Ma'aseh*[64] 12:19, 21-23).

- The Apostle *Shawol*[16] returned from his second and third missionary journeys to the port of Caesarea (*Ma'aseh*[64] 18:22; 21:8). After his third journey, *Shawol* stayed in the city with Philip and his four virgin daughters who were prophetesses. *Boulos*[7] then proceeded to *Or-Shlem* with several disciples from Caesarea. (*Ma'aseh*[64] 21:9-16).

- Because of danger to his life, the Roman authorities in *Or-Shlem* sent Saul *Shawol* to *Caesarea* for trial. The apostle gave a bold witness to *Yeshua* during his hearings before Felix, Festus, and King *Agrippa*. Under house arrest for two years at *Caesarea*, *Shawol* eventually used his Roman citizenship to appeal to Caesar for a hearing. (*Ma'aseh*[64] 23:23- 26:32).

Caesarea to Tel Aviv

The coastal runs through the *Tel-Abib*[160] main promenade where the group can see the Mediterranean shore. *Tel-Abib,* the name is a biblical name, but *Tel-Abib* in the Bible was in Babylon. *Tel-Abib,* in Hebrew means "hill of the new spring." An ancient city from the Babylonian exile on the *Kebar*[161] Canal, near *Nippur*[162] in what is now Iraq. *Tel-Abib* is mentioned in the book of (*Khazkiel*[163] 3:15).

Then I came to them of the captivity at *Tel-Abib*, that lived by the river *Chebar*, and to where they lived; and I sat there overwhelmed among them seven days."

Over the past many years, this waterfront has been so much developed into a very beautiful beach.

Tel-Abib was founded in 1909 as a new Jewish suburb north of the ancient Mediterranean port of *Yuffi*[158]. Sixty-six families gathered on the sand dunes south of *Yuffi* and selected lots for property in a new neighborhood. They gathered sixty-six gray seashells and sixty-six white seashells. They printed the names of the participants on the white shells and the plot numbers on the gray shells. That's how they selected the plots.

By calling their new city *Tel-Abib*, the early immigrants to Palestine appear to have expressed their determination to rebuild the harvest *Yahweh* intended *Yesrael* to become. It would be new and alive.

Tel-Abib became the first modern Jewish city in Palestine. *Tel Abib's* most significant architectural heritage consists of buildings from the 1930s and '40s, designed in the International Style, which was influenced by the Bauhaus school. *Tel-Abib* is considered to have the greatest concentration of such buildings worldwide. We have another name for *Tel-Abib*: The White City. The White City was designated a UNESCO World Heritage site in 2003.

By the beginning of the twenty-first century, the modern city of *Tel-Abib* had developed into a major economic and cultural center. *Tel-Abib* is headquarters for a number of government ministries, including the Ministry of Defense, as well as other public organizations. Most of the foreign embassies in *Yesrael* are also located in the city. In addition, most of *Yesrael*'s large corporations are headquartered in *Tel-Abib*.

Tel-Abib is depicted as "the city that never sleeps," a thriving, vibrant, modern, dynamic, and multicultural, generally characterized as tolerant, secular, and liberal, while also materialistic city of the present, lacking deep historical roots. By contrast, *Or-Shlem* is considered eternal, holy, and conservative.

We have a saying in *Yesrael*, "While *Or-Shlem* prays, *Tel-Aviv* plays, and Haifa works!" *Or-Shlem* is a religious city where three monotheistic religions started. *Tel-Abib* is secular. Haifa is very technologically advanced.

Another saying: "*Or-Shlem* is the past, *Tel-Abib* the present and Haifa the future." *Or-Shlem* is the past, because of its history and archaeology. *Tel-Abib* is the present because it is very secular and business oriented. It represents the young entrepreneur spirit. Haifa is the future because of the seaport exports and imports and its industrial importance. Exposed to the West because of its location, there is a great deal of modern influence there.

Yuffi

Going from *Tel-Abib* to *Yuffi*[158] is a move from the modern back to ancient times.

Tradition says that *Yuffi* was named after Noah's son, *Yaphet*[164] (who built *Yuffi* after the Flood). It is also possible that the name is derived from the Hebrew *Jaffeh*, or Aramaic *Yuffi*, meaning *"to open"*. Ancient papyrus documents reveal that *Yuffi* existed as a seaport more than 4,000 years ago, and as such, it is said to be the world's oldest harbor in continual use. Greek legend mentions a ravishing Andromeda chained to the breakwaters of *Yuffi's* seaport.

The Andromeda Rocks, Yuffi

Greek Mythology

The King of *Yuffi*[158], Cepheus, and his wife, Queen Casiopeia, had a daughter, Andromeda. She was famous for her great beauty. Queen Casiopeia boasted that she and her daughter were more beautiful than the mermaids. Her arrogance enraged the gods. They appealed to Poseidon, God of the Sea, and asked him to punish the arrogant humans. Poseidon agreed and sent a flood of water and a sea monster to destroy the lands of the Philistines and *Yuffi*.

King Cepheus, after consulting with the oracle and under pressure from the residents, decided to sacrifice his Andromeda in hopes of appeasing Poseidon by sacrificing her to the sea monster. Beautiful Andromeda was tied to the rocks on the shore of *Yuffi* and left there.

Perseus, son of Zeus, chief of the gods, was passing through, saw Andromeda, and fell in love with her. The king and queen promised him their daughter as his wife if he could rescue her from the monster. Perseus chopped off the head of the sea monster, which fell into the water, and became the famous sea rocks of *Yuffi*.

The Bible speaks of *Yuffi* many times. In the Old Testament, we have two stories. The city was the seaport used by King *Shelmon* while he was building the *Hayklo*. King *Hiram* of Tyre sent cedar logs for the *Hayklo* to *Yuffi* where they were hauled ashore and transported to *Or-Shlem* (2 *Metlata*[165] 2:16) and it was in *Yuffi that Yonon* left for Tarshish while attempting to flee *Yahweh's* command and was consequently tossed overboard for the whale (*Yonon* 1:3).

In the New Testament, there are a couple more stories. *Tabitha*[166] was brought back to life by *Kepha* in *Yuffi* (*Ma'aseh*[64] 9:36). Soon after, *Yahweh* gave *Kepha* the vision of the unclean animals and commanded him to preach the Gospel to Gentiles and Jews alike. (*Ma'aseh* 11:4-17).

Downtown *Yuffi*[158]

While driving through the streets of *Yuffi*, you will see the clock tower in the center of the city. The *Yuffi* clock tower is one of seven built in Palestine during the Ottoman period. The others are located in *Tsfat*[167], *A'cco*[168], *Natseret*[33], *Haifa,* and *Shechem*[169]. *Or-Shlem*[5] also had a clock tower built during the Ottoman period on top of the *Yuffi* gate. It no longer exists; The clock tower was torn down by the British in the 1920s.

On the north-eastern corner of the clock is the *Saraya*[170], a Turkish word for "a palace of royalty." The *Saraya* was designed in a classic eastern look. The front has four marble poles, a beautiful entrance with arches, also made from marble. What is left today is a reconstruction of the entrance of the *Saraya*. Unfortunately, the *Saraya* was destroyed during the 1948 war. We see a reconstruction of the façade in white marble poles.

*The Saraya (left) with the marble poles –
Jaffa clock tower (center)*

The *Yuffi* flea market is a wonderful place to experience local life. It offers a treasure of antiques, handmade, and second-hand items. "Flea market" in Hebrew is s*huk hapishpeshim*[171].This portside neighborhood of alleyways, covered walkways, and outdoor verandas has been operating for more than 100 years across the same streets. Open six days a week, Sunday through Friday, from morning through early evening hours, is a wonderful place to find antiques if you are a collector.

The year was 1915. In the mountains of *Tur Abdeen*[172], the ancient heartland of the Syriac people, in Turkeye whispers of massacre carried from village to village. My great-grandfather was a young man then, living among the stone monasteries and vineyards where our people had spoken Aramaic since the days of the apostles. But the Turks called it *Sayfo*[173] literally means "the sword" and it came swiftly. Villages burned. Monks were slain. Families vanished overnight.

One evening, elders gathered in the dim candlelight of a church carved into the rock. They whispered that the only hope was to leave. Some spoke of the long road south, to Aleppo, Damascus, and finally the Mediterranean coast where ships and trains could carry the survivors toward safety. My great-grandfather, clutching only a small cross and a few coins, joined others in silence. Behind him, he left vineyards, carved crosses, and the graves of his fathers.

The train was iron and smoke, a beast roaring through lands he had never seen. From Mardin down toward Aleppo, every stop was dangerous, soldiers searched carriages, demanding papers, sometimes dragging men away. But fortune carried him forward. The train was crowded with Armenians, Syriacs, and Greeks, all running from the same fate. Their languages mingled, but their tears were the same.

Weeks later, dusty and weary, he reached the port city of *Yuffi*, a place alive with citrus groves and the smell of the sea. There, among Jews, Arabs, and Christians, he found a fragile peace. The sound of Aramaic prayers in small chapels reminded him of home, though home was now only a memory. He built a new life by the sea, carrying with him the echo of *Tur Abdin's* mountains and the sorrow of *Sayfo*[173].

From him, we are here today. His journey was not just survival; it was the carrying of a language, a faith, and a people across the edge of extinction into new soil where it could still breathe.

The Frere School *De La Salle* is a French international school established in 1882. Incidentally, this is where my father, Yousef Antone Moubarak, attended school. He was born in *Yuffi*, and much of his family still lives there.

Collège des Frères de Jaffa

Simon the Tanner's House

After walking through the old city of *Yuffi*, you will reach Simon the Tanner's house. This is where *Kepha* was staying when Cornelius sent for him – the one "whose house is near the seacoast." (*Ma'aseh*[64] 10:5-7)

> "Now send men to *Yuffi* to call for a man named Simon who is called *Kepha*. He is staying with

> *Kepha* the tanner, whose house is near the seacoast." When the angel who spoke to him had gone, Cornelius called two of his servants and a devout soldier from among his attendants.

Kepha is a masculine name of Aramaic origin, meaning "little rock" or "stone." *Kepha* is a biblical name known for its connection to Peter from the Greek word for "rock," *petros*. When the disciples wanted to tease Peter, they called him *Kepha* because he was a stubborn man. (Many of us have nicknames for our friends. Not all of them are kind.)

Today, the house is owned by an Armenian family, *Zakarian*, and is closed to visitors. On the roof of the house, the British mandate constructed a lighthouse serving the ships entering the harbor. Near the lighthouse is a small mosque, *Jamea El-Botrus*[174]. It was constructed in 1730 and accompanied by a guardhouse intended to defend the city against attacks from the sea.

This is where one of the most significant events in Christian history took place. *Kepha's* vision led him to proclaim the Gospel to the Gentiles, allowing them to join the Early Church and its communities.

Kepha's Vision

Read (*Ma'aseh*[64] 10:9-16):

> The next day, while they were on their journey, drawing near to the city, *Kepha* went up upon the housetop to pray about noontime. And he became hungry, and wanted to eat; but while they were

preparing food for him, he fell into a trance.

And he saw the heaven open and something fastened at the four corners, resembling a large linen cloth, was let down from heaven to the earth; And there were in it all kinds of four-footed beasts and creeping things of the earth and birds of the air. And there came a voice to him, saying, "*Kepha,* rise; kill and eat." But *Kepha* said, "Far be it, my *Adonai,* for I have never eaten anything which was unclean and defiled." And again the voice came to him a second time, "What *Yahweh* has cleansed, you should not call unclean." This happened the third time; then the cloth was lifted up to the heaven.

Kepha, as already pointed out, was a loyal and observant Jew who kept the *Torah* and never ate anything that wasn't kosher. A stubborn man, he does not want to spread the message of *Yahweh* to Gentiles. Gentiles were considered pagans, and it would have been unseemly for a good Jew to mingle with them.

During *Kepha's* vision, a voice commanded him to "rise, kill, and eat" the unclean animals. *Kepha* was confused by the instruction. He kept saying, "By no means, *Adonai*; for I have never eaten anything that is unclean or defiled." The voice in the vision repeated the instruction, instructing *Kepha* a total of three times. At no point did *Kepha* break *Yahweh's* written commandment from (*Dbarim*[14] 14:1-21) by eating unclean animals.

The purpose of *Kepha's* vision was not meant to support the idea that *Yahweh* had done away with Old Testament dietary laws. The passage in (*Ma'aseh* 10) explains the exact purpose and reason for *Kepha's* vision.

What is Kosher food?

Kosher refers to the Jewish laws dealing with what foods can and cannot be eaten and how those foods must be prepared. Traditional Jewish practice forbids the consumption of some types of food (certain varieties of animals, animals slaughtered by any but the accepted method, the blood of mammals or birds) and some combinations of foods (roughly, meat with milk products).

Let me put it in Western words for you. *Kepha* saw a vision of a Big Mac cheeseburger with bacon coming down from heaven – a non-kosher food. One of the important aspects of observing kosher is keeping milk and meat properly separated. This prohibition is derived from the verse, "Do not cook a kid in its mother's milk." This verse appears in the *Torah* three times, twice in (*Shemoth*[22] 23:19 and 34:26) and once in (*Dbarim*[14] 14:21).

Some Jewish authorities give reasons for this prohibition. One reason is that it is cruel to cook a baby in the very milk intended to nourish it. The *Torah* forbids the cooking and consumption of any milk with any meat to prevent one from cooking a kid in its mother's milk. But *Yeshua* and the *Roho-Kodsho* have redeemed the baby and his mother's milk by the blood of Christ.

Simon the Tanner's house in Yuffi

Cornelius's Invitation

The Gentile men sent from Cornelius tell *Kepha* the divine reason for their coming. Cornelius was directed through a heavenly vision and a voice to send for *Kepha* so that Cornelius's house might hear about *Yahweh*: the word of the Good News and the salvation birthed by the Spirit of *Yeshua*.

Read (*Ma'aseh*[64] 10:23-29):

> So *Kepha* brought them into the place where he was staying and welcomed them. The next day he arose and went with them, and a few men from amongst the brethren of *Yuffi* accompanied him. And the next day they entered Caesarea. And Cornelius was waiting for them, and all his relatives and also his dear friends were assembled with him. And just as *Kepha* was entering, Cornelius met him and threw himself at his feet and worshipped him. But *Kepha* raised him, saying, "Stand up; I am but a man also." And after he had talked with him, he went in and found a great many people had come there.

Obedient to the voice of the *Roho-Kodsho*[8], *Kepha* makes the journey north to *Caesarea* and arrives at the house of Cornelius. As *Kepha* enters, he finds a gathering of Cornelius's relatives and close friends eagerly awaiting the divine message from *Yahweh*.

Kepha begins by telling them about the meaning of the vision *Yahweh* gave to him while on the roof praying in

Yuffi. *Kepha* tells those listening the true meaning of his divine vision: "*Yahweh* has shown me that I should not call any person unclean or defiled."

The purpose and meaning of *Kepha's* vision are quite clear. *Kepha* (and all Jews) should no longer believe that Gentiles coming to faith in *Yahweh* are unclean (unacceptable by *Yahweh*) or defiled (unholy). The reality is that *Yahweh* has, in fact, accepted Gentiles coming to faith in Him. They do not need to undergo a man-made ritual conversion to become a legal Jew.

This idea of Gentiles being unclean (unacceptable) was so ingrained in Jewish thought that Judaism of the day deems it to be "unlawful" for a Jew to associate with or enter the house of a Gentile. This is why, when *Kepha* enters the house of Cornelius, he says: "You yourselves know how unlawful it is for a Jew to associate with or to visit anyone of another nation." (*Ma'aseh*[64] 10:28)

Kepha then turns his attention to his host, Cornelius the Gentile, and asks, "So when I was sent for, I came without objection. I ask then why you sent for me?"

Read (*Ma'aseh*[64] 10:30-33):

> Then Cornelius said to him, "Four days I have been fasting; and at three o'clock in the afternoon while I was praying in my house, a man dressed in white garments stood before me, And said to me, 'Cornelius your prayer has been heard, and your alms are a memorial before *Yahweh*. But send to the city of *Yuffi* and bring Simon, who is called

> *Kepha*; behold he is staying in the house of Simon the Tanner, by the seaside; and he will come and talk with you.' At that very time I sent for you, and you have done well to come. Behold we are all here present before you, and we wish to hear everything commanded you from *Yahweh*."

Cornelius answers *Kepha's* question by explaining to him the divine vision he had also received, then concluding with an invitation for *Kepha* to share the message then *Kepha* had called them all together to hear. And while *Kepha* finished teaching, looked what happened (*Ma'aseh*[64] 10:44-48).

> While *Kepha* spoke these words, the *Roho-Kodsho*[8] descended on all who heard the word. And the Jewish converts who had come with him were seized with amazement because the gift of the *Roho-Kodsho* was poured out on the Gentiles also; For they heard them speak with different tongues, and magnify *Yahweh*. Then *Kepha* said to them, "Can any man forbid water, that these people who have received the *Roho-Kodsho,* just as we have, should not be baptized?" And he commanded them to be baptized in the name of our *Morio*[25] *Yeshua Mshiho*[10]. And they urged him to remain with them a few days.

The *Roho-Kodsho*[8] fell on the Romans! Was that possible? They were not Jews. This is the Second Pentecost, the Gentile Pentecost. The first Pentecost took place 14 years earlier in *Or-Shlem* in the Upper Room. This one launched the Gentile Church. It is shocking to *Kepha* and his Jewish companions, but it opened their eyes to *Yahweh's* will. How could they deny that *Yahweh* had also chosen the Gentiles when they saw such evident working of the *Roho-Kodsho*? Thus, the Gentile Church was born.

Then *Kepha* returns to *Or-Shlem,* and Church Elders debate the issue. The event was unprecedented. They didn't know what to do with the Gentiles. *Yuffi* was the place where *Yahweh* extended his mercy to the Gentile people. If you read the book of *Roma'yeh*[57], it was always *Yahweh's* plan to include the Gentiles.

Here in *Yuffi,* as described in (*Ma'aseh*[64] 10), the Jewish people fulfilled *Yahweh's* promise to *Ob-Rohom* that he would be a blessing to all the nations of the world. *Yuffi* is the spot where *Yesrael* fulfilled the prophecy of being a light to the nations.

Now it's time to head for *Or-Shlem.*

The Drive up to Or-Shlem[5]

In the ancient world, city streets and gates were often named after the destinations they led to. For example, Hebron Road in *Or-Shlem* pointed travelers toward Hebron. In the same way, the Jaffa Gate the main western entrance into *Or-Shlem* was named because it faced the road leading directly to the port city of *Yuffi* on the Mediterranean coast.

The drive up from *Yuffi* to *Or-Shlem* takes about 40 miles. The group will be in the city for three nights.

The Land of Yesrael

The stretch of land from the Mediterranean coastal plain up through the *Shephelah*[176] and into the hill country of Judah and Ephraim is among the most fertile and strategic regions in the ancient world. This natural rise from the sea to the mountains gave Israel access to rich soil, varied crops, and secure strongholds.

The "Seven Species" of the Land, mentioned in (*Dbraim*[12] 8:7–8). These seven are central symbols of the fertility and blessing of the Promised Land.

> "For the LORD your God is bringing you into a good land, a land of brooks of water, of fountains and springs, flowing out in the valleys and hills with a land of wheat and barley, of vines and fig trees and pomegranates, a land of olive oil and honey."

Olives and Olive Oil

Olives and olive oil are an important part of the area's culture and economy even today. Olive oil is the foundation of most Mediterranean foods. Olive oil cleanses the liver and loosens stools. Drinking a teaspoon of olive oil every morning before eating can, can help to prevent stones in the urinary tract. Olive oil protects against heart disease by lowering blood pressure and has strong anti-bacterial properties. It also contains several antioxidants to help fight cancer. Thus, olive oil can truly be called the foundation of life.

The olive tree is a symbol of life (at least according to my grandfather). As believers, we are like olive trees. We bring life to this world. Olive trees live for an extremely long time and represent eternal life in this way. It is also very hard to kill an olive tree.

Olive tree

Chronic inflammation is thought to be a leading driver of diseases, such as cancer, heart disease, metabolic syndrome, type-2 diabetes, Alzheimer's, arthritis and even obesity. Extra-virgin olive oil can reduce inflammation, which may be one of the main reasons for its health benefits.

The main anti-inflammatory effects are mediated by the antioxidants. Key among them is oleocanthal, which has been shown to work similarly to ibuprofen, an anti-inflammatory drug.

Grapes and Vineyards

In the Eastern Mediterranean basin, wine has been made for thousands of years. In ancient times, this region was the equivalent of today's France and Italy, both in terms of quantity and quality. Indeed, the Eastern Mediterranean was where wine culture was born, shaped by the Canaanites, Israelites, Phoenicians, Ancient Greeks and Romans, and then nurtured by Judaism and Christianity.

Grapes grow in beautiful clusters and correspond to beauty. From grapes, we get wine. The first century wine was so important as was learned when we visited the church in *Kanna* where *Yeshua* turned the water to wine. Grapes include both nourishing and eliminating qualities.

Grape-seed oil nourishes the skin, while also containing a very high content of antioxidants that help in eliminating free radicals. Grapes possess a diuretic quality, yet they are very nutritious, being replete with vitamins A, B, and C, while also treating blood and energy deficiency.

Grapes are a good source of potassium, a mineral that helps balance fluids in your body. Potassium can help bring down high blood pressure and lower your risk of heart disease and stroke. Most people don't get enough of this nutrient, so eating grapes can help fill the gap.

The vine leaf is another grape byproduct. In the spring and early summer, the leaves may be carefully picked and put aside to make stuffed or rolled vine leaf dishes. Many of the domestic vineyards or wild vines in the Eastern Mediterranean were looked after by the woman in the family; domestic winemaking was their responsibility. It was easy for them to make use of the vine leaves to make dishes that became associated with the region. My mother used to cook for us a lot of Vine Leaves, they are so Juicy. The most famous are Greek *dolmas* (or *dolmades*), which are stuffed or filled grape leaves. The filling may be rice, meat, fresh herbs and spices, made in full flavored bite-sized pieces. They are delicious and nutritious, and though most associated with Greece, they are also commonly used in *Cypriot, Lebanese, Turkish, Palestinian, Yesraeli* and Druze cooking.

Vineyards in the Judean hills

Figs and Fig Trees

The fig tree symbolizes prosperity, peace and leadership. Prosperity because of the abundance of sweet juicy figs, peace because of the tree's refreshing shade, and leadership in that the fig tree itself grows to be a large, magnificent tree, often referred to as "the king of trees."

First century *Talmidim*[177] would follow their rabbi as he walked throughout the land, teaching with both word and action. The Bible describes learning from a rabbi as "sitting at his feet," which was often done in the synagogue as well as in the *Hayklo*[3] colonnades. Sitting at the rabbi's feet was often done under a fig tree, not only because of the shade it provided but also because of the tree's sweet fruit. Soon "under the fig tree" became an idiom for one who sits under the shade of a Rabbi's teaching, enjoying the "sweet" fruit of his instruction and wisdom.

There are two prophecies talking about resting under the fig tree (*Mikha*[79] 4:4 and *Zechariah*[66] 3:10). Both passages deal with the end of exile, the forgiveness of sins, and restoration of the covenantal people the consolation and redemption of *Yesrael* which was the expectations of the people during the first century. This was the vocation of *Yeshua*. He ended the exile. He restored the mountain (kingdom) of *Yahweh*. And the *Hayklo*[3] is built up in the body of *Yeshua*.

Fig trees are native to the Mediterranean area, although they may be found more extensively from Asiatic Turkey to northern India. Today, they are also found growing on a commercial basis in numerous other countries around the world. They are also often grown as large decorative potted trees in greenhouses or "sunrooms" in cold climates.

The fig plant is cultivated as a bush from 1 meter (3 feet) tall, to large trees over 10 meters (33 feet) tall. Their wide, coarse deciduous leaves are easily identified. The sweet fruit develops above the points of shed leaves, or in the axil of leaves of the current year, with one or two figs set together. Depending upon local temperature and rainfall, there may be one or two crops harvested per year.

Figs have been a major food for people of the Mediterranean and Middle East for thousands of years. Their ability to store easily by drying made them, along with various grains and raisins, a dependable long-term food source. The same can just as truly be said about them today.

Figs are mentioned from beginning to end throughout the Bible. Virtually everyone in the Bible ate, or at least was familiar with, figs.

Fresh Figs

Modern science affirms the nutritional benefits of figs: they are very rich in minerals, especially potassium, iron, and calcium, and they contain omega-3 and omega-6 fatty acids. Figs also contain phytosterols, which inhibit the absorption of dietary cholesterol, thus decreasing the total levels of cholesterol. Moreover, they may help prevent certain types of cancers.

Pomegranates

The pomegranate is a fruit-bearing, deciduous shrub or small tree that grows between five and ten meters tall. The tree is native to the Mediterranean and Middle East but is now cultivated for its delicious fruit throughout the world.

A pomegranate is a very beautiful and majestic fruit; it even has a crown. It represents majesty and glory. The fruit is rich in vitamins (E, C, A) and folic acid while recent research work indicates that the pomegranate is a potential asset in preventing heart attacks.

Pomegranate juice contains an antioxidant that is particularly strong and is more effective in preventing heart attacks than red wine, green tea or tomatoes. It is full of antioxidants and good for our immune system. A healthy immune system is so important, especially since the COVID-19 pandemic, because pomegranates boost our immune system. Pomegranate seed oil causes cancer cells to self-destruct; the juice of the fruit is toxic to most breast cancer cells yet has almost no effect on healthy cells. Pomegranate juice has also been proven to decrease heart disease by decreasing LDL ("bad cholesterol") and increasing HDL ("good cholesterol").

Eating pomegranates on a daily basis or drinking the juice can be an excellent aid for your immunity, fight Type-2 diabetes, keep blood pressure in check, smoothen digestion and make your skin glow too.

Pomegranate tree

Dates

Dates are the fruit of the date palm tree, which is grown in the Middle East. In the Aramaic way of thinking, the tree in the Garden of Eden from which Adam and Eve ate was a date palm. *Eden*[177] is a physical place in the Middle Eastern portion of Iraq, a very lush area with rivers. A Palm tree has leaves large enough to provide covering. Adam and Eve "clothed" themselves after they sinned.

According to Scripture, honey was made from dates. Dates have become quite popular in *Yesrael* in recent years. Eating dates may help improve brain function. They are high in several nutrients, fiber, and antioxidants, all of which may provide health benefits ranging from improved digestion to a reduced risk of disease.

The fiber and nutrients in *Medjool* dates can help with weight management, but portion control is important. They are high in calories and should be consumed in moderation to avoid unwanted weight gain. *Medjool* dates are an excellent source of potassium, which is lacking in most people's diets.

Eating dates may help improve brain function. Laboratory studies have found dates to be helpful for lowering inflammatory markers, such as interleukin 6 (IL-6), in the brain. High levels of IL-6 are associated with a higher risk of neurodegenerative diseases like Alzheimer's.

Other studies have shown dates to be helpful for reducing the activity of amyloid beta proteins, which can form plaque in the brain. When plaque accumulates in the brain, it can disturb communication between brain cells, which can ultimately lead to brain cell death and Alzheimer's.

One study found that mice used food mixed with dates to measure the animals' memory and learning ability. The mice that ate the mixture improved in those areas and also exhibited fewer anxiety-related behaviors compared to those eating regular food.

Palm tree

Wheat and Barley

There are a lot of fields of wheat and barley in the area. Wheat was one of the first cereal crops cultivated by man. The most common variety on the market is soft wheat, which is mostly used in milling. It is used to make flour, bread, biscuits, and so on.

During the Neolithic Period (6,000 years BC), wheat was cultivated in the Fertile Crescent, in what is now known as the Middle East. Mixed with water and cooked on hot stones, dry flatbread was first leavened by the Egyptians, who would add water from the Nile, which was rich in the natural ferments contained in yeast.

Barley was originally cultivated for making bread and gruel. Nowadays, barley is mostly used as the main ingredient in beer. One day in Mesopotamia, or so the story goes, someone prepared a barley gruel and then forgot about it. This mixture started fermenting spontaneously in the open air, giving rise to the first beer. Capable of adapting to any climate, barley is now cultivated in both temperate and cold regions, on plains, and at high altitudes.

Wheat fields

Summary of the Seven Species of the Land

Even when there is a drought in *Yesrael*, these seven species of crops will grow and give produce. This illustrates *Yahweh*'s Word. His Word is so sufficient to our lives, whatever our spiritual journey may bring.

The *Torah* mention of the seven species of crops is not incidental. Rather, these foods are central to a Jewish spiritual path that strives to elevate the physical through intentional living. Eating the seven species in a conscious way can promote our well-being, help us connect to the land of *Yesrael*, and deepen our relationship with *Yahweh*. Each of the seven species contains deep lessons about

Yahweh and our spiritual lives. Every time we eat them, we have the opportunity to tune into their spiritual messages, eat consciously, and bring the world a step closer to its perfected state.

Here is what each of them symbolizes.

- Wheat: Kindness
- Barley: Severity
- Grapes: Harmony
- Figs: Perseverance, Endurance
- Pomegranates: Humility
- Olives: Foundation
- Dates: Royalty

Approaching *Or-Shlem*

Fifteen minutes before arriving at the southeastern entrance of *Or-Shlem*, play Michael Marbrick's "The Holy City." It is an emotional moment as *Or-Shlem* comes into view.

> Last night I lay sleeping
> There came a dream so fair
> I stood in old Jerusalem
> Beside the temple there
> I heard the children singing
> And ever as they sang
> Methought the voice of Angels
> From Heaven in answer rang

"Jerusalem, Jerusalem!
Lift up your gates and sing,
Hosanna in the highest.
Hosanna to your King!"

And then methought my dream was changed
The streets no longer rang
Hushed were the glad Hosannas
The little children sang
The sun grew dark with mystery
The morn was cold and chill
As the shadow of a cross arose
Upon a lonely hill

"Jerusalem, Jerusalem!
Hark! How the Angels sing,
Hosanna in the highest,
Hosanna to your King!"

And once again the scene was changed
New earth there seemed to be
I saw the Holy City
Beside the tideless sea
The light of God was on its streets
The gates were open wide
And all who would might enter
And no one was denied
No need of moon or stars by night
Or sun to shine by day
It was the new Jerusalem
That would not pass away

> "Jerusalem! Jerusalem
> Sing for the night is o'er
> Hosanna in the highest
> Hosanna for evermore!"

Or-Shlem[5] or *Shlem* in Aramaic means "peace." This is the City of Peace. The word *Shlem* comes from the verb, meaning "to complete or to perfect." *Shlemut* means "to fulfill oneself, to achieve a level of completion in one's life." So, *Or-Shlem* is "the City of Completion." *Or* means "light". It symbolizes that nothing is missing or broken in your life. You are full of light, and you become complete because of *Yeshua*. *Shlama*[179] is a blessing of peace that people often say to one another. I use it a lot.

The whole concept of *shlama* is not the peace, the light that is outside or surrounding you only, but rather of inner peace, health, and contentment from inside your life. It radiates from your very being everywhere you go, exactly like *Or-Shlem*.

You will check in the hotel in *Or-Shlem* for three nights. Have a good rest because the tour of *Or-Shlem* is most walking. You will study about the city and what happened here for the next three days. And I will cover that information in *Volume III* of this series.

The final Book Volume III in the series is dedicated to the profound and emotional climax of *Yeshua's* life, his crucifixion, his death, and his triumphant resurrection. We will have a tour for the Last week of Jesus in *Or-Shlem*. You will explore the events leading to his crucifixion, the significance of the cross, and the ultimate redemption through his resurrection. You will witness the sacrifice and the power that have been at the core of Christianity for centuries. *Crucifixion and Resurrection* offers a poignant and inspiring conclusion to this incredible journey.

End of Volume II

What's Next?

I hope you enjoyed Volume II. My deepest prayer is that my efforts will enrich your understanding and deepen your faith. Here's what's coming next.

Our journey culminates in **Volume III**, where the focus shifts to the final and most profound week of *Yeshua's* life in *Or-Shlem*. This volume is dedicated to the emotional and spiritual climax of his story: his crucifixion, death, and triumphant resurrection. We will explore the events leading up to his crucifixion, understand the profound significance of the cross, and experience the ultimate redemption through his resurrection. "Crucifixion and Resurrection" provides a poignant and inspiring conclusion to his incredible journey, highlighting the sacrifice and enduring power that have been central to Christianity for centuries.

Join us as we continue this journey through the life of *Yeshua*, from his humble beginnings to his transformative ministry and the ultimate sacrifice and triumph destined to change the world.

Additional Information and Resources

Stay Connected with Twins Tours:

Website: Visit www.twinstours.com for more information.

YouTube: Search for "Twins Tours Academy" on YouTube to access a wide range of teachings. Don't forget to subscribe to the video channel.

https://www.youtube.com/twinstours

Podcasts: Enjoy all the teachings from this book and more on Andre's podcast. Listen here:

https://podcasts.apple.com/us/podcast/israel-walking-the-holy-land/id1437523827

WhatsApp: Contact Andre at +1 830-318-0650

Telegram: **https://telegram.org/dl**

Email: **info@twinstours.com**

Subscribe to Online Video Courses: Access online video courses at www.twinsbiblicalacademy.com/academy

Instagram: **https://instagram.com/twinstours**

Facebook:

https://www.facebook.com/TwinsToursTravel/

X: Follow Andre on at **https://x.com/twinstours**

Three Recommended Books to deepen your understanding (all by Andre Moubarak):

Heading to the Holy Land: How to Pray, Plan and Prepare for a Life-Changing Journey

Study Reader Israel: Twins Tours

One Friday in Jerusalem

You can find these books on Amazon or on our website: **https://www.twinsbiblicalacademy.com/shop**

Our Story

When the October 07, 2023, war took place in Israel, travel groups stopped coming to the country, leaving me with nothing to do. As someone who loves my work and is passionate about it, I was disheartened by this sudden halt.

In my desire to help during this challenging time, I turned to God and sought guidance through prayer. After three days of earnest prayer, I felt led to create "Twins Biblical Academy" and develop video courses that allow virtual visits to sites in Israel over ten days. These courses follow a chronological order, starting from *Yeshua's* birth and concluding with his resurrection. To my knowledge, no other tour guide or travel agency provides a comprehensive ten-day tour in chronological order.

Through these online video teachings, I aim to impart the heart and mind of Jesus while providing insight into the culture, customs, and context of Scripture. Over the course of many years, I poured my heart, hard work, and dedication into developing these deep online video teachings, even without expecting monetary compensation. The Academy represents my 20 years of experience as a guide, incorporating abundant resources and information to help you internalize God's Word. Furthermore, it offers a creative way to explore the land when physical visits are not feasible.

Understanding that a ten-day tour in Israel can be financially burdensome, I made these online courses freely accessible through the website. However, if the content has blessed you and you wish to support our ministry, I invite you to consider becoming a monthly partner. By making a monthly donation, you will gain unlimited access to my future media projects and books.

If you are unable to contribute financially, I kindly request your help in spreading the word about the website to your friends at work, extended family, church members, and on social media.

https://www.twinsbiblicalacademy.com/give

Twins Biblical Academy Online Courses

Living in Israel, we have had the privilege of guiding Christian groups through the Holy Land on a daily basis. However, not everyone has the opportunity to embark on this journey due to various reasons:

1. **Financial constraints:** Traveling to Israel can be expensive, often requiring years of savings to afford the trip.
2. **Physical challenges:** The long flight, extensive walking, and lack of wheelchair accessibility at many Israeli tourist sites make it strenuous and exhausting for some individuals to participate in organized group tours.
3. **Time constraints:** Taking a trip to Israel typically requires a minimum of eight days, not including travel time, which may be difficult for those unable to take an extended break from work or family obligations.
4. **Concerns about the Middle East**: Ongoing uprisings and regional conflicts in the surrounding countries often create anxiety and hesitation about traveling to the Middle East.

5. **Health considerations:** The recent global pandemic and potential future requirements for proof of vaccination or quarantine pose additional challenges to international travel.

We would like to provide you with an immersive online experience that allows you to explore the Holy Land virtually. It is essential to emphasize that numerous groups visiting Israel have unfortunately missed out on receiving high-quality educational content during their tours despite visiting renowned tourist sites. Rather than having the opportunity to delve deeper into each location, they were hurriedly moved from one place to another to fulfill their itinerary.

https://www.twinstours.com/virtual-tours

Why Another Online Course: "Twins Biblical Academy"

In these online courses, you will have the flexibility to learn at your own pace as they are designed to be easily accessible on your devices. Regardless of your location, you can explore the wonders of the Holy Land at your preferred time, in the comfort and convenience of your own surroundings.

Through these courses, you will have the opportunity to virtually visit significant biblical sites and gain profound insights. The teachings offered will present the mind and heart of Jesus through the lens of Middle Eastern perspectives and the cultural and contextual backdrop of the first-century Aramaic Hebraic world. Our faith finds its roots in the historical, geographical, and archaeological significance of the Holy Land, encompassing modern-day Israel, Jordan, Lebanon, Syria, Iraq, and Egypt. This region, often referred to as the "Levant," serves as a geological bridge connecting.

Africa, Asia, and Europe. It stands as the epicenter of the world, where God chose to show himself, and the accounts of this divine revelation are recorded within the pages of the Bible. It is a story of salvation that unfolded among real people during a specific time in history within this particular region. While the message of salvation spread throughout the world, some indigenous Christians have remained in the Holy Land. I am privileged to be descended from these indigenous Christians and honored to share a part of my personal testimony with you.

Tony and Andre, both born and raised in Jerusalem, have spoken the Semitic languages like Jesus and his disciples. The streets of the Old City of Jerusalem served as their childhood playground, where they knew that Jesus performed miracles and taught parables in their own neighborhood. Their family resided along the Via Dolorosa; the path *Yeshua* walked while carrying His cross to *Golgotha.*

Some Background about the Maronite Community

Our family belongs to the Maronite Aramaic-speaking Christian community, and we consider ourselves indigenous to the Holy Land. We have an ancient and unbroken lineage of following in the footsteps of Jesus and the teachings of the Bible, starting from the Early Church until the present day. All of our ancestors were Christians from Lebanon, tracing our roots back to the early days of the Church. Our language is Aramaic, specifically with a Syrian dialect that closely

resembles the Aramaic spoken by Jesus Himself in his Galilean dialect. Additionally, I have also learned to speak Hebrew, which came naturally to me as Hebrew, Aramaic, and Arabic are all Semitic languages closely related to one another.

Understanding these languages helps me gain a deeper comprehension of scripture, as Jesus himself would have spoken Hebrew and Aramaic in His daily life. The Maronite Church was established by believers who lived in the ancient region of Greater Syria, near the church of Antioch, where the followers of Jesus were first called "Christians." Located in the present-day regions of Lebanon and Syria, they were the immediate neighbors of the Jewish believers in Israel, and from the very beginning, they adopted the prayer style of the Jerusalem Church. This prayer tradition, known as the "Liturgy of Saint James," has been continuously practiced by the Maronite Church from its founding to this day, preserving its Aramaic form without external influences from the West.

The Maronite tradition is rooted in the practices of the original Jerusalem church, which was led by Jewish disciples of Jesus shortly after his resurrection. In the Book of Acts, we learn that the disciples and believers who remained in Jerusalem continued to pray in the Temple, observe Jewish prayers, honor the Jewish patriarchs, and experienced the excitement of recognizing Jesus as their Messiah within the Jewish context.

As Aramean Christians, we have carefully preserved the ancient prayers and ways of thinking from the first century. Therefore, I am able to teach the original Hebraic context of scripture, as I belong to this ancient Semitic linguistic heritage and Middle Eastern way of thinking.

It's important to note that Maronites are not Arabs or Palestinians; we are descendants of the Arameans, a group that originated in modern-day Syria several thousand years before Christ. Aramaic, the language spoken by *Yeshua*, has gradually faded away over the centuries, but our

Maronite identity and national heritage are firmly rooted in Aramaic Phoenician culture. Interestingly, I have taken a DNA ancestry test that confirmed I am 100% from the Middle East,

specifically, from modern-day Lebanon and Syria. This means my ancestors were originally Phoenicians.

Due to my deep connection to the customs, culture, and context of scripture, I can explain and provide insights into these aspects. We Maronites are not only heirs to an ancient Christian lineage through our ancestry, but we are also Spirit-filled believers and followers of Jesus Christ. We firmly believe in the power of the unchanging Word of *Yahweh*. My approach to teaching scripture is grounded in a profound understanding and reverence for the Word of *Yahweh*.

What You Will Learn in the Online Courses

Through these online courses, we aim to take you on a transformative journey, enabling you to see the land of the Bible through the lens of Jesus' Middle Eastern perspective. With our 20 years of experience as indigenous believers who speak and comprehend the languages of Jesus, we will guide you through an exploration of the first century lifestyle in Israel.

During the courses, we will delve into the intricate details of how the people of the first century lived, including their daily routines, dietary practices, attire, occupations, modes of transportation, worship traditions, and methods of communication. By immersing ourselves in their culture, customs, and the broader context of their mindset, we will gain a comprehensive understanding of life during that time. We refer to these as the three C's: culture, customs, and context.

Our ultimate aspiration is that these courses will offer you a deeper comprehension of Jesus, leading to a more profound connection with him. As a result, we hope that these teachings will bring clarity to your understanding, provide necessary corrections where needed, and offer confirmation to strengthen your personal journey with Jesus. Please let us know if there's anything else we can assist you with or any specific topics you would like us to cover in these courses.

First C: Culture

Indeed, culture plays a significant role in shaping people's lives, influencing their perspectives, values, humor, loyalties, fears, and hopes. Understanding the cultural context is crucial for grasping the specific meanings of words and expressions within a language. This is especially true when studying the Hebrew language and Jewish culture of Jesus. During the first century, *Yeshua* lived in a time when the Temple and its sacrificial system were still operational while the entire region was under Roman rule.

Yeshua, born into a Jewish family in Bethlehem, was raised in Nazareth and immersed in Jewish traditions. He studied the Torah in the local synagogue, adhering to the practices of a Middle Eastern, Galilean, and Torah-observant Jew. He and his family journeyed to the Temple in Jerusalem for the three pilgrimage feasts. Jesus served as a rabbi in Galilee, teaching in various synagogues. He returned to Jerusalem during the holy festival of Passover, where He ultimately became the sacrificial Lamb of Judah. It is believed that He will return as the victorious Lion of Judah in the future.

When engaging with scripture and seeking to deepen our relationship with *Yeshua's* understanding, his Jewish identity and cultural background become invaluable. It gives us a perspective that differs from our own Western and modern culture. These online courses aim to offer practical insights and information on comprehending *Yeshua* within the context of his first century culture.

Furthermore, it is worth mentioning that I also have a comprehensive online course available that explores the differences between Eastern and Western cultures.

Second C: Customs

Customs are fundamental aspects of a culture, comprising patterns of behavior that are followed and upheld by its members. Often, individuals adhere to customs without fully comprehending their origins or underlying reasons. Customs serve a crucial role in fostering a sense of affiliation and belonging within communities, groups, and organizations, contributing to social cohesion. As customs are deeply ingrained in societal dynamics, they gradually evolve into the accepted norms of a given society.

By embracing and practicing customs, individuals participate in shared traditions, rituals, and behaviors that strengthen the bonds among community members. These customs help to establish a collective identity, preserve cultural heritage, and maintain social order. They provide individuals with a sense of continuity, connecting them to the past and shaping the present and future of their culture. Understanding customs within a specific cultural context allows for a deeper appreciation of the values, beliefs, and social dynamics of a society. It enables individuals to engage with others more effectively, respect diversity, and foster social harmony.

Third C: Context

Understanding the context of words and passages is indeed crucial when interpreting Scripture. Each verse in the Bible carries a specific historical context, encompassing cultural elements, customs, the time period, the author, the intended audience, and geographical and political circumstances as well as the occasion and purpose of the writing. Examining the historical context allows for a clearer understanding of the circumstances surrounding events and teachings that may be unfamiliar to us in our current time.

In your signature course, "The Lord's Prayer in Aramaic," participants will have the opportunity to learn how to read and write Aramaic. This will enable them to recite the Lord's Prayer in Jesus' own language, experiencing the depth and beauty of the original Aramaic sentences spoken by *Yeshua* himself, just as he did 2000 years ago.

Additionally, there is another course available for learning biblical Hebrew, consisting of seven lessons. Biblical Hebrew is the primary language used in the 39 books of the *Tanach* (Hebrew Bible), also known as the Old Testament. Hebrew is written and read from right to left, with its unique alphabet. Hebrew letters do not have uppercase and lowercase forms. The Babylonian script, commonly used in modern Hebrew Bibles, is employed in this course. Vowel points are utilized to indicate vowel sounds, and it should be noted that Hebrew letters and vowels can be pronounced in different ways due to various dialects. The course teaches the modern dialect, which

is considered the standard way of speaking Hebrew in present-day Israel.

The objective of these language courses is to provide beginners with a solid foundation in understanding and utilizing Aramaic and Hebrew. They aim to equip participants with essential knowledge that can serve as a basis for more advanced language studies in the future.

Moreover, there will be additional courses available, including the historical geography of the land of the Bible, exploring the differences between Eastern and Western cultures, and delving into the

significance of the *Shema*, the most important Jewish prayer in the Old Testament. These courses will offer opportunities to learn phrases in Aramaic and Hebrew that scholars agree were likely spoken by *Yeshua* himself.

https://www.twinsbiblicalacademy.com

Acquired Learning

By engaging in these courses, you will gain valuable insights into how God has worked throughout history, archaeology, and the geography of the land of the Bible. The transformative power of these teachings lies in their ability to help you think more like Middle Eastern *Yeshua*. As you delve into the culture, customs, and context of *Yeshua's* time, you will develop a deeper understanding of His identity. This understanding, in turn, will enable you to grasp the significance of your own life in relation to Him.

The courses aim to bring about a transformation in your thinking and perspective, aligning it with the teachings and mindset of *Yeshua*. This process of renewal aligns with the scriptural exhortation to be transformed by the renewing of your mind (Romans 12:2). By immersing yourself in these teachings, you will experience a profound impact, particularly if you have a hunger to deepen your spiritual walk and gain a greater understanding of the stories within the Bible.

Embarking on this journey through the online courses will yield three significant results: clarity, correction, and confirmation. The teachings will bring clarity to your understanding, allowing you to grasp the deeper meaning and significance of biblical narratives. They will also provide correction, aligning your perspectives with the truth and authenticity of Jesus' teachings and life. Finally, these courses will cover confirmation, strengthening your faith and affirming the truths you already hold.

Clarity

These online courses provide clarity in your Christian Walk by helping you understand Scripture in a clearer way, eliminating confusion and bringing focus to your life.

Correction

Through these online courses, your understanding of the Word of God will be corrected. Sadly, our current culture often rejects correction, emphasizing self-centeredness and resistance to guidance. Even within the Christian community, the desire for personal autonomy can hinder the acceptance of correction. Yet, a gentle rebuke has the power to positively impact the soul.

This truth applies to all believers as we navigate relationships that sometimes call for biblical correction. While it may be challenging, it is an integral part of expressing love in accordance with scripture (2 Timothy 3:16-17).

Confirmation

Enrolling in these courses will bring confirmation to your faith. The Holy Spirit empowers us to live out our faith in every aspect of life and to bear witness to Christ in all circumstances.

In our present culture, characterized by anxiety, disagreements, doubts, and the denial of Christian beliefs, the challenge lies in whether we will obey Christ or conform to the prevailing culture. These online courses will anchor you and instill greater confidence in your Christian journey.

Confirmation of the Word of God serves to establish a stronger connection with the Holy Spirit and fosters a deeper sense of unity within the church community, our fellow brothers and sisters in Christ (Hebrews 4:12).

It is crucial to embrace both the Word and the Spirit. We cannot prioritize the Holy Spirit while disregarding the Word of *Yahweh*. Both aspects are essential as the Word itself is the expression of the Spirit. Scripture, the Word of God, affirms our faith, nurturing its growth, depth, and maturity within the core of our being.

How the Courses Work

I will serve as your personal tour guide and instructor in the video courses. They are structured into multiple lessons and offer a comprehensive learning experience. Packed with insightful teachings, maps, presentations, and captivating pictures of the Holy Land, they will enhance your understanding of the Bible. To ensure a continuous learning journey, a new video teaching will be delivered to your email inbox every month. This regular distribution of content will enable you to steadily deepen your knowledge and engagement with the material.

Who Benefits from the Courses

These online courses are specifically designed for church leaders, ministry leaders, elders, pastors, and individuals seeking to deepen their spiritual walk through a comprehensive understanding of Scripture. Drawing from my extensive experience guiding believers on

tours of the Holy Land, I have dedicated countless hours to curating and developing these courses to be accessible and easily comprehensible.

The "Twins Biblical Academy" courses offer a transformative spiritual journey through the land of the Bible, with a focus on personal growth and a deeper relationship with God. You can join me in these enlightening Zoom classes, and I invite you to RSVP for the next free lesson at

https://www.twinsbiblicalacademy.com/webinars

More Books For Your Reading Pleasure

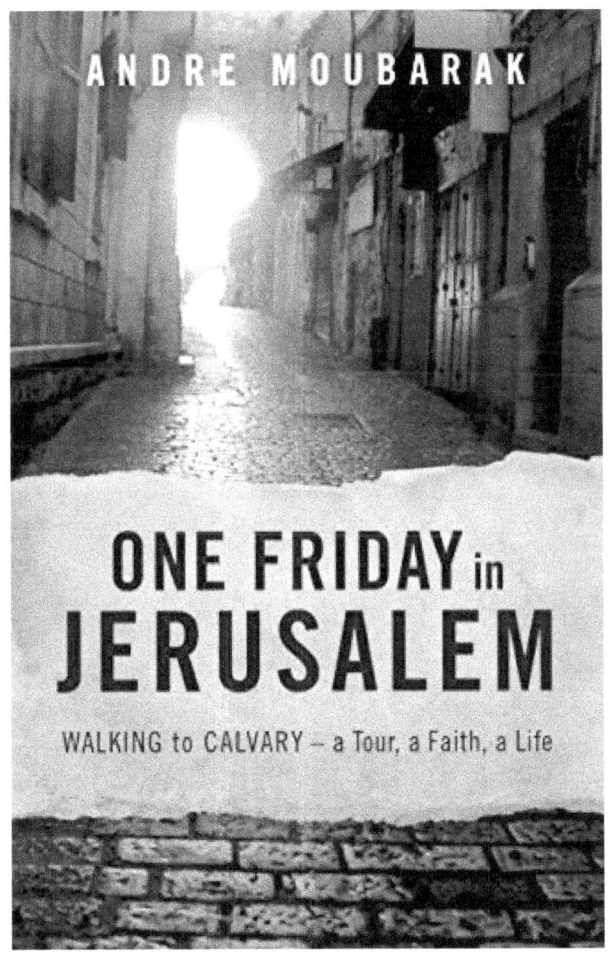

Step into the sandals of Jesus and experience the profound journey of *One Friday in Jerusalem*. This captivating tour book immerses you in the sights, sounds, and emotions as Jesus carries His cross along the arduous half-mile path to Calvary. Feel the sweat on your brow, inhale the scents of the bustling crowd, hear the commanding voices of soldiers, and confront the agonizing reality of the crucifixion. Andre, a member of a marginalized community in a land divided by ethnicity, shares why each station of the cross holds deep significance.

One Friday in Jerusalem goes beyond a mere tour guide, offering unique Middle Eastern perspectives on the Bible. Packed with historical, cultural, geographical, archaeological, and spiritual insights, it takes you on a profound reflection of Jesus' Passion. Through the remarkable and true stories of Andre, who intimately understands the sorrows and struggles of the Via Dolorosa, you will also encounter the transformative power of the risen Christ – a source of joy, hope, and life-changing impact.

Heading to the Holy Land is a must-have guide for tour leaders, pastors, and anyone planning to bring a group to Israel. This concise book covers everything from legal and ethical considerations to cultural insights, providing you with the necessary tools to become a skilled and equipped Tour Leader. Whether managing a group in Israel or the West Bank, touring the Holy Land will help you navigate the process and ensure a successful and impactful experience for your group.

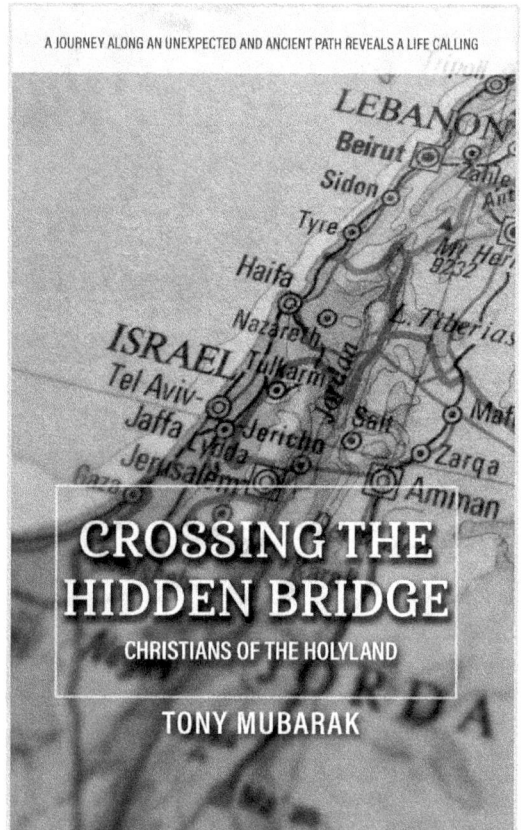

This book is written for those who are interested in learning more about the Holy Land experience and having a deeper contemporary look at the challenging issues of this land.

Also, the book will help you understand more about what it is like for the Christians to live here. How do we, the Christians of the Holy Land: this hidden bridge contribute to the conflict? And what is our connection to the Bible as well?

This new Holy Land guide invites readers to discover the hidden bridge – Christians of the Holy Land. Although their presence has been hidden by a century of conflict, they have something profound to teach us. The journey combines Biblical insights with reflections on the contemporary hopes and challenges of Christians living in different parts of Israel and Palestine, along with personal stories from the author woven throughout. What does living faithfully for Christ in such a contested land look like? That question drives the story forward. The journey begins on an afternoon stroll in the wilderness of Mount Carmel and the discovery of something hidden in the distance!

Visit our website, **https://www.twinsbiblicalacademy.com/shop** or find the book on platforms like Amazon.

Invite us to share the Word with your ministry.

As licensed tour guides in Israel, The Twins' passion and calling is to bridge the gap between the Middle Eastern and Western churches in the U.S. by teaching the roots of the Bible from the Aramaic/Hebraic mindset. We pursue unity in Christ between the Western and Eastern Churches by building bridges through personal interactions and seminars.

With our unique perspective, we specialize in bringing this understanding of the roots of the first century culture, customs, and context to churches and their members across the United States.

Twins Tours Academy provides the following teachings:

1. Understanding the Arab/Israeli Conflict

2. The Church's role during the war
3. The Christians of the Holy Land
3. Jesus' Languages - Hebrew & Aramaic – Customs
4. Jesus as a Man - The Historical Jesus – - ntext
5. Jesus as a Rabbi - The Spiritual Jesus – Culture
6. Educational online Virtual Tours

Andre is based in New Braunfels, Texas for the next few years. Tony travels twice a year to the U.S. from Israel. Both of us give seminars and conferences at churches to help people see the Bible through Jesus' Middle Eastern eyes. We are both available to travel to your church, on an agreed upon schedule, to share the topics you are most interested in during a worship service, conference, or special event.

We can do each teaching in 45 minutes. A full day meeting can be divided into different sessions depending on your need. Also, we are happy to preach during your Sunday morning services.

We ask that you cover transportation costs (flying or driving within the U.S.), food, and lodging while we are with you. We welcome staying in host homes if this helps make our visit more affordable.

We do not require any honorarium for the teachings, but a love offering is appreciated.

For those interested in travelling to Israel in the future, we also mentor group leaders to develop their Christian tour packages either as a combination of sites or hands-on mission work.

Thank you for your interest in our ministry. If you have any questions, please contact us:

Email: **twinsbiblicalacademy@gmail.com**

Phone: (830) 318-0650

(Endnotes)

1. "Jesus" in Aramaic
2. "Peter" in Aramaic
3. "Temple" in Aramaic
4. "Matthew" in Aramaic.
5. "Jerusalem" in Aramaic
6. is the common dialect of the Greek language
7. "Paul" in Aramaic
8. "Holy Spirit" in Aramaic
9. "Kingdom of Heaven" in Aramaic
10. "Messiah" in Aramaic.
12. "Mark" in Aramaic.
13. "Luke" in Aramaic.
14. "Deuteronomy" in Aramaic.
15. "Heaven" in Aramaic.
16. "Saul" in Aramaic. Saul is better known to Christians as "Paul."
17. "Ephesians" in Aramaic."
18. "The sacred" covenant name of God in Hebrew
19. "King" in Aramaic.
20. "Kingdom" in Aramaic.
21. "Citizen" in Aramaic.
22. "Exodus" in Aramaic.
23. "The Lord shall reign forever and ever." In Hebrew.

24 "Egypt" in Aramaic.
25 "Lord" in Aramaic.
26 "Deserted" in Greek.
27 "Israel" in Aramaic.
28 "John" in Aramaic.
29 "Father" in Aramaic.
30 "Seven Springs" in Greek.
31 "Sea Road" in Latin.
32 "Jordan River" in Aramaic.
33 "Nazareth" in Aramaic.
34 "Chorazin" in Aramaic.
35 "Bethsaida" in Aramaic.
36 "Capernaum" in Aramaic.
38 "Andrew" in Aramaic.
39 "Jacob" in Hebrew.
40 "the one whom Yahweh has given" In Hebrew.
41 "Philip" in Aramaic.
42 "Moses" in Aramaic.
43 "The Gardens of the Kings" in Aramaic
44 A rabbi.
45 "Twin" in Aramaic, Thomas in English.
46 "God has given" or "Gift of God" In Hebrew
47 "The love of *Yahweh*" in Aramaic.
48 "Womb love" in Aramaic.
49 "Human love or affection" in Aramaic.
50 "Reed" or "measuring rod" in Aramaic.
51 "House of gathering" in Hebrew.
52 "Isaiah's" in Aramaic.
53 "Judah" in Aramaic.
54 "Satan" in Aramaic.

55 "Passover" in Aramaic.
56 "Philip" in Greek – there is no corresponding Aramaic name.
57 "Romans" in Aramaic.
58 "Corinthians" in Aramaic.
59 "Island" pure Latin not Greek or Aramaic.
60 "Kataluma" is "a place to stop, to rest, to lodge" In Greek.
61 "Joseph" and "Mary" in Aramaic.
63 "Bethlehem" in Aramaic.
64 "Acts" in Aramaic.
65 He who replaces" "Successor" or "The exchanged one" In Aramaic "Halpai" the Greek "Alphaíos" is not originally Greek. It's the Greek transliteration of an Aramaic (and Hebrew) name.
66 "Zechariah" in Hebrew.
67 "Horse" in Greek.
68 "Gergesa" the land of the Gerasenes.
69 "The Dead Sea" in Aramaic.
70 "Grain" "produce" of the LORD" or "Crops belonging to Yahweh" in Hebrew.
71 "Tower" in Aramaic
72 "John the Baptizer" in Aramaic.
73 "Dead Sea" in Aramaic.
74 "Jordan" in Aramaic.
75 "Job" in Aramaic.
76 Literally, "walks on water."
77 "Valley of the Doves" in Aramaic.
78 The Jewish oral law.
79 "Micah" in Aramaic.
81 "Hebrews" in Aramaic.
82 "Abraham's" in Aramaic.
84 "The place of ambush" "place of blending" or "shadowy place" In Aramaic.

85   "He will build" or "He shall cause to be built" In Aramaic.
86   "Jeremiah" in Aramaic.
87   "Elijah" in Aramaic.
88   "The book of Kings" in Aramaic.
89   "To cover" to "shade" to "hang over" to "drape" In Hebrew.
90   "A tunic" "shirt" or "inner garment" something separate, divided from the outer covering in Hebrew.
91   "The son of the Star" in Aramaic.
92   "Orders" in Hebrew.
93   "Tractates" in Hebrew.
94   "Verses" in Hebrew.
95   "Six Orders of the Mishnah" in Hebrew.
96   "Genesis" in Hebrew.
97   "He who praises" in Hebrew.
98   "Cyrene" a major Greek colony in Libya.
99   "Hosea" in Aramaic.
101 "Psalms" in Aramaic.
102 "The blowing of the wind" in Aramaic.
103 "The fertile land" "the place of rich soil" or "the land of fatness "in Aramaic.
104 "Joshua" in Aramaic.
105 "The exalted one" or "the circular / mighty one" In Aramaic.
106 "Numbers" in Aramaic.
107 "The high place" or "the raised stream" in Aramaic.
108 "The Circle" "The Hollow" or "The Basin" in Aramaic.
109 "The river of life and fullness in the mercy of the King" in Aramaic.
111 "The fortified place" or "the walled settlement" in Aramaic
112 "The tower/elevation of the Sun" in Aramaic.
113 "To learn" "to study" or "to teach" In Hebrew.
114 "The devoted mountain" "The consecrated one" in Aramaic.

115 "View" in Arabic.
116 "White" "to be white" or "to make pure" In Aramaic.
117 "Field of Streams" in Aramaic.
118 "Stream of the Springs" or "River of the Eyes" In Aramaic.
119 "The Party of God" in Arabic.
120 "Place of brightness" in Aramaic
121 "Judges" in Aramaic.
122 Hebrew
123 "Hezekiah" in Aramaic.
124 "Jeroboam" in Aramaic.
125 "David's" in Aramaic.
126 "Rehoboam "to be wide, spacious, broad, enlarged" in Hebrew
127 "Aaron" in Hebrew.
128 "The Feast of Tabernacles."
131 "Samuel" in Aramaic.
132 "Absalom" in Aramaic.
133 "Pentecost" in Aramaic.
134 "Glory" in Aramaic.
135 "a bridge" "an arch" or "a small bridge over a stream" In Arabic.
137 "Jericho."
138 "Bubbling stream" in Aramaic.
139 "Jonathan" in Aramaic
140 "Gideon's" in Aramaic.
141 "Jezebel" in Aramaic.
142 "Carmel" in Aramaic.
143 "*Yahweh* will sow" in Aramaic.
144 "Asyria" in Aramaic.
145 "The Two Rivers, Tigris & Euphrates in Aramaic"
147 "Jonah" in Aramaic.
148 "Solomon" in Aramaic

149 "Proverbs" in Aramaic.

151 "Naar" Young Men in Hebrew

152 "Role Away, Swift" in Hebrew.

153 "Mountain of the Druze" in Arabic.

154 "God" in Arabic

155 "God" in Arabic

156 "Obadiah" in Aramaic.

157 "Holy Land" in Aramaic.

158 "Jaffa" in Aramaic.

160 "Tel Aviv."

161 "Kebar" is mentioned prominently in *Ezekiel 1:1–3* as the place where the prophet Ezekiel received his visions while in exile

162 "Nippur" Nippur was one of the most important religious cities of Mesopotamia, about 100 miles southeast of modern Baghdad

163 "Ezekiel."

164 "Yaphet" in Hebrew comes from the Semitic root (*pataḥ*), meaning to open, *to make spacious, to enlarge.*

165 "Chronicles."

166 "Dorcas."

167 "Safed" in English a religious Jewish city near the Golan heights.

168 "Ackre" in English a seaport crusader city in the North of Israel.

169 "Nablus" A Palestinian city in west bank.

170 "Saraya" a Turkish word for "a palace of royalty".

171 "Flea market" in Hebrew.

172 "Tur Abdeen" an Aramaic Town in Turkey.

173 "The Sword" in Aramaic the Turkish genocide for the Aramean Christians.

174 "The Mosque of Peter" in Arabic.

176 "Lowlands" in Hebrew

177 "Dsciples" in Hebrew

178 "Eden" in Aramaic.

179 "Peace" in Aramaic

www.ingramcontent.com/pod-product-compliance
Lightning Source LLC
Chambersburg PA
CBHW071804080526
44589CB00012B/673